Offender Rehabilitation

Offender Rehabilitation

Theory, Research and Practice

Gwen Robinson
Iain Crow

Los Angeles • London • New Delhi • Singapore • Washington DC

SAGE Publications Ltd
1 Oliver's Yard
55 City Road
London EC1Y 1SP

SAGE Publications Inc.
2455 Teller Road
Thousand Oaks, California 91320

SAGE Publications India Pvt Ltd
B 1/I 1 Mohan Cooperative Industrial Area
Mathura Road
New Delhi 110 044

SAGE Publications Asia-Pacific Pte Ltd
33 Pekin Street #02-01
Far East Square
Singapore 048763

Library of Congress Control Number 2008931097

British Library Cataloguing in Publication data

A catalogue record for this book is available
from the British Library

ISBN 978-1-4129-4770-1
ISBN 978-1-4129-4771-8 (pdk)

Typeset by C&M Digitals (P) Ltd., Chennai, India
Printed in Great Britain by CPI Antony Rowe, Chippenham, Wiltshire
Printed on paper from sustainable resources

Contents

List of Tables and Figures

Tables

Figures

Preface

The notion of rehabilitation is a broad one, and can be applied in a variety of settings, such as the rehabilitation of the sick. In this book we are specifically concerned with the rehabilitation of offenders. This is something that has had a chequered history over the last century or so, having developed towards the end of the nineteenth century, flourished in the mid-twentieth century, suffered an eclipse in the 1970s, but then achieved something of a revival towards the end of the century. During this time, the term has been used in different ways, and as a result of its changing status and developments in the practice of rehabilitation, there has sometimes been confusion about what it means and what it entails.

Our main intention in writing this book has been to establish some clarity about what rehabilitation is, how it has been applied and with what consequences, and where it stands in the early years of the twenty-first century. To do this we have looked at the theoretical, historical and methodological contexts of rehabilitation. We have also considered in some detail the principal contemporary practices associated with offender rehabilitation: assessment, the delivery of 'programmes' of intervention, and what we refer to as social and relational rehabilitation.

One of the problems faced by anyone setting out to write about offender rehabilitation is that, as with criminal justice policy in general, it is a topic that can experience rapid changes. This means that any book stands the risk of becoming out of date quite quickly. While we cannot avoid this happening altogether we have tried to reach beyond the shifting sands of criminal justice policy by adopting a thematic approach to our topic. Throughout the book we refer to particular groups of offenders, such as sexual offenders, and offenders with drug problems, but it has not been our intention to study these groups in themselves (there is, however, some reference to other texts that do so). In terms of geographical context, our main point of reference is England and Wales but, throughout the book, we refer to developments and examples of practice from a number of parts of the world, including Scotland, North

America and Australia. There is also a focus on adult offenders, although we refer to juvenile offenders in a number of chapters.

While we hope that this book will contribute to a better understanding of offender rehabilitation in general, it is important to say that the book itself has a context, and this is the undergraduate module that the two of us have taught together for some five years. This book had a predecessor (*The Treatment and Rehabilitation of Offenders*, Crow, 2001), which was written because there was a need for a text for students to use. However, the present book was not intended as a second edition of its forerunner. Not only have there been many developments since that book was written, but since we have begun to work together the module has changed in many ways, and we wanted to present a new text which reflects these changes.

With this in mind Chapter 1 starts with a consideration of the theoretical context of rehabilitation and how the term is defined. Rehabilitation is one of a number of terms (such as reintegration and resettlement) that start with the prefix 're-', and it is important to untangle just what that means and how useful it is in the specific context of offending. The chapter also looks at the theoretical justifications for rehabilitation and its significance in the criminal justice process, and ends by considering some of the criticisms that have been levelled at offender rehabilitation.

In Chapter 2 we move on to examine the appearance of rehabilitation as a modern concept that developed first from the use of imprisonment, as an alternative to corporal or physical punishments, and then alongside the emergence of positivist criminology. The first half of the twentieth century saw the 'rehabilitative ideal' becoming the dominant penal paradigm, followed by a swift collapse, producing an ideological vacuum, which was only partially filled by a variety of other concerns.

Chapter 3 looks at how rehabilitation has been delivered in both custodial and community settings, with examples of work from the prison system, the Probation Service, and the independent sector.

One of the key recurrent questions posed of rehabilitation is whether it 'works'. What this means, and the methodology involved in determining the effectiveness of rehabilitation is considered in Chapter 4.

Chapter 5 takes up the story of how the 'new rehabilitationism', and the policy related 'What Works?' movement, grew out of the ashes of the old rehabilitative ideal during the 1980s and 1990s, and influenced practice at the end of the twentieth century. The chapter ends with some reflections on the results and implications of this initiative.

In Chapter 6 the focus shifts somewhat to look at the mechanics of rehabilitation by examining how the assessment of offenders has developed. This involves assessing the risks that offenders pose, their needs, their likely response to rehabilitative interventions, and the probability of reconviction.

The evolution of the various instruments that have been used in assessing offenders is described. The chapter includes a consideration of an alternative to the risk/needs model of intervention, which stresses the importance of assessing offenders' strengths and abilities.

Following this, some of the structured programmes that have been employed in trying to change offenders' behaviour and reduce reoffending are considered in Chapter 7. The chapter focuses mainly on the cognitive behavioural programmes that have become so predominant in offender interventions since the 1990s. The development of general offending behaviour programmes is reviewed, and the effectiveness of some of these programmes (in both custodial and community contexts) is also considered.

Much offender rehabilitation, such as assessment and offending behaviour programmes, focuses on the individual offender, but the importance of the social context in which offending occurs also has to be recognised. This is discussed in Chapter 8. What we refer to as social rehabilitation can involve many aspects of social policy, so we have concentrated on those matters, such as housing and employment, which have been seen as being particularly important in relation to the rehabilitation of offenders. The chapter also looks at the policy and developments that have taken place in relation to such matters in England and Wales since the beginning of the present century, which have focused in particular on the resettlement of ex-prisoners.

In Chapter 9 we reflect on observations by several commentators that rehabilitation is a process which takes place in the context of relationships of various kinds. This takes account of the relationship between the offender and his or her supervisor in the context of mandated or statutory rehabilitation, the possibilities for mentoring relationships, and the role that the courts can play in offender rehabilitation. The chapter also looks at the potential of restorative justice approaches in rebuilding the relationships between offenders, victims and communities. Finally, it considers the specific example of a new initiative which seeks to safely manage sex offenders in the community with the aid of community volunteers.

In Chapter 10, we conclude by considering the contemporary relevance of rehabilitation, and return to the question of how it is defined and how it could be justified as a strategy in the twenty-first century.

Acknowledgements

We would like to dedicate this book to our students – past, present and future – at the University of Sheffield. Some of them have helped us to see this subject in new and refreshing ways.

Iain would particularly like to acknowledge the continuing support he has received from Margaret in this and other endeavours.

Gwen would like to take the opportunity to thank Iain for his generosity, patience and good humour as a colleague for the past five years. The publication of this book coincides with Iain's retirement from the University and it is hoped that he has many happy years of relaxation ahead.

In writing this book we have drawn on the work we have done with many academic colleagues and practitioners, but the results are solely our responsibility. We are particularly grateful to Caroline Porter and her associates at Sage Publications for the help we have received in bringing this book to completion.

ONE

Introducing Rehabilitation: The Theoretical Context

Introduction

In this chapter we begin our exploration of offender rehabilitation by considering the ways in which rehabilitation has been represented and understood in the context of offending. This takes us into theoretical territory, as we consider the criminological assumptions which lie behind ideas about offender rehabilitation. We go on to consider the relevance of rehabilitation in the offender's journey through the criminal justice process: is rehabilitation best understood as a *type* of punishment; as an *alternative* to punishment; or something which most appropriately *follows* punishment? We then turn our attention to the various theoretical justifications for rehabilitative approaches. On what grounds – and in whose interests – have such approaches been promoted or considered desirable? Do offenders have a right to be rehabilitated? In the final part of the chapter we identify and outline some of the main critiques of offender rehabilitation. These centre on questions about justice for offenders; about the use of coercive strategies to change people; and about the degree to which we can justify 'helping' offenders when other disadvantaged groups within society may not be able to access the services they need. The chapter closes by posing a number of questions for discussion or further reflection.

The Concept of Rehabilitation

Ideas and practices associated with the rehabilitation of offenders have a long history, stretching back at least as far as the eighteenth century. However, as a concept, rehabilitation is surprisingly difficult to pin down, such that when different writers, theorists or practitioners refer to it, there is quite a good chance that they are not talking about precisely the same thing. This is at least in part because 'rehabilitation' can be understood both as a general objective or goal, and as a process or set of practices (Rotman, 1990); but attempts to define rehabilitation are also complicated by a proliferation of related terms. Some of these (such as 'reform' and 'redemption') have a long history; others (such as 'reintegration', 'resettlement' and 're-entry') have more recent origins.

Clearly what all of these terms share in common is their prefix 're', which implies a return to a previous condition. It is perhaps unsurprising then to learn that according to a general, dictionary definition, rehabilitation is closely associated with the notion of 'restoration', which denotes a return to a former (desirable) state or status. Thinking about rehabilitation as a process of restoration certainly seems to make good sense in medical contexts, where we often talk about the rehabilitation of a person following a physical injury sustained in an accident. Here, there is a clear sense in which the process of rehabilitation involves assisting the individual to get 'back to normal'. He or she may need to re-learn motor skills, such as how to walk (in the case of a broken limb); or seek to recover cognitive skills, such as memory (in the case of a head injury). In either scenario, rehabilitation implies returning to a former, favourable state.

This is arguably a useful starting point for thinking about the rehabilitation of offenders. If asked to describe a 'rehabilitated offender', it is likely that the majority of lay people would indicate a person with some history of offending behaviour which has now ceased. We might think of this as a return to 'normal', law-abiding behaviour. This is clearly a behavioural definition: it is about a change in the way a person behaves. So the action of rehabilitation might involve the provision of interventions to remove the propensity, desire or necessity to offend.

But the notion of rehabilitation also has a symbolic dimension, such that it implies a return to a former status: that of a law-abiding citizen who is accepted by and enjoys the same rights as other members of the community. In other words, offender rehabilitation can imply not just behavioural change, but also a symbolic process whereby an individual is permitted to shed the negative label of 'offender' and be reinstated within the community after a period of exclusion or censure. Indeed, as Garland (1985) has observed, the concept of rehabilitation was first conceived in French law in the second half of the seventeenth century and was used to refer to the destruction or 'undoing' of a criminal conviction. Mannheim (1939: 151) describes the act of rehabilitation in its original context as 'a deletion of all entries regarding the conviction in the records'.

In England and Wales, this symbolic restoration of the former offender is at the heart of the 1974 Rehabilitation of Offenders Act. The Act was passed largely in response to the recommendations of a committee set up in the early

1970s to consider the problems of a criminal record to 'rehabilitated persons', defined as the large number of people 'who offend once, or a few times, pay the penalty which the courts impose on them, and then settle down to become hard-working and respectable citizens' (JUSTICE et al., 1972: 5). Recognising the stigma associated with having a criminal conviction, and the barriers thereby erected in respect of gaining employment in particular, the committee's report argued that there was a need for 'rehabilitation laws' which would treat the majority of old convictions, after a period of time had elapsed, as 'spent and irrelevant', thereby enabling the social reintegration of the offender.[1]

There are, then, good grounds for thinking about offender rehabilitation in terms of restoration. However, that is not to say that the equation of the two concepts is unproblematic. As both Rotman (1990) and Raynor (2004a) have argued, we need to be careful *not* to confine the concept to the sense of restoration to a pre-existing condition of adequacy. For Raynor, this is principally because we cannot always assume that offenders were ever in a desirable state to which we would wish to restore them. For Rotman, the notion of a return to a former condition is too narrow because it does 'not cover the achievement of totally new social or psychological developments or the acquisition of new skills' (1990: 3–4). For both, then, it is arguable that rehabilitation sometimes needs to go further than 'restoration', by actually improving upon (as opposed to reverting to) an offender's original state. So this would suggest a definition of offender rehabilitation as 'change *for the better*'.

The Human and Criminological Subject of Rehabilitation

In this section we confront the criminological assumptions which lie behind 'rehabilitative' practices and interventions, and posit that *all* such practices are founded on a particular understanding of the offending subject. In other words, whatever their shape, approaches to rehabilitation are never theory-free. They reflect particular criminological theories (about *why* people offend) and, even more broadly, theories about the nature of human behaviour. In this section, then, we address the following question: who is the human and criminological subject of rehabilitation?

Criminological theories tend to view the human subject – the offender in other words – on a core continuum with, at one extreme, active agents who create and shape their world and bear responsibility for the choices and decisions they make; and, at the other, passive subjects whose behaviour is shaped by a variety of forces largely beyond their control (Henry and Milovanovic, 1996: 16). These extreme positions are sometimes characterised in terms of the dichotomy of 'freedom' and 'determinism', and in criminology they are mirrored, respectively, in the *classical* and *positivist* schools of criminology.

The classical tradition, with its roots in eighteenth-century Europe (Beccaria, 1963 [1764]), is founded on a view of the offender as a rational actor and emphasises the role of free will in dictating behaviour (including offending). According to the classical perspective, offending behaviour is a result of the application of choice on the part of the individual: specifically a calculation of the costs and benefits of a particular course of action. Offending, in common with any other form of human behaviour, is motivated by the will to pleasure. In other words, human behaviour is motivated above all else by a desire to seek pleasure and enjoyment, and to avoid pain. As a rational actor, free to choose his or her course of action in any given situation, the offender bears full responsibility for his or her behaviour. Classicism draws no distinction between those who offend and those who do not: we are all thought to be driven by the same impulses and subject to similar temptations.

In contrast positivism – in its extreme manifestation – views the offender as a 'puppet' or entirely passive victim of external or internal forces. When viewed in this way, the offender tends to be seen as bearing little or no responsibility for his or her actions. As a consequence, it follows that he ought to be 'treated' or 'helped', much like someone suffering from a physical illness, in an attempt to remove the causes of his offending. It was this set of assumptions which animated the so-called 'treatment model' which dominated the way offenders were dealt with in the mid-part of the twentieth century, and which we shall encounter in greater detail in Chapter 2. Less extreme versions of positivism contend that offenders' behaviour is not entirely determined but nonetheless their ability to exercise free will is likely to have been constrained by factors not entirely within their control (e.g. poverty; mental illness; or attitudes learned from antisocial/pro-criminal peers or family members). In this scenario it follows that whilst offenders bear *some* responsibility for their offending, they can claim some mitigation for their behaviour and it might be possible to prevent reoffending if the factors which led them to offend are tackled or confronted.

Positivist criminology has its roots in the work of Italians Cesare Lombroso, Enrico Ferri and Raffaele Garofalo. Lombroso, whose highly influential book *L'Uomo Delinquente* ('The Criminal Man') was first published in 1876, is best known for his Darwinian theory that offenders were atavistic 'throwbacks' to an earlier stage of evolution: that is, biologically inferior subjects. However, not all positivist explanations rest on biological assumptions. There are in fact three main types[2] of positivist explanation: (i) biological; (ii) psychological; and (iii) social/environmental. Thus, positivist assumptions may recommend interventions aimed at changing people and/or their social/environmental circumstances.

A positivist perspective then, tends to recommend 'expert' intervention to deal with offending behaviour: that is, some intervention likely to involve the identification of the causes of offending ('diagnosis') and their subsequent 'removal'. One possible exception to this is some versions of biological positivism: if it is theorised that offending is a result of some biological abnormality for which there is no cure then there are fewer grounds for optimism.

In Britain and elsewhere, the history of attempts to rehabilitate offenders is intimately entwined with the emergence and development of positivist criminology, and a view of offending behaviour as determined (to a greater or lesser extent) by factors which lie outside the individual's control (e.g. Hollin, 2004). During the 1950s and 1960s, in the USA and Britain, positivism came to dominate criminological thinking and the 'treatment model' associated with it reflected a common belief that both the causes of – and the cure for – crime would ultimately be discovered, relieving society of the problem of crime forever. Allen (1959) famously referred to this as the *rehabilitative ideal*. Correspondingly, the decline of the treatment model in the latter part of the twentieth century is associated with the critique of positivist criminology and the emergence of a neo-classical perspective on offending behaviour, which revived the image of the rational offender exercising more or less free choices.

It is however important to note that attempts to rehabilitate offenders both pre-date 'mainstream' positivist criminology and have survived its decline in the latter part of the twentieth century. As Clive Hollin (2004) has noted, and as we shall see in later chapters, the revival of a neo-classical perspective has been linked with a revival of rehabilitative optimism. So whilst the link between rehabilitation and positivist criminology must certainly be acknowledged, we should not assume an entirely dependent relationship. Later in this chapter we explore the various theoretical justifications for rehabilitation, which go a long way to explaining how and why rehabilitative approaches have such a long history and show no signs of extinction.

Rehabilitation and the Criminal Justice Process

We have already noted, above, that the notion of rehabilitation is not confined to offenders. Thus, for example, we commonly refer to the rehabilitation of persons who have been injured or are otherwise 'debilitated' by some medical condition. Even more generally, we talk about the rehabilitation (as in 'revival') of particular fashions, whether it be the mini-skirt, the wedge heel, or 'flares'.

Of course, none of these contexts is of focal concern in this book. Rather, our principal focus is the applicability of the notion of rehabilitation to offenders: namely, individuals who have broken the law. This however begs certain questions about how and in what contexts 'rehabilitation' becomes relevant to such individuals. For example, does it imply a particular type of punishment or sanction? Is it best understood as a type of punishment or an alternative to punishment? Or is it perhaps better summed up as a process which *follows* punishment? There is no single 'correct' answer to any of these questions:

rather, there are a number of different 'ways of seeing' rehabilitation in the context of punishment or penal sanctions.

Rehabilitation and diversion

The first point to make is that access to services or sources of help which can broadly be described as 'rehabilitative' is not necessarily contingent upon an offender having been processed by the criminal justice system. A good example is people who misuse drugs. By virtue of their consumption of illegal substances, such individuals may well have broken the law on many occasions; but it is perfectly possible not only that such individuals may evade detection, but also that they may enter into treatment voluntarily.[3] When celebrities enter 'rehab', for example – typically because of problems associated with the consumption of illegal drugs – it is often in the absence of any criminal proceedings against them.

It is also sometimes the case that an offender whose offending *has* been detected may avoid prosecution or criminal sanctions but nonetheless be referred by a criminal justice agency to rehabilitative help. One such example is the use of diversion schemes, whereby offenders (typically juveniles or mentally disordered offenders) are sometimes referred to sources of help or treatment-type interventions as an alternative to prosecution. Since the 1970s a variety of diversionary schemes and measures have been introduced, in Britain and elsewhere, under the influence of labelling theory. Labelling theory emphasises the damaging and stigmatising effects of a criminal label on young offenders and thus recommends 'diversionary' measures to keep them out of the criminal justice system for as long as possible. Other offenders may get as far as court and be diverted from there. For example, in 1990 the Home Office provided guidance on the policy of diversion and aimed to ensure that, where possible, mentally disordered offenders were referred to health and social services for support and treatment rather than punished via prosecution and criminal sanctions (Home Office, 1990). Courts can thus opt for a disposal under the Mental Health Act 1983, such as a Hospital Order, in place of a criminal justice disposal (such as prison) where the offender has been assessed as having a mental disorder.

Rehabilitative punishment

For those who are not diverted prior to sentencing, there are a number of ways in which rehabilitation can become relevant. First of all, the sentence of the court may reflect – in whole or in part – a desire to bring about the rehabilitation of the offender. This is often referred to as 'rehabilitative punishment', or 'penal rehabilitationism' (von Hirsch and Maher, 1992).

Sentencing decisions are guided by principles or 'philosophies' which serve to justify the punishments imposed by the criminal courts.[4] Consequentialism (or reductionism) and retributivism are the two main philosophies relevant to sentencing and punishment – although there are others (see Cavadino and Dignan, 2007: Chapter 2; Zedner, 2004: Chapter 3; Hudson, 2003: Part 1). When a sentence with a rehabilitative component is passed, the sentencer is being guided, to some extent at least, by a *consequentialist* philosophy. Consequentialism justifies punishment with reference to the desirability of its future consequences. Rehabilitation is one of three main consequentialist strategies, sitting alongside *deterrence* and *incapacitation*. All three strategies share a forward-looking orientation, each aiming to achieve the goal or 'end' of crime reduction. Incapacitation is consequentialist in that it seeks to prevent reoffending by physically restraining or removing the offender from society, thereby removing his or her opportunities to offend. Deterrence also seeks to prevent reoffending, but by different means: namely, by ensuring that punishment is suitably unattractive to the would-be offender. Rehabilitation, in common with both of these strategies, seeks to reduce the likelihood of reoffending, but via instituting changes in the offender. These 'changes' are usually couched in positive terms. For example, Cavadino and Dignan explain that rehabilitation seeks to 'improve the individual offender's character or behaviour and make him or her less likely to re-offend in future' (2007: 41–2).

In contrast, *retributivism* essentially describes the principle that wrongdoers should be punished because they deserve it, by virtue of the wrong that they have done. Unlike consequentialism it is a backward-looking strategy: it looks back to the offence or offences committed and considers the amount of deserved punishment. In other words, it specifies punishments which 'fit the crime', with little or no reference to the future consequences of that punishment. Retributivists are principally concerned with ideas of *desert* and *proportionality*, which concern the amount or degree of punishment prescribed: this, they argue, should reflect the seriousness of the offence(s) committed and not exceed what is deserved. Convictions of a similar type should therefore attract similar sentences.

Sentencing with a view to offender rehabilitation does not, however, recommend a specific sanction. As we shall see in later chapters, there has never been a consensus on this issue. Opinion has been, and remains, particularly divided on the issue of whether prison is an appropriate context for rehabilitation.

Rehabilitation beyond punishment

'Penal rehabilitation', then, describes any penal sanction – whether custodial or community-based – which is designed (in whole or in part) with the objective or 'end' of offender rehabilitation in mind. However, the idea of rehabilitative punishment is not uncontroversial. For some theorists, rehabilitation is conceptually divorced from punishment, such that it is not understood as an objective or quality of a positive process of punishment, but rather as an *antidote* to punishment: or, more precisely, the potentially harmful effects of punishment (e.g. Cullen and Gilbert, 1982; Rotman, 1990; McWilliams and Pease, 1990). According to this view, just as retributive punishment may be deserved, so the offender deserves not to be unduly damaged by the experience of punishment. Any handicaps or damage inflicted on the offender in the process of punishing him or her ought to be offset or mitigated by rehabilitative measures. Rotman's position is often referred to as *rights-based rehabilitation*, which we shall revisit in the following section.

Regardless of one's theoretical position in respect of rehabilitative punishment or sanctions, however, we must also note that for many offenders it will be at the end of their journey through the criminal justice process that rehabilitation becomes relevant. For example, prisoners serving longer prison sentences tend to be subject to a period of supervision in the community (on licence or parole) after release from custody; a time during which they may receive help and assistance from a probation officer (or similar) with a view to preventing the likelihood of reoffending and easing the transition to life 'outside'. Similarly, offenders serving shorter sentences (for whom there is no statutory or compulsory period of supervision post-release) may seek or access help of various kinds, either from statutory agencies such as the probation service, or from non-statutory agencies and organisations (e.g. NACRO). This process of adjustment to life after prison is commonly referred to as 'resettlement' (in the UK) or 're-entry' (in the USA). It is also worth noting that to the extent that rehabilitation refers to a symbolic process – a return to citizenship – it is difficult to envisage such a process occurring until an offender has completed his or her sentence or punishment.

Theoretical Justifications for Rehabilitation

For more than two hundred years, penal reformers and theorists have advocated rehabilitation as an essentially *humanitarian* response to wrongdoing, and a means of bringing about the improvement or humanisation of criminal sanctions. Writing in the late eighteenth century, the penal reformer John Howard developed his own ideas about the reform of offenders as an alternative to what he saw as an overly punitive and disproportionate response to offending behaviour at that time (Howard 1929 [1777]). More recently, writers including Cullen and Gilbert (1982) and Rotman (1990) have continued to advocate rehabilitation on similar grounds. Rotman for example claims that:

> The rehabilitation of criminal offenders offers the criminal justice system a unique avenue of improvement [and] has enormous potential for humanizing and civilizing social reaction

against crime. Modern rehabilitative policies challenge the fantasy that the dark side of society can be forgotten and that deviants can be simply packed off to prison. They propose instead to offer inmates a sound and trustworthy opportunity to remake their lives (Rotman, 1990: 1).

Another way to justify the practices associated with offender rehabilitation is with reference to the positivist position, outlined above. If we accept the view that to a large extent offenders are victims of forces beyond their control, we can clearly justify the argument that they therefore merit whatever help might be available to prevent further offending and facilitate a 'normal' life – much in the same way that we might justify the provision of physiotherapy to a person with a broken limb.

We can take this argument further. If we accept that crime is caused, at least in part, by social deprivation (e.g. poverty) or other problems which society has failed to address (e.g. mental illness) such that the individual's capacity to avoid crime has been compromised, then it is possible to argue that society has an *obligation* to intervene or help the offender out of the situation (Cullen and Gilbert, 1982; Carlen, 1989). Put another way, we might argue that the offender has a right to receive help to avoid further offending. This is one version of 'rights-based' or 'state-obligated' rehabilitation. The other (weaker) version of this position takes us back to the notion of rehabilitation as restoration, and is usually invoked in respect of offenders who have served sentences of imprisonment. As we saw in the previous section, Rotman (1990) argues that just as the state has a right to punish the offender for his or her wrongdoing, so the offender has a right not to be debilitated by the effects of punishment. In other words, the offender should not find himself in a worse position (economically, socially, psychologically etc.) after a period of punishment than prior to it. Thus, for example, Rotman includes in his definition of rehabilitation the provision in prisons of educational opportunities; vocational training; appropriate psychological or psychiatric treatment; and the maintenance of family and community links. He also argues that the offender's right to rehabilitation is consistent with the full restoration of prisoners' civil and political rights of citizenship after release from prison (Rotman 1990: 184).

It is, however, also possible to justify rehabilitation with reference to *utilitarian* arguments. Utilitarianism is a philosophy which originates in the work of the English philosopher Jeremy Bentham (1748–1832) and which was subsequently developed by John Stuart Mill (1806–73) (see Cavadino and Dignan 2007: 52–3). The utilitarians argued that an action is ethically or morally right if it produces 'the greatest happiness' for the greatest number – i.e. the best overall consequences. The utilitarian justification for rehabilitation is therefore that the transformation of offenders into law-abiding members of the community serves the interests of society as a whole. Insofar as it is possible to make 'honest citizens' of former offenders, rehabilitative practices not only maximise the availability of useful, contributing members of society, but also protect society from future crime and victimisation (see also Raynor and Robinson, 2005: Chapter 2).

It might of course be argued that we could achieve the same end by locking up offenders en masse and keeping them there indefinitely. Indeed, incapacitation is making a comeback in the form of public protection sentences for certain categories of dangerous offenders. This is not, however, a wholesale answer to the problem of crime for most people. For one thing it would raise important questions about justice. For proponents of retributivism, proportionality (or 'just deserts') in punishment is of primary importance: in other words, sanctions for criminal behaviour ought to be in proportion to the amount of wrongdoing. For another, incapacitation would be a very expensive solution. Economy is thus another possible justification for a rehabilitative approach to punishment. And even if we cannot demonstrate that rehabilitative interventions have crime-reduction effects, we can invoke a weaker version of the utilitarian position to argue that of the two approaches, rehabilitation is preferable because it at least involves the avoidance of unnecessary harm from excessive penalties.

Rehabilitation and its Critics

So far we have represented rehabilitation as a 'force for good'. Conceptually, it has been noted that rehabilitation is associated with the positive notion of restoration; but that it can also imply a process oriented toward improving the offender's former standing: a 'change for the better'. We have also noted that ideas associated with the rehabilitation of offenders have tended to be motivated by humanitarian concerns: that is, with a view to 'humanising' the criminal justice system and rendering the experience of criminal sanctions a more positive and constructive one for the offender.

Rehabilitative punishment and questions of justice

However, that is not to imply that there are not problems with rehabilitation. In particular, the notion of *rehabilitative punishment* (see above) has met with strong criticism. Firstly, it has been argued that sentencing offenders with a view to rehabilitation is problematic on the grounds that it can lead to disproportionate sentences and, more generally, inequity. Proponents of retributive justice and desert-based sentencing argue that allowing sentencing decisions to be influenced by a desire to change or rehabilitate offenders invites extended periods of punishment which go beyond what is deserved (in respect of the seriousness of the crime committed). As we shall see in Chapter 2, this has been a valid criticism of rehabilitative punishment in the past. But it is worth reiterating the point that even some of the proponents of rehabilitation have raised strong objections to the idea of rehabilitative punishment and the risks of injustice which it poses. For example, Raynor (1997: 253) has argued that 'the presumed benefits of a [rehabilitative] programme should not be used to justify an increased sentence as being "good for" an offender': rather, a rehabilitative sentence should be limited by the principle of desert (see also Rex, 1998: 38–9). Similarly, Rotman (1990: 14) has argued that 'No one should endure a longer sentence in "order to be rehabilitated".' Where the two differ is that whilst Raynor considers rehabilitation a legitimate goal of sentencing and punishment, Rotman – as we have seen – rejects this view.

Dubious practices?

A second criticism concerns the *content* of 'rehabilitative' interventions. As we shall see in subsequent chapters, faith in rehabilitation has manifested itself in a wide variety of practices for which 'rehabilitative effects' have been claimed, from the treadmill and the crank through extended periods of solitary confinement, to psychosurgical and medical interventions. For Rotman (1990: 102), the most important 'therapeutic' abuses perpetrated in the guise of rehabilitation have involved the use of biochemical means to control and/or 'recondition' the offender. The history of rehabilitation includes the use of drugs to 'chemically castrate' sexual offenders; to tranquilise 'dangerous' offenders; and to arouse pain and fear in the context of 'aversion therapy'. Judged against today's standards, such interventions hardly fit the description of 'humane' approaches to punishment (see in particular von Hirsch and Maher, 1992). Particular questions have been raised about the *moral* content of certain rehabilitative interventions. Rotman asks:

> Should rehabilitation be defined to include efforts to produce a moral change in offenders, or should it rather be confined to the acquisition of the capacity to abstain from future crimes? (Rotman, 1990: 6)

Rotman's own answer to this important question is that attempts to inculcate particular moral values in offenders contradict the basic freedoms enjoyed by individuals in modern pluralistic societies. Rotman promotes a vision of rehabilitation which 'enhances human freedom instead of narrowing it' and 'excludes from its goals any imposition of moral systems based on particular religious or political ideologies' (1990: 7).[5]

Is coercion justified?

Rotman (1990: 8) draws a distinction between *authoritarian* and *anthropocentric* models of rehabilitation, which he sees as, respectively, authoritarian/oppressive, and liberty-centred/humanist. The authoritarian model, he argues, sees rehabilitation as a technology designed to 'mould' the offender and encourage conformity to some predesigned pattern of thought and behaviour; whilst the second, in contrast, is client-centred and – importantly – voluntary. For Rotman, rehabilitation is not something which should ever be imposed on the offender:

> The humanistic model of rehabilitation excludes all manipulative schemes to alter the offender's personality or behaviour and demands fully informed consent and willing intelligent participation. ... Instead of stamping the mind of the offender with a predetermined constellation of behavioural patterns, it should become a guide toward the creative possibilities of thought and new channels of action. (Rotman, 1990: 8–9)

For Rotman, then, attempts to rehabilitate offenders should be subject to the offender's consent and should invite the active participation of offenders in their own process of rehabilitation.

However, not everyone has objected to the idea of obliging or coercing offenders to engage with rehabilitative interventions. For example, Carlen's (1989: 20–1) own vision of *state-obligated rehabilitation* includes the principle that offenders *could* be obliged to engage in a programme of rehabilitation offered by the state, and she argues that no such programme should be rejected on the grounds that it violates the offender's civil liberties. She offers the examples of recidivist 'white collar', driving or sexual offenders, all of whom, she argues, could be coerced into accepting a 'rehabilitative' or 're-educative' community-based sentence.

Day et al. (2004) have noted that coercing offenders to attend rehabilitative programmes is increasingly regarded as an acceptable course of action, particularly for offenders who are considered to present a high risk of harm to the public (e.g. sexual, violent and substance misusing offenders). Typically, they note, interventions offered to these groups are coercive *not* in the sense that individual offenders have no choice but to cooperate, but rather in the sense that there are likely to be negative consequences for non-participation.[6] This might mean, for example, a lower likelihood of securing parole or early release from custody; or, in the case of community-based sentences, a return to court for re-sentencing if the offender fails to comply with a treatment programme ordered by the court. Day et al. argue that coercion is not inherently unethical: rather, what is important is (i) whether professionals involved in rehabilitation programmes exercise coercion in an ethical or an abusive way; and (ii) the impact of coercion on programme effectiveness. They also point to the *subjective* dimension of coercion: for example, a person may be *objectively* coerced (e.g. when a court makes rehabilitation a component of a sentence) but not feel coerced (e.g. if she or he accepts that rehabilitation is a legitimate or welcome course of action). Alternatively, a person who perceives entry into a rehabilitative programme as coerced may well change their opinion as the programme progresses: where internal motivation increases in the course of an intervention which is perceived in positive terms, perceptions of coercion may decrease.

Day et al. note that despite a limited evidence base from which to draw conclusions about the effectiveness of coerced offender rehabilitation, what research there is indicates that coercion is successful in both getting offenders into treatment and keeping them there (see also Farabee et al., 1998). They conclude their review of research thus: 'coercing offenders into attending rehabilitation programmes (or placing legal pressure on them to attend) is unlikely in itself to lead to poorer outcomes' (2004: 266).

'Less eligibility'

A final criticism of offender rehabilitation – whether voluntary or coerced – points to the problems inherent in offering rehabilitative resources and 'help' to offenders, whilst such assistance remains unavailable to others in society who have not offended but may well be experiencing some of the same personal problems and social/economic disadvantages. Where this occurs, rehabilitation offends the principle of 'less eligibility'. Formulated by Bentham in the late eighteenth century, this principle states that 'saving the regard due to life, health and bodily ease, the ordinary conditions of a convict doomed to punishment' shall not be made 'more eligible than that of the poorest class of citizens in a state of innocence and liberty' (Bentham, 1791, quoted in Rotman, 1990: 112). In other words, those convicted of offences should not enjoy conditions more favourable than those enjoyed (or endured) by the poorest independent labourer.

Peter Raynor (1997: 259) attempts to get round the problems posed by a principle of 'less eligibility' in two ways. First, he argues, improved opportunities should be part of a general social policy agenda, such that socially disadvantaged non-offenders ought to enjoy the same access to appropriate sources of help. His second argument is that rehabilitation should not consist in *conferring* but rather *offering* opportunities to offenders: in other words, offenders should be expected to engage with and participate in – as well as consent to – their own rehabilitation.

Conclusion

Our purpose in this introductory chapter has been to consider the key theoretical issues and debates relevant to the rehabilitation of offenders. It will now be clear that what at first sight appears to be a relatively straightforward concept is in fact rather more complex. Just what is meant by it, what we think it entails and how we justify doing or attempting it depends to a great extent on the theoretical stance(s) we adopt. It is for this reason that there is no single 'vision' of offender rehabilitation, but rather a collection of views, some of which appear to have relatively little in common and even at times to be in conflict.

In Chapter 2 we move on to consider in more depth the history of offender rehabilitation, and in this context we will see quite clearly some of the key ways in which 'visions' of rehabilitation have changed from one century – and even at times from one decade – to the next.

Questions to Consider

1 Can you find – or devise for yourself – a satisfactory definition of offender rehabilitation?
2 How do you understand the relationship between *behavioural* and *symbolic* rehabilitation? Is it possible to achieve one without the other?
3 'Success in rehabilitation involves *changing* offenders' (von Hirsch and Ashworth 1998: 1). Do you agree? Why/why not?
4 Is rehabilitation best conceived as a right of the offender, or a privilege of the state?
5 How useful is Rotman's distinction between *authoritarian* and *anthropocentric* rehabilitation? To what extent do you think current penal practice represents one or other of these models?

Suggested Further Reading

Chapter 1 of von Hirsch and Ashworth's edited collection *Principled Sentencing* (1998) contains a selection of useful readings on rehabilitation, including an excerpt from Cullen and Gilbert's (1982) *Reaffirming Rehabilitation*; von Hirsch and Maher's essay 'Should penal rehabilitationism be revived?'; and Sue Rex's essay 'A new form of rehabilitation?' Rotman's (1990) book *Beyond Punishment: A New View of the Rehabilitation of Offenders* (Chapter 1 of which is reproduced in *A Reader on Punishment* (1994) edited by Duff and Garland) elaborates his authoritarian and anthropocentric models as well as providing a useful historical introduction to the topic. Definitions of rehabilitation and justifications for rehabilitative practices are also discussed by Raynor and Robinson (2005), Chapters 1 and 2.

Notes

1 Not all jurisdictions have such 'rehabilitation laws' and in some parts of the world it is particularly difficult for former offenders to earn their status as equal citizens. For example, in the USA, an estimated 5.3 million people are denied the right to vote because of laws that prohibit voting by people with felony convictions, and the

American Civil Liberties Union (ACLU) reports that in 11 states offenders can lose their right to vote for life. [http://www.aclu.org/votingrights/exoffenders/ index.html]

2 It is important to recognise that these are 'ideal types' which in the real world tend to overlap, reflecting familiar 'nature vs nurture' debates in psychology. Thus for example social psychological accounts of offending consider how a person's behaviour comes to be shaped by observing the behaviour of others around him through 'modelling', indicating an acknowledgement that sometimes internal and external factors coincide.

3 It should be noted however that research has shown that drug-using offenders are not generally inclined to seek help voluntarily (e.g. Bennett, 1998).

4 In England and Wales, the 'purposes of sentencing' have been set out in the Criminal Justice Act 2003, s. 142. 'The reform and rehabilitation of offenders' is one of five such purposes set out in relation to offenders aged 18 and over.

5 Readers are referred to Anthony Burgess's 1962 novel *A Clockwork Orange* for an extreme example of 'brainwashing' in the name of 'rehabilitation'.

6 Day et al. (2004) explain that they prefer the term 'pressured' rather than 'coerced' in that a choice is exercised on the part of the offender, but that choice is likely to be constrained by the consequences of refusal or non-cooperation.

TWO

Rehabilitation in an Historical Context

Introduction

In this chapter we review the development of rehabilitation up to the 1980s, covering its early roots, the period of its rising influence in the early and middle part of the twentieth century, and its decline in penal policy from the 1970s onwards. In the last part of the chapter we look at what followed this decline.

Early Indications

As noted in Chapter 1, the term rehabilitation has been used in different ways, and it is also worth noting that rehabilitation has meant different things at different times. What we understand by rehabilitation today is likely to be different to what the term might have meant to someone in the nineteenth century. Because of this, it is hard to determine just when rehabilitation emerged as a feature of how offenders were dealt with in any contemporary sense. The development of rehabilitation can be seen as a series of emerging distinctions occurring at various points in time:

classical to positivist
corporal to carceral
carceral to community

However, these were not necessarily sequential developments, and distinctions can also be made within these.

Classical to positivist

The first of these, the shift from classical to positivist thinking, is most commonly traced back to the work of Cesare Lombroso in the latter part of the nineteenth century. As we explained in Chapter 1, the positivist school of Lombroso stood in contrast to the classicism of Beccaria and Bentham that had preceded it. Whereas 'classical' criminology emphasised dealing with the offence, the positivists focused more on the offender. Classical thinkers emphasised the importance of reasoning, justice and uniformity of sentencing. The positivists placed more emphasis on offenders as fundamentally different from non-offenders (Fattah, 1997: 214), and as people who could not help being who they were. However, Garland (1997: 31) points out that, although Lombroso's work gave rise to a scientific approach to criminality, it required much shaping and refashioning before it could form the basis for a realistic policy. Nonetheless, 'criminal justice was to cease being a punitive reactive system and was to become instead a scientifically informed apparatus for the prevention, treatment and elimination of criminality' (Garland, 1997: 32). As Bottoms has noted, by denying the 'meaning content' of human action positivism tends to regard offenders as being pre-determinedly 'crime-prone'; it treats crime as a naturally occurring phenomenon and hence sees the role of the organs of the state as unproblematic, and it relies on the ability of behavioural science 'experts' to accurately predict and treat the problem behaviour (Bottoms, 1977: 81–2).

Corporal to carceral

Another significant development in the way that offenders have been dealt with has been identified as the shift from corporal to carceral punishment, from physical punishment to incarceration, which took place around the end of the eighteenth century. This change has been described by Michel Foucault (1977), who referred to prison as 'the gentle way in punishment'. Prior to this the most common way of dealing with offenders was by physical punishment ranging from the stocks through to hanging. Places of confinement such as lock-ups and bridewells were largely temporary measures pending trial and sentence, and when prisons were used as a punishment they were only intended to be retributive and deterrent. From 1848 transportation was increasingly replaced by a national system of prisons where convicts serving three to five years of *penal servitude* would carry out hard labour.

As important as the emergence of the Lombrosian School of scientific inquiry, was the growth during the eighteenth and nineteenth centuries of new institutions and forms of administration, not just of justice and punishment, but of health and manufacture. The development of the prison, the factory, and the lunatic asylum had much in common (Melossi and Pavarini, 1981), and this nexus was related to ideas about spiritual and moral well-being. Penal reformers were aided by nonconformist industrialists and manufacturers of the time, such as Jedediah Strutt who helped Richard Arkwright set up a model cotton spinning factory at Cromford, near Matlock in 1771. Strutt claimed that the establishment of the factory with its regular work and wages, together with the stabilising influence of a closely supervised village community had transformed the behaviour of the local inhabitants, which had previously been characterised by vice and immorality (Fisk, 1998). Thus, 'In that first generation of industrialisation, factories could still be justified not simply as technical achievements, but as moral ones as well' (Ignatieff, 1978: 63) and, 'It was no accident that penitentiaries, asylums, workhouses, monitorial schools, night refuges, and reformatories looked alike, or that their charges marched to the same disciplinary cadence' (Ignatieff, 1978: 214–5). Behind this similarity of institutional structures was the idea that 'science', whether in medicine or the new forms of 'scientific management', could answer all society's needs, and we shall return to this shortly.

An important development within carceral regimes occurred during the nineteenth century with the idea that they might incorporate features intended to bring about *reform* amongst inmates, and this notion of reform is probably the closest one gets to the concept of trying to rehabilitate offenders until towards the end of the nineteenth century. These changes came about largely as a result of the work of the Quakers John Howard and Elizabeth Fry. Their work was partly based on their wish to ameliorate the harsh conditions in the convict prisons, but was also based on a moral and religious impulse: convicts should be treated humanely, but in order to achieve reform they should contemplate the error of their ways under appropriate moral guidance, and in isolation from the distracting influence of other felons. The penal reformers[1] of the nineteenth century have tended to be seen as enlightened and well-meaning individuals, concerned with the rights and welfare of people who were victims of an unjust and oppressive society as much as they were offenders. But, as Ignatieff, Foucault and others have pointed out with the benefit of hindsight, their reforms often led, unwittingly, to new forms of repression, including extended periods of solitary confinement. Cruel physical punishments, such as whippings and beatings, continued within the new institutions, usually without any due process as to their administration, but the institutions themselves introduced a new form of social and moral control over the poorer classes of society, whether they were criminals, lunatics or just impoverished:

> The new martyrs do not die a slow death in the torture chamber but instead waste away spiritually as invisible victims in the great prison buildings which differ in little but name from madhouses. (Horkheimer and Adorno, 1973: 228)

In fact Howard's ideas were criticised at the time. In his *Enquiry Concerning Political Justice* (1793), William Godwin, a leading rationalist of the time, argued that solitude was in its way just as brutal as corporal punishment, arousing resentment rather than acquiescence.[2] Godwin claimed that people could not be reformed in solitude, since reformation was a social process depending on persuasion and example.

While Howard and Fry are most commonly associated with penal reform in the nineteenth century, their main concern was with penal institutions. However, there are indications that the reform of offenders also aroused the concern of philanthropists more generally, and in a broader social context. John Ruskin, for example, was invited to join a committee in 1868 to look into how the 'improvident and more or less vicious persons' should be helped (Dearden, 2004: 38–9). He wrote *Notes on the General Principles of Employment for the Destitute and Criminal Classes* for the committee in which he suggested suitable occupations for such people, including road-making, harbour-making, porterage, dressmaking, and works of art, such as pottery, metalwork, sculpture and painting – probably the nearest one can come to a contemporary understanding of rehabilitation, and underlining the point above that the distinctions we are making are not necessarily chronological.

The Gladstone Committee

A significant step towards the development of rehabilitation occurred with the *Report from the Departmental Committee on Prisons* in 1895, known as the Gladstone Report. The Committee was a response to widespread concern about prison administration and conditions, but the members decided to extend their brief 'to discover whether any and what better system and methods of treatment could be adopted' (para. 4).

The report does not use the term rehabilitation. It refers to 'treatment' in the general sense of how prisoners were treated in the context of prison conditions at the time, and to reformation, which it concludes 'is quite impracticable in prison' (para. 25), and that, 'The present system, while admirable for coercion and repression, is excessively deficient on the reformatory side' (para. 33). The committee therefore concentrated on 'a proper classification of prisoners' (para. 27) as a basis for treating people as individuals, distinguishing between offence and offenders: 'While sentences may roughly speaking be the measure of particular offences, they are not the measure of the characters of the offenders' (para. 20). In particular the report identifies the separate needs of first-time offenders, young prisoners, habitual criminals, habitual drunkards, females and infants, debtors, unconvicted prisoners, and lunatics and the 'weak minded' (paras. 81–93).

The report also stressed the importance of links with the outside world, by extending visits and communications (paras. 32–3), and by what happened after prison. Attention was paid to the need to develop the role of Prisoners' Aid Societies, which were local voluntary associations, to 'see a uniform system established' (para. 34). The report also referred to the role that education and productive labour could play, stressing that unproductive labour was of little value:

> We start from the principle that prison treatment should have as its primary and concurrent objects, deterrence and reformation. It follows, therefore, that it is desirable to provide labour which in conjunction with the general prison discipline does not impair the one, and which does include the other. (para. 47)

The significance of the Gladstone Report lies in its argument that the reform of offenders should have the same weight as deterrence in penal policy. Not surprisingly in view of its remit most of the Gladstone Committee's recommendations were concerned with the amelioration of prison conditions, but it is the sentiments that underlie the Committee's aspirations that were to be its most lasting legacy, summed up in the following:

> There are but few prisoners other than those who are in a hopeless state through physical or mental deficiencies who are irreclaimable. Even in the case of habitual criminals there appears to come a time when repeated imprisonments or the gradual awakening of better feelings wean them from habitual crime. (para. 33)

Raynor and Robinson (2005: 48) amongst others have pointed out that the importance of the Gladstone Committee is disputed, with some seeing it as a radical departure, heralding the approach of the 'rehabilitative ideal', while others see it as a continuation of a penal system primarily concerned with deterrence and retribution, which by reforming the system made it more acceptable. In our view the Gladstone Committee was not itself a major contributor to the rehabilitative ideal, but did lay down some foundations on which others could build.

The Early Twentieth Century: Rising Aspirations

In the previous section we referred to the distinctions between classical and positivist thinking, and between corporal and carceral treatment. The other distinction referred to which contributed to what became known as the 'rehabilitative ideal'[3] was between custody and community. This was something that, although it had its beginnings in the latter part of the nineteenth century, began to manifest itself more as the twentieth century progressed, and became increasingly linked to the development of probation. Here we begin to encounter rehabilitation as something in its own right, rather than as a concomitant of punishment. However it is important to note that the emergence of the probation service which, like penal reform, had its roots in moral and religious zeal was not an isolated phenomenon. There were several elements which came together in the forging of the rehabilitative ideal. For a start there was a reforming ethos in the early years of the twentieth century which favoured such developments. Changes in criminal justice should not be seen in isolation from the wider political and social context of which they are a part, and the first decade or so of the twentieth century saw a reforming administration which introduced progressive measures such as an Education Act, a Children's Act, an Old Age Pensions Act, and an Insurance Act. This administration included a Home Secretary who made one of the more remarkable contributions to the rehabilitative impulse:

> The mood and temper of the public in regard to the treatment of crime and criminals is one of the most unfailing tests of the civilisation of any country. A calm and dispassionate recognition of the rights of the accused, and even of convicted criminals, against the state, a constant heart-searching by all charged with the duty of punishment, a desire and eagerness to rehabilitate in the world of industry all those who have paid their dues in the hard coinage of punishment, tireless efforts towards the discovery of curative and regenerating processes, and an unfaltering faith that there is a treasure, if you can only find it, in the heart of every man [sic] – these are the symbols which in the treatment of crime and criminals mark and measure the stored-up strength of a nation, and are the sign and proof of the living virtue in it. (Winston Churchill, HC Debates, col. 1354, 20 July 1910)

This quotation echoes the sentiments of the Gladstone Committee cited earlier, and suggests that this was a time when there was a willingness to look for the good in people. It reflects a view of human nature which Ward and Maruna regard as fundamental to a good theory of rehabilitation (2007: 34), and stands in contrast to the 'penal populism' that ended the twentieth century, reflected in the comments of a Minister at the Home Office who had responsibility for promoting the changes which led to the Criminal Justice Act 1991:

> Any general theory of punishment would have to start with the recognition that people sometimes freely choose to be bad, by quite deliberately harming other people or their property. There may be explanations, or mitigations, for it but badness is at the root. (Patten, 1991)

The medical contribution

We referred earlier to the institutional convergence of prisons, factories and asylums. But British penal institutions were also shaped by medical practitioners as much as by penal reformers. Ignatieff points out that penal reformers, such as John Howard, were supported by physicians like the Quaker John Fothergill who worked in penitentiaries:

> These doctors regarded the hygienic reform of institutions as a moral, no less than a medical crusade. The sicknesses of the poor were interpreted as the outward sign of their inward want of discipline, morality and honour. (Ignatieff, 1978: 60)

Some of these medical practitioners were also keen to translate their practical experience into academic work, and this helped to contribute to the emergence of the so-called 'medical model' in offender rehabilitation. The academic interests of such people as the psychiatrist Henry Maudsley, who made a study of the criminals who constituted the patients under his care tended to run alongside dealing with individual offenders. Maudsley was succeeded in the twentieth century by others, such as Hamblin Smith (a prison doctor whose interest was in the psychiatric assessment of inmates), Norwood East (who undertook an experiment in psychological therapy at Wormwood Scrubs prison in the 1930s), and Trevor Gibbens at the Institute of Psychiatry (who had a particular interest in the psychology of young delinquents).

Garland (1997) has suggested that the development of British criminology can be seen as having several 'streams'. Norwood East represented the mainstream of medico-psychiatric criminology. A more radical offshoot of this was the clinical psychoanalytic school centred on the Institute for the Scientific Treatment of Delinquency (ISTD) set up in 1932, which had close links with the Tavistock Institute. A rather different stream was that initiated in 1913 when Charles Goring published *The English Convict: A Statistical Study*. This was the first work to put forward a conception of criminality as normal rather than pathological, but it did not initially have much influence. Its detractors, such as W. C. Sullivan, medical superintendent at Broadmoor, argued that clinical rather than statistical methods were the only reliable basis for policy. It was Goring, however, who laid the foundations for the kind of statistical prediction studies which later underlay the work of the Home Office Research Unit. A third stream of development was what Garland describes as 'the 'eclectic', multifactorial, social-psychological' research exemplified by Sir Cyril Burt in his 1925 study *The Young Delinquent*.

The 1950s saw the founding of the *British Journal of Delinquency* (now the *British Journal of Criminology*), which initially had a predominantly medical emphasis. In 1955 a special number of the journal contained papers presented at a Symposium on Predictive Methods in the Treatment of Delinquency, held at the Medical Society of London. An article in this issue by Edward Glover, one of the leading criminologists of the time and an editor of the journal, shows how firmly crime was associated with pathology. He explained that to people like him notions of recidivism and the prediction of recidivism were 'redundant, misleading and tendentious', and that they were more used to thinking in terms of relapse. Glover went on to say:

> There is no more reason to describe the symptoms of pathological delinquency as recidivism than to say that tubercular symptoms which persist beyond the average time range in spite of various measures of treatment are signs of recidivism. It would be equally absurd to describe the victim of a skin disease as a recidivist because his rash continued after tentative steps had been taken to control it. (Glover, 1955: 121)

The Symposium papers clearly reflect a difference between those with a psychiatric background, such as Glover, and those like Leslie Wilkins, who brought a more sociological perspective to bear on criminological inquiry. In the same year publication of *Prediction Methods in Relation to Borstal Training* (Mannheim and Wilkins, 1955) by the Home Office Research Unit saw the beginning of the process of evaluating the effects of training and treatment. This raised questions about whether the results achieved by borstal training were anything more than a reflection of the selection procedure. It was this kind of analysis which in due course undermined the treatment ideology. The late 1950s also saw the formation of the British Society of Criminology as a breakaway from the ISTD's dominance by psychiatry and psychoanalysis. Garland has described the scientific criminology that developed in Britain between the 1890s and the Second World War as 'heavily dominated by a medico-psychological approach, focused upon the individual offender and tied into a correctionalist penal-welfare policy' (1997: 44). This approach flourished during the 1920s and 1930s and was at its height in the period following the Second World War. It had always had its competitors, and already at the time of its greatest success during the 1950s the seeds of its downfall were being sown. The opening of Grendon Underwood, a therapeutic prison, in 1962, and of the new Holloway prison for women built almost as a secure hospital (Rock, 1996), could be regarded as the high points of the rehabilitative ideal, but they were also amongst the last fruits of the traditional treatment approach in British penal policy.

Rehabilitation in the community

In describing the medico-psychological approach to the rehabilitation of offenders we have briefly scanned through the late nineteenth to mid-twentieth century, so it is time to return to the development of a community-based response to offenders and the emergence of the Probation Service, which itself contained quasi-medical features.

There are indications of people being released from court on some form of condition of behaving themselves prior to the nineteenth century (Vanstone, 2004). Alternatives to punishment were being used in North America in the early nineteenth century, and the legal basis for probation was developed in Massachusetts in the 1860s. In Britain some individual magistrates in Warwickshire in the 1820s sought to temper the harsh penalties then imposed by giving young offenders a nominal day's imprisonment, after which their parents and employers were to supervise their behaviour to ensure they did not return to court. The Probation Service had its roots in the work of Church of England Temperance Society missionaries who started working in what were then Police Courts in the 1870s. This work was undertaken on a voluntary basis initially, first in London, then elsewhere. To start with, probation was associated with releasing offenders under recognisance to be of good behaviour. Early work included investigations, recommendations to the courts, home visiting and matrimonial conciliation, but soon involved prison after-care as well. Alcohol played a large part in the lives of those with whom the early Police Court missionaries worked, and this formed the focus of much of their work. The role of the missionaries resulted in the development of probation being seen as a mixture of humanitarian concern and religious commitment. However, Vanstone suggests that there was more to it than this and that, as we have indicated above, penal developments need to be seen in their wider social and political context. Vanstone argues that 'the concept of probation and its practice is best understood within a synthesis of the influences and pressures (political, social and cultural) that were dominant at the end of the 19th century and the beginning of the 20th century' (2004: vii). Vanstone is referring here to a fear of widespread public disorder during late Victorian times, and a worry that repressive penal conditions might prompt such disorder.

In 1887 the work of the Police Court missionaries received their first official recognition in the Probation of First Offenders Act, which enabled courts to release offenders 'on probation' to the missionaries. This was followed in 1907 by the Probation of Offenders Act, which provided a statutory basis for probation work to replace the use of recognisance. But the Act's essentially permissive nature meant that the appointment of officers and use of probation developed very unevenly. The service was still only partly funded by public money, and at this stage much of the work done by officers was concerned with social factors, such as finding homes and jobs for offenders.

The after-care of prisoners by probation officers developed as a result of the Prevention of Crime Act 1908, which also established borstal institutions, with a period of licence to follow training. The setting up of a Departmental Committee of the Home Office in 1922 to consider the 'Training, Appointment and Payment of Probation Officers' was followed by the Criminal Justice Act 1925, subsequently amended by the Criminal Justice (Amendment) Act 1926. Following this Probation Committees were set up on a local basis. At least one probation officer had to be available to every Petty Sessional Division, and rules were introduced which governed the appointment and conditions of probation officers. These developments meant that probation moved from being something whose use had been permitted and encouraged, towards something that was increasingly regulated, with officers' duties being progressively more defined, and the Home Office beginning to play a greater role.

The use of probation increased during the 1920s and 1930s, extending to more matrimonial work, to acting as guardians *ad litem* in adoption cases, and to the supervision of people who failed to pay their fines. During this time also there was an important shift in the approach of probation work, away from the moral and material well-being of offenders and towards the treatment of individuals. This period, running between the 1930s and 1960s, is described by McWilliams as moving from the missionary phase of special pleading to the 'diagnostic phase' of probation work, and it is particularly important because this was the time when the medical model of offending became fully developed. The basis for probation work shifted from metaphysics to science, the status of the offender changed from 'sinner' to 'patient', and the social enquiry report was 'transformed from a special plea for mercy to an instrument of objective professional appraisal' (McWilliams, 1986: 241). King describes the change as follows:

> The growth of other social services and the improvement of social conditions towards the end of this period (the 1930s) gradually made the old emphasis on work to deal with drunkenness and sheer poverty less necessary.... Interest in the medical and psychological aspects of crime and social inadequacy was growing fast.... This brought an increased emphasis on the importance of the personal and mental factors in delinquency and its treatment as opposed to the purely environmental.... The importance of diagnosis was increasingly recognised, and the gradual change in the attitude to treatment, once started, was to play a growing part in determining the nature of probation work in future. (1964: 22–3).

A Departmental Committee of the Home Office was established during 1934–36 to undertake a wide-ranging review of social services in courts of summary jurisdiction. This Committee reviewed the whole position of probation at the time, proposing an official system of inspection of the work of probation officers and considering the organisation of the Service and the appointment and training of officers. It also proposed that the increasing demands being made of the Service were such that it should now become a full-time public service and the remaining missionaries, selected and paid for by voluntary societies, were to disappear. Moreover, the use of recognisance as a basis for probation, without proceeding to conviction, was felt to be unsatisfactory and was to be replaced by a legal order 'which nevertheless should preserve the valuable element of "consent" which distinguished probation from all other forms of treatment of offenders' (King, 1964: 25).

Joan King's book, *The Probation Service* (1958 and 1964) epitomises the mid-twentieth century casework model of probation and the 'treatment model' in general. However, King starts her chapter on the Principles and Methods of Social Casework with the recognition that, 'Social work, being concerned with social ills, is an expression both of society's altruism and society's fear' (1964: 51). Casework is based on 'social diagnosis' and 'the interview is the medium through which case work operates' (1964: 84). King stresses the importance of early childhood – 'the client, for his part … finds himself in a somewhat dependent position which reminds him of childhood experiences'[4] (1964: 60) – and the close relationship between casework and psychotherapy (1964: 58). The early work of the missionaries and Probation Service included responding to offenders' material well-being, but King notes that with the advent of the welfare state to assist with material needs there came an opportunity to concentrate on the inner person, enabling clients to get a clearer picture of themselves and develop insight into their behaviour. King sees probationers as in one respect little different from non-offenders, noting that 'people come to the attention of caseworkers for a wide variety of reasons and with many differing problems', but probationers are different to the extent that 'the same man might come to the attention of the probation officer because he had resorted to crime in a mistaken attempt to solve his problems' (1964: 64). As a means to rehabilitation the casework model is based on an underlying theory that probation officers 'have to work with those whose consciences are defective as a result of their early experiences' (1964: 76). This model held sway for several decades during the twentieth century and was at the core of the rehabilitative ideal.

Although the modern probation service could be said to have been largely established by the time the Second World War arrived, changes have continued up to the present. For example, until the Criminal Justice Act 1991 offenders were given a probation *order*, which was imposed in place of a sentence. The 1991 Act made probation into a sentence in its own right, and paved the way for the setting of nationally required standards of work. Subsequently, section 38 of the Crime (Sentences) Act 1997 removed the necessity to obtain an offender's consent to probation and other community sentences. Although these changes tended to increase further the extent to which probation was becoming a centrally regulated service, this was not new, but something that had been an element in the development of the service throughout its history. We shall take up the story of more recent developments in the next chapter.

The Late Twentieth Century: Falling Aspirations

Before going further it should be noted that by the mid-twentieth century the notion of rehabilitation had become very much identified with the treatment model, so much so that the terms 'treatment' and 'rehabilitation' have often been used interchangeably. This is an unfortunate association because, as we explained in Chapter 1, rehabilitation implies so much more than individualised treatment. While the idea of rehabilitation prospered in the early part of the twentieth century through this association, it suffered subsequently because of it. The latter part of the 1960s and the 1970s saw the treatment model coming under attack from several directions: theoretically, ethically and empirically. Most attention has tended to focus on the last of these, particularly on certain well-known and frequently cited studies, but this attention tends to overshadow the fact that the empirical findings reveal the flawed theoretical basis of the medical model. A criminology dominated by those running the system was being challenged at a theoretical level by Becker (1963) and other labelling theorists (e.g. Matza, 1969), and by the 'new' criminologists (Taylor et al., 1973; 1975). Apart from critiques of the disease analogy, a frequent theme of this era was that, because the treatment approach focused on changing the individual, a criminology associated with it effectively operated in the service of the state and neglected the need for change in society.

Alongside this was a growing disquiet about the implications of a clinically based approach for the institutions of justice. While formal sentencing was clearly in the hands of the courts, the logic of a treatment approach was that people should be 'treated' until they got 'better'. As a consequence the executive (as opposed to the judicial) arm of criminal justice had considerable discretion regarding the nature and extent of a particular penal disposal. In the early 1970s the American Friends Service Committee (1971) challenged the assumptions underlying treatment ideology, and criticised it both on the grounds that it was based on a determinist model of human behaviour, and because of its frequent association with injustice and neglect of the rights of the individual. This focused in particular on indeterminate sentencing, which often led to people being detained for longer periods than their offences warranted, on the basis that they were undergoing a form of therapy: 'The concept of individualisation has been used to justify secret procedures, unreviewable decision making, and an unwillingness to formulate anything other than the most general rules or policy' (1971: 40). The rationale was that the length of treatment should be decided by individual needs and individual responsiveness to it, and this could not be determined in advance. However, whereas a sentence was announced in a public forum where all the information was available for scrutiny and according to due legal process, subsequent decisions which prolonged incarceration and other forms of 'treatment' were often taken without such public scrutiny and due process: a prisoner who did not co-operate could be portrayed as not responding to treatment. This was more of an issue in the USA, where indeterminate sentencing was more common, than elsewhere. But even as the effectiveness of treatment was coming under attack in the 1970s, the Butler Committee (1975) was proposing a new form of indeterminate, 'reviewable' sentence for England and Wales for 'dangerous' offenders, and an important element of the parole system centred on whether the prisoner had demonstrated change or willingness to change.

In the UK the main custodial sentence affected by indeterminacy was that of borstal training, although the indeterminate element of the sentence was limited, so that young offenders aged between 15 and 21 served a minimum of six months and up to two years, the actual date of release being determined by the Home Secretary 'as soon as he is satisfied that the objects of the training have been achieved' (Home Office, 1971, para. 107). Nonetheless, the consequence of the concerns raised by the American Friends Service Committee report and others (von Hirsch, 1976) was to draw attention to numerous instances where doctors, social workers, and other professionals took executive decisions which directly or indirectly affected people's freedom and autonomy without being able to be effectively challenged. This happened because the treatment approach was imbued with notions of paternalism and authority, of 'doctor knows best'. The challenge to the treatment approach was part of the breakdown of such assumptions. However, it was the interpretation of the results from a number of empirical studies that proved most conclusive in dislodging the treatment model from its position of pre-eminence, and it is to some of these that we now turn.

'Nothing works'

During the 1960s a team of researchers undertook a review for the New York State Governor's Committee on Criminal Offences to assist the planning of rehabilitative programmes. It looked at 231 studies reported between 1945 and 1967. However, the conclusions the review came to were more uncomfortable than the Committee had anticipated; so much so that publication was delayed for some time. Eventually one of the research team published a journal article that proved to be a watershed for the treatment approach, and consequently for the rehabilitative ideal (Martinson, 1974). The article's broad conclusion that 'nothing works' became synonymous with a way of characterising the treatment/rehabilitation approach for a generation. The article looked first at various types of intervention in custodial institutions, including education and training, individual and group counselling, medical treatment (drugs and surgery), the 'therapeutic' environment, and the length and security of imprisonment. Martinson also considered non-institutional programmes, including psychotherapy, probation and parole, and intensive supervision. He concluded that, while programmes in the community did not 'work' in terms of reducing offending, at least most did not make things worse,[5] and they cost less than prison.

If nothing works, what are the implications? Martinson suggested that there were three possible considerations:

1 flawed methodology – some treatment programmes may be working to some extent, but research was not capable of identifying this;
2 flawed treatment – the programmes were not yet good enough;
3 flawed theory – this would be the case if crime was a social phenomenon rather than a disease.

Martinson concluded by suggesting that this left a deterrent strategy as the apparently best option, but that since at that time relatively little was known about the efficacy of deterrent effects, more studies were needed.

Martinson's article has been criticised over the years on a number of grounds. One of the main ones is that the study used a very limited measure of recidivism as the criterion of effectiveness, looking simply at whether or not reconviction had occurred, rather than at the nature of any reconviction. Arguably if someone was reconvicted of a lesser crime than previously, or the treatment intervention was followed by a longer period of non-offending than was the case prior to intervention, it could be said to have had some effect. The study has also been criticised on the basis that by the time it was published the studies on which it was based were so out of date as not to be relevant to the kinds of things that were happening by the mid-1970s. It has also been suggested that Martinson quite simply overstated the case and failed to distinguish that there were promising programmes that were worth consider-ing further. Related to this is the further point that some things may have worked for some offenders, and that the work by Martinson and others failed to distinguish this differential effectiveness (Palmer, 1975).

In the UK also there had been some investment in evaluating the effective-ness of measures for dealing with offenders. As mentioned earlier, the Home Office Research Unit had begun to consider questions related to treatment effectiveness. With growing attention focusing on 'alternatives to custody', an important question was whether certain kinds of intensive community based treatment, of the kind that were needed for those who might otherwise go to prison, would work. Shortly after Martinson's work was published the results of a Home Office Research Unit study which examined the effects of an inten-sive form of probation supervision was produced (Folkard et al., 1976).

The 'intensive probation' examined in this study was quite intrusive, provid-ing intensive practical intervention in the family, work and leisure situations of probationers. Such a high degree of intervention in itself raises questions about whether there are limits to the extent to which intrusion in various aspects of a person's life in the name of rehabilitation can be justified, but this tended to be accepted at the time as part of the prevailing positivist orthodoxy. The 'IMPACT' study (Intensive Matched Probation After-Care and Treatment) was conducted in four areas on males aged 17 and over, randomly allocated to experimental and control groups during 1971–72, with approximately 500 young males in each of the experimental and control groups. The findings were consistent with Martinson's conclusion that no general treatment effect could be demonstrated, but not inconsistent with Palmer's (1975) view that some pointers could be provided to suggest differential effects for different types of offender. The researchers looked for interaction effects, i.e. whether things like social back-ground and personality variables affected outcomes. A personality inventory (the

Mooney Inventory) and pre-trial assessment of criminal tendencies did show a tendency to discriminate: there was some indication (though not statistically significant) that offenders assessed as having low criminal tendencies and more personal problems did better in intensive treatment.

Around the same time the Home Office published a study (Brody, 1976) which like that by Martinson and his colleagues was a review of existing work, and covered many of the same studies. However, the focus was more broadly on *sentencing* policy than specific forms of treatment. Its findings reinforced the rapidly developing 'nothing works' ethos, but Brody also said that some kinds of treatment seemed to work for certain offenders: intensive counselling and supervision were mentioned for example (Brody, 1976: 40). This again underlines the importance of interaction effects – 'the matching of appropriate treatment to different types of offender' (Brody, 1976: 41).

Empirical studies undoubtedly played a major part in the demise of rehabilitation (as embodied in the treatment model) as a central plank of criminal justice policy. But as we have already explained, they were not the only factor involved, and by the late 1970s in the UK and the USA the political tide was turning against such reformist ideology. Garland has suggested that:

> Perhaps we should see the collapse of faith in rehabilitation as being literally that: not a reasoned criticism, not an adjustment to negative finding, but something akin to a stockmarket crash. That confidence in the system could so suddenly collapse in this way suggests that the structural underpinnings of the system were already seriously eroded. (2001: 69)

The collapse can also be seen in relation to the political context of the time (Mair, 1991). The studies referred to came out in the mid-1970s, at a time when a Labour Government with a small minority was encountering economic and other difficulties, unemployment was rising, and trade unions were proving to be a problem. It was possible for those on the political right to characterise this as part of a wider social malaise affecting the UK and Western society in general. The rehabilitative ideal was part of a broader liberal ideology, and its failure could be seen as a weakness in the social fabric of the time (Cavadino et al., 1999). Consequently by 1979 it was possible for the Conservative Party to be making an issue out of law and order, something that had not happened to any great extent previously. There was a call for a return to a stricter, more authoritarian approach, epitomised by the Shadow Home Secretary, William Whitelaw's promise of the re-introduction of tougher regimes in detention centres for young offenders, generally referred to as the 'short, sharp, shock'.

After 'Nothing works'

The decline of rehabilitation as the central focus of penal policy had a considerable impact on criminal justice. Kuhn (1970) describes how, in certain conditions a prevailing paradigm can be replaced by another paradigm, with far-reaching consequences. But in the case of the rehabilitative ideal and the treatment model there was no alternative paradigm waiting in the wings, and this was recognised at the time: 'It is abundantly clear that there is no adequate overarching penal theory to replace the collapsed rehabilitative consensus of fifteen years ago' (Bottoms, 1977: 91).

There was then no single initiative or school of thought that was ready to move unequivocally into the gap in criminal justice policy left by the virtual demise of the treatment model. Instead, several developments occurred, although not necessarily as direct and explicit responses to 'nothing works'. Some of these developments involved a shift of emphasis towards functions of sentencing other than rehabilitation, while others centred more on what needed to be done regarding crime control if measures to reduce offending amongst known offenders could not be relied upon to work.

One response to 'nothing works' was the idea that even if imprisonment could not provide an effective solution to offending, at least it could prevent the offender from committing further crimes during the period of his or her incarceration. This is known as 'containment' or 'incapacitation' (Tarling, 1979). Although this view had a certain popular appeal, it has been pointed out that 'incapacitation is impossibly open-ended as a general principle of criminal punishment' (Zimring and Hawkins, 1995: ix). Furthermore, much depends on incarcerating the right group of people. Incapacitation assumes that a high proportion of the crimes that would otherwise be committed are prevented by being able to lock up those who would have committed them. It is at least possible that a high proportion of offences are committed by people who never get caught or who, if caught, would be unlikely to offend again. For example, Van Dine et al. (1977) found in a study that they conducted that over two-thirds of their sample were first offenders, and therefore many offences would not have been prevented by imposing incapacitating sentences at a previous conviction. Pease and Wolfson (1979) point out that the assumptions on which studies of incapacitation are based are therefore critical.

The appeal of incapacitation was also restrained, for a time at least, by the realisation that massive amounts of money would have to be spent on locking people up to have even a modest impact on offending rates (Tarling, 1979). Nonetheless, incapacitation attracted some support in the USA (Shinnar and Shinnar, 1975). But even there the impact was limited, as research on incarceration in California found (Zimring and Hawkins, 1995), and an American commentator pointed to the short-sighted nature of the policy:

> To say that we are winning the war on crime because we've had to put everyone in prison, in short, is like saying that we're winning the war on disease because we've had to put everyone in hospital. (Currie, 1996:10)[6]

Another response to 'nothing works' was to argue for the greater use and development of non-custodial sentences for certain offenders, on the grounds that if everything was equally ineffective, then at least non-custodial methods had the advantage of being much cheaper (Shaw, 1980).[7] It was in this context that a number of new 'reparative' penalties were introduced, in which the emphasis was not on trying to change offenders, but rather encouraging them to make amends for the harm caused by their offending. These measures included the introduction of compensation orders (involving the offender making financial reparation to his or her victim) and of indirect reparation in the form of the community service order, requiring offenders to perform unpaid work in the community.

Although no more a replacement for the treatment paradigm than any other development, another policy pursued in the wake of 'nothing works' was to combine different approaches to dealing with offenders by, on the one hand punishing and incapacitating very serious offenders as much as possible, while on the other hand developing more limited forms of non-custodial measures for the less serious offenders: a *bifurcated* approach towards dealing with offenders. In 1977 Tony Bottoms explained what he referred to as 'the renaissance of dangerousness' in the context of the 'decline of the rehabilitative ethic' (Bottoms, 1977). In such a climate he suggested that it was not surprising that there should be a 'switch of attention from treatment to prevention and containment, with a particular emphasis on the notion of dangerous offenders'. This prompted the emergence of a bifurcation in penal policy 'between, on the one hand, the so-called "really serious offender" for whom very tough measures are typically advocated, and on the other hand, the "ordinary" offender for whom, it is felt, we can afford to take a much more lenient line' (Bottoms, 1977: 88). The consequence, Bottoms suggested, would be a penal policy in which there were the 'mad' and the 'bad', against whom we wish to take serious action, and the 'rest', for whom 'situational' theories of crime, relating to poverty and bad housing and so on are appropriate, for whom we are prepared to reduce penalties. It was in respect of this latter group, Bottoms argued, that we could expect to see continued efforts at rehabilitation – albeit not necessarily of a variety with much in common with the discredited 'treatment model'. In the next chapter we shall consider the extent to which rehabilitation continued to be a focus of work with prisoners and those serving community sentences, and some of the ways in which ideas and approaches associated with rehabilitation shifted, developed and changed focus after 'nothing works'.

Conclusion

In this chapter we have seen that the belief that a major part of the response to crime should be to rehabilitate individual offenders emerged in the latter part of the nineteenth century, and reached its peak around the middle of the twentieth century. It was then challenged theoretically, ethically and empirically, leading to the simplistic conclusion that 'nothing works'. This created a vacuum that led to various other policy options being explored, although nothing quite occupied the central role in criminal justice policy that the rehabilitative ideal had achieved. Nonetheless, the rehabilitation of offenders never disappeared from the agenda, and in later chapters we consider the ways in which rehabilitation developed, adapted, and ultimately survived – albeit in an irrevocably changed penal and political context.

Questions to Consider

1 Why did the rehabilitation of offenders become so closely associated with the medical model?
2 What are the main weaknesses or criticisms of the treatment model?
3 Is the criminal justice system better off without the 'treatment' of offenders?
4 Was the conclusion that 'nothing works' well founded?
5 Can and should offenders be given rehabilitative sentences?

Suggested Further Reading

Other accounts of the emergence and development of rehabilitation can be found in Cavadino and Dignan (2007), Garland (1985, 2001), Raynor and Robinson (2005). For a more detailed consideration of the medical model of crime see Gerry Johnstone's book *Medical Concepts and Penal Policy* (1996). Raynor and Robinson (2005: Chapter 4) contains a fuller disucussion of the theoretical weaknesses of the medical model.

Notes

1 It is useful to distinguish between the commonly used term 'reformers', which here refers to those who sought to improve conditions, and the reform of individual offenders.
2 Cited in Ignatieff, 1978: 117–8.
3 A term first coined by Allen, 1959.
4 The book refers to the probationer as 'him' throughout.
5 Although he also cited several programmes that did (Martinson, 1974: 39–40).
6 As this quotation indicates, the medical analogy did not die out altogether.
7 As with other developments the decline of the rehabilitative ideal was not the only factor involved; prison overcrowding and unrest within prisons also played their part.

THREE

Delivering Rehabilitation: Custodial and Community Contexts

Introduction

In this chapter we consider the extent to which prison and community sentences play a role in rehabilitation. We also look at the work of independent agencies, commonly referred to as the Community and Voluntary Sector (CVS). The work of therapeutic communities is also considered, using a prison-based example (Grendon Underwood) and a community-based example (the Phoenix House programme for drug addicts).

This may look like a wide range of topics for a single chapter, but the underlying theme is the settings in which rehabilitation occurs, and this inevitably raises the question of just how important is the setting in which rehabilitation takes place to its success. At first glance it may also appear that there is a spectrum here, ranging from incarceration at one extreme, where rehabilitation seems to be at its most problematic, to the therapeutic community at the other, where rehabilitation is the main focus. However, we would argue that each of the settings described can contribute to the process of rehabilitation.

Rehabilitation in the Context of Prison

The purpose of prison

As mentioned in Chapter 2, the prison system we are familiar with today has not always been in existence, and only came to be one of the main ways of dealing with offenders just over two hundred years ago. Historically the legal functions have been custodial, coercive and punitive (Morgan and Liebling, 2007: 1107–8). The *custodial* function is that of holding a person where necessary pending trial and sentence. A person may be held *coercively* in order to get them to comply with a court order, most often these days because they have defaulted on payment of a fine. But the most common function is *punitive*, as a result of conviction for an offence. Although prison tends to be thought of primarily as a punishment, sentences of imprisonment have been considered in modern times to have several purposes: retribution, deterrence, incapacitation, and rehabilitation. Alexander Paterson, a reforming Prison Commissioner, best known for having pronounced that 'Men come to prison *as* a punishment, not *for* punishment', also said that:

> In order to afford anything in the nature of permanent protection, either the prison must keep the offender within its walls for the term of his natural life, or it must bring such influence to bear upon him while in custody that he will, on the day of his discharge, be an honest, hard-working and self-controlled man [sic], fit for freedom, and no longer an enemy of society. (Paterson, 1951: 24)

Which of the four purposes referred to above is accorded the highest priority will vary depending on the prevailing penal philosophy of the time, and there has been much debate about the way in which prison operates.

At the time during the twentieth century when the rehabilitative ideal was at its strongest the treatment and training potential of prison was enshrined in what was then Rule 1 of the Prison Service, which advocated prisons as a place where inmates were encouraged towards the leading of 'good and useful lives'. The system of parole was also very much part of this conception of prison, with its notion that release should in part depend on the extent to which an offender had responded positively to efforts to reform him or her. At the high point of the rehabilitative ideal the 'treatment model' was expressed most clearly in the UK prison system during the 1960s by the building of Grendon Underwood prison, described later in this chapter, and the planned conversion of Holloway, the main prison for women in Britain, into a secure psychiatric establishment. Rock describes how it was intended to convert the old Holloway into a new establishment 'to be arrayed as a therapeutic continuum, a string of small, linked, flexible spaces that would plot a moral career for the inmate' (Rock, 1996: 9). As a result of numerous delays the project was not completed until 1985, by which time a change in the penological climate meant that 'a collection of special therapeutic spaces' was used instead for the purposes of control, containment and discipline.

As elsewhere the loss of confidence in the rehabilitative ideal during the 1970s led to a re-appraisal of the role of prisons, and this culminated in the work of the May Committee (1979) towards the end of the decade. In their evidence to the May Committee, King and Morgan (1980) suggested as an alternative to Rule 1 the term 'humane containment'. But the May Committee and others were not happy with this because of its negative implications, suggestive of a policy of 'warehousing' criminals in circumstances that lacked moral justification. May therefore adopted the phrase 'positive custody', but the concept never really achieved any meaningful development in practice. As Morgan put it, '"humane containment" has been judged too stark a prospect, and "positive custody" too woolly' (Morgan, 1994: 901).

In this rather uncertain climate imprisonment made its way through the 1980s, on the one hand extolled (especially for more serious offenders) by a Government of the day which laid claim to 'law and order' credentials, but on the other hand recognised as expensive and ineffective (Windlesham, 1993: 239). Consequently the Home Office began to develop a policy which, by focusing more on the punitive aspects of community-based sentences, would reduce reliance on imprisonment. This subsequently produced the Criminal Justice Act 1991, with its sentencing framework of incremental loss of liberty based on a 'just deserts' approach. As far as prisons were concerned, the period of ambiguity about their role was brought to an abrupt end in April 1990 with the Strangeways riot and disturbances at other prisons, and the subsequent report by Lord Justice Woolf and Judge Stephen Tumim. The report (Woolf and Tumim, 1991) was a largely pragmatic and managerialist response to the circumstances which gave rise to the 1991 riots, and it sought ways to avoid a recurrence, rather than to look for a new creed for the prison system.

The recommendations of Woolf and Tumim covered such matters as closer co-operation between the different parts of the criminal justice system, an enhanced role for prison officers, levels of certified normal accommodation, access to sanitation, and improved standards of justice. Regarding rehabilitation, Woolf and Tumim favoured the formulation 'that the prisoner is properly prepared for his return to society' (para. 10.29), and Recommendation 72 stated that, 'The Prison Service and the Probation Service must work together to achieve the common objective of helping offenders to lead law-abiding lives' (Woolf and Tumim, 1991: 440). But it was emphasised that this 'does not mean a return to what came to be known as the treatment model' (para. 10.34). Under the old model of treatment 'it was thought appropriate to sentence an offender to a custodial sentence for reformative treatment, as if being a criminal was a curative condition.' While an offender should not be sentenced to imprisonment for reformative treatment, Woolf and Tumim did regard it as part of the Prison Service's role to ensure, wherever practicable, that while serving a sentence a prisoner should have the opportunity of 'training'. Woolf and Tumim also referred to the need to give special attention to certain groups of prisoners, including mentally disordered offenders, sex offenders and drug abusers. Although widely regarded as the way forward for the Prison Service at the time, the recommendations of Woolf were not fully implemented (Morgan and Liebling, 2007: 1112–13).

Following the Woolf report, with its emphasis on trying to ensure good standards, good managerial practice and fairness for prisoners, rehabilitation became something that prison could and should address, but the idea was to *facilitate* rather than coerce treatment or training, so that prisoners would have the opportunity of addressing personal shortcomings and social disadvantages associated with their offending. Morgan suggested that on this basis there was 'a real prospect of forging an alliance between "new realism" in sentencing theory and a "neo-rehabilitative" approach to prisons administration, with justice as the underlying leitmotif' (Morgan, 1997: 1150). Rotman had described this as an 'anthropocentric' model of rehabilitation, 'humanistic and liberty centred' as opposed to authoritarian and paternalistic (Rotman, 1990; see also Chapter 1). Garland expressed it in similar terms: 'The inmate is now said to be responsible for making use of any reformative opportunities that the prison might offer' (Garland, 1996: 458). Coyle, a former prison governor, also recognised that a new framework had emerged, based on the recognition that the *act* of imprisonment is always negative, but that every attempt should be made to make the *experience* of imprisonment as positive as possible. This recognised, among other things, the obligation to offer prisoners the *opportunity* to spend time in prison constructively and to prepare themselves for release:

> The concept of 'opportunity' is a recognition that in respect of rehabilitation, that is, of change from within, the prisoner is master of his own destiny. He is a human being with a free will, with rights and with responsibilities. The need is to give the prisoner, and for him to take, as much responsibility as possible for his own life and actions. (Coyle, 1992: 6)

Thus the closing years of the twentieth century saw an emphasis on purposeful activities:

> to reduce crime by providing constructive regimes which address offending behaviour, improve educational and work skills and promote law abiding behaviour in custody and after release. (HM Prison Service, 1999: 8)

This sounds hopeful, but the question remained as to what extent prison is a place where progress can actually be made towards rehabilitation in practice.

Rehabilitative work in prison

Efforts to treat prisoners so that they leave prison with some chance of being rehabilitated in wider society and less likely to reoffend can be seen as taking three main forms. The first is that involving **special provision and places**, such as special hospitals for the mentally disordered, and specialised therapeutic wings and institutions at Wormwood Scrubs in London and Grendon Underwood in Oxfordshire. We consider Grendon in more detail towards the end of this chapter, but it is worth noting here that one of the main issues underlying such special facilities has often been the tension that exists between the therapeutic and custodial functions of such provision.

The second type of activity is that which involves **programmes** designed to address specific issues and offenders, such as anger management, drug misuse and sex offences. These have often involved various kinds of groupwork and cognitive skills training (see further Chapter 7). Following the decline of the treatment model such programmes tended to be rather ad hoc in nature, occurring only where there were initiatives by particular individuals or institutions. But during the 1990s this began to change with more integrated programmes being developed on a wider basis, especially in relation to tackling sex offending and drug misuse.

In 1989 the Prison Department commissioned a survey which showed that 63 prisons in England and Wales were operating some kind of specialist provision for sex offenders, although it was likely that the nature and quality of initiatives at this time was very variable (Sampson, 1994). Following this survey, in 1991, the Prison Service announced the introduction of the Sex Offender Treatment Programme (SOTP) for sex offenders in custody. The programme is designed to challenge offenders' denial of their behaviour. There is a core programme consisting of 200 hours of structured treatment, which can be supplemented by an extended programme for those who present the greatest risk. The success of such treatment is often gauged by changes in offenders' attitudes and cognition, and there were indications that the programme had a positive effect on those who had taken part (Vennard and Hedderman, 1998: 107). However, the results of programmes for sexual offenders have to be regarded with caution since, in the absence of any intervention, sexual offenders are generally reconvicted for sexual offences at a very low rate anyway, and a follow-up period of more than two years is advisable.

Similar developments occurred regarding the treatment of those with drug problems. The Annual Report of the Chief Inspector of Prisons for 1993–94 said, 'The treatment of those prisoners addicted to hard drugs ... leaves much to be desired.' Inspectors at that time did not find any local prison with a regime for drug withdrawal that met the standards applied in NHS drug dependency clinics. Following this report, however, changes came about as a consequence of growing concern about drug use within prison, as well as a more general concern about drug related crime. A 1995 White Paper, *Tackling Drugs Together*, made a commitment to improving the availability of effective treatment for drug misusers in prison, and in the same year the Prison Service published a policy document, *Drug Misuse in Prison*, which aimed to reduce both the demand for, and supply of drugs in prison, and to address the potential for harm reduction. A key part of this strategy was the introduction of mandatory drug testing (MDT), first on a limited basis, and subsequently in all prisons during March 1996. A survey carried out in 2001–2002 came to the conclusion that since testing began in 1996 MDT, along with other strategies, had substantially reduced cannabis use within prisons but had had little effect on the use of heroin (Singleton et al., 2005).

Alongside the development of testing, treatment programmes were also introduced. A programme run by the Rehabilitation for Addicted Prisoners Trust (RAPT) at Downview prison was based on a 12-step approach to abstinence similar to that of Alcoholics Anonymous. Following a study by Player and Martin (1996), the programme was extended to more prisons by the Home Office. However, the research indicated that the programme only attracted and retained the more serious and persistent offenders serving medium term sentences, with long histories of substance abuse (Martin, 1996). In 1996 funding for treatment was increased to £5.1m and 59 establishments were involved (Tilt, 1997). Despite this, concerns about the Prison Service's ability to deal with drug dependent prisoners was voiced by the All Party Parliamentary Drugs Misuse Group. Although the Group was impressed by the Prison Service's efforts at tackling drug misuse, it was in no doubt that, in 1998 at least, provision was far from adequate. The group concluded that 'The throughcare and aftercare of drug misusing prisoners is appalling – there is no other way to describe it' (para. 2.1.iv). It said there was a lack of accessibility to treatment programmes for the majority of prisoners (para. 3.2.vi), and that more treatment programmes were needed in prisons (para. 3.3.ii).

The issue of throughcare was subsequently addressed by research that studied prisoners from 17 establishments who received drug treatment while in prison who were released between October 1998 and January 1999 (Burrows et al., 2000). This found that although half the prisoners concerned were offered help to obtain treatment on release, only 11% had a fixed appointment with a drugs agency; most were given more indirect help, such as the name of a drug service near their home, or being told to contact a probation officer. The study also identified shortcomings in throughcare provision because effective throughcare depends on multi-agency co-operation, but it was not clear which agency has overall responsibility.

The Prison Service's drug strategy was reviewed in May 1998 and it was concluded that 'An ambitious project of expanding drug treatment in prisons has been achieved at a time when population pressures have reached unprecedented levels.' However, 'The monitoring of in-treatment progress and outcomes was generally poor and measures of change were seldom used' (HM Prison Service, 1998a: 2). The Prison Service published a revised drugs strategy, *Tackling Drugs in Prison* (1998b), and in 1999 the Prison Service launched CARAT (Counselling, Assessment, Referral, Advice and Throughcare). This aimed to provide a range of interventions, starting with an initial assessment on a prisoner's entry into custody, and linking prisons with community agencies in order to ensure continuity of care. Information on prisoners using the

CARAT's services has been collected since April 2002, and the results have been used to strengthen throughcare arrangements, but have also highlighted the need to make greater provision for the needs of crack or poly-drug users and short-term prisoners, and the lack of resources for aftercare (May, 2006). Work relating to drug use amongst prisoners was reviewed in a report summarising the results of seven studies (Ramsay, 2003), which said that although good quality treatment can be effective in reducing drug use and reoffending, treatment needed to be tailored to individual need, to be of adequate duration, and to be followed up with high quality aftercare.

Aside from programmes addressing problems such as sex offending and drug misuse, prisons also benefited from the implementation of the 'What Works?' agenda by the Labour Government from the late 1990s onwards, which concentrated on cognitive behavioural treatment. Initially the results were promising (Friendship et al., 2002b) but subsequent follow-up research found little difference between those receiving treatment and those who did not (Friendship et al., 2003; Cann et al., 2003). These programmes are discussed in more detail in Chapter 7, but the net result was that CBT programmes for the general prison population (as opposed to sex offenders) could not be shown to have been effective in reducing reconviction rates. The research did, however, suggest that this could change if various factors in the way programmes were implemented and studied could be altered. It is also worth noting that these were behavioural initiatives, and their lack of success does not rule out the prospects for other ways of approaching rehabilitation within custodial establishments.

This is therefore a good point at which to refer to the third main area of activity, **social rehabilitation**, which includes the provision of education, training, social skills programmes, and work preparation intended to prepare offenders for when they are released. This is in contrast to what one commentator has referred to as 'therapeutic rehabilitation' (Duff, 2005), and it is important because incarceration in itself creates the need for rehabilitation following release by removing people from society. In doing this they are likely to lose jobs, housing and to have their relationships adversely affected. We consider social rehabilitation in more detail in Chapter 8, but would note here that an important feature of attempts to provide for the rehabilitation of ex-prisoners is the notion of throughcare (which as we have seen has been a particular source of concern in relation to those with drug problems). This is a process which is supposed to begin at the point of sentence and continue through until an offender completes a period on licence following their release. The term 'embraces all the assistance given to offenders and their families by the Prison and Probation Services and outside agencies and ties in with all the training, education and work experience they are given' (HM Prison Service, 1993: 5–6).

Throughcare acquired more significance following the introduction of early release provisions in the Criminal Justice Act 1991, which led to the drawing-up of a national framework for throughcare. This framework set out key through-care tasks required for successful resettlement, which included addressing addictions, budgeting, accommodation, employment problems, problems with reading and writing, relationship and family problems, low self-esteem, lack of relevant training, work experience or qualifications, lack of parenting skills, and discrimination experienced by the offender (HM Prison Service, 1993: 11). Such plans subsequently became part of a wider strategy for prisoner resettlement, with more emphasis placed on 'joined up rehabilitation' (considered further in Chapter 8).

Although custodial institutions have a role to play in the rehabilitation of offenders, it also has to be recognised that they have to contend with powerful countervailing tendencies. Foremost amongst these is the pre-eminent concern with security. This was underlined during the 1990s following an escape by armed prisoners from Whitemoor prison in 1994, followed by the discovery of Semtex explosives at the prison, and the escape of three life-sentence prisoners from Parkhurst prison on the Isle of Wight in 1995. Inquiries were set up to investigate these incidents (Woodcock, 1994; Learmont, 1995) and the result-ing pre-occupation with security made it difficult to pursue more positive endeavours. Cavadino and Dignan suggested that 'following the Woodcock and Learmont reports, the emphasis within prisons seems to be firmly on security at the expense of justice and humanity' (Cavadino and Dignan, 1997: 119), and in his annual report for 1996–97 HM Chief Inspector of Prisons, Sir David Ramsbotham, said:

> While money has been made available to implement recommendations made in the Woodcock and Learmont reports, it has been cut, and continues to be cut, despite the pro-vision of some extra financial resources, from activities designed to help prisoners lead law abiding and useful lives in custody and after release ... In sum, while money and attention have been directed at the security part of the mission, the reverse has been true of the reha-bilitation. (HM Chief Inspector of Prisons, 1998)

The other constraining factor has been the continuing growth in the prison population and consequent overcrowding (Cavadino and Dignan, 2007), which often means that work directed towards rehabilitation is subordinated to efforts to manage the prison population on a day-to-day basis. Speaking at a confer-ence in 2000 the then Lord Chief Justice, Lord Bingham, called for more reme-dial treatment for persistent offenders at a time when only about 3,000 prisoners out of what was then a total population of 66,000 (less than 5 per cent) were involved in treatment and rehabilitation programmes.[1] A population of 48,000 in the early 1990s had risen to 64,000 by the end of the century, and reached 80,000 in 2007. In June 2007 it was reported that two prisoners were preparing a legal challenge because overcrowding meant they had not been able to gain access to courses which they needed to complete in order to persuade the parole board they had addressed their offending behaviour and were no longer a risk to the public.[2] Finally, it has been argued that if prisons are regarded as sites for effective rehabilitation, there is a risk that even more use will be made of custodial sentences than at present. As Nellis (1999) has argued, the notion of prison as a 'positive good' poses a significant threat to the tradition of penal reductionism and diverts attention away from the obvious harm that prison can do.

Rehabilitation in the Context of Community Penalties

Reconfiguring probation from the 1970s

In Chapter 2 we described the early origins of the Probation Service, and its association with the rehabilitative ideal. The demise of the treatment model, with which rehabilitation had become so closely linked, forced a major rethink in the service about the basis for its work. Several attempts were made to develop new models for probation practice. One was proposed by a group of probation officers who advanced the idea of what they referred to as 'Sentenced to Social Work' (Bryant et al., 1978). The 'medical model where the officer is expected to cure the offender's criminality' would be replaced by a clear distinction between the requirements placed on the offender by the court on the one hand, and the offering of services to help the offender (or 'client', as they were known in those days) on the other. It was argued that under such an arrangement the court would have more confidence in the level of supervision and:

> The offender would be treated as a more responsible individual, and by allowing him to choose social work help, the dignity inherent in self-determination would be recognised. (Bryant, et al., 1978: 112)

This 'Sentenced to Social Work' approach was tried briefly over about two years in three different petty sessional divisions in Hampshire with, it was claimed, some success (Coker, 1984). Although it never became the norm for probation service practice, some of the proposals regarding the setting out of the requirements of a probation order were to be found some fifteen years later in the establishment of national standards for probation.

The best known alternative to the treatment model, however, was that put forward in the late 1970s for 'A non-treatment paradigm for probation practice' (Bottoms and McWilliams, 1979). This was based on four key principles:

1 Treatment would be replaced by the provision of practical help for offenders, such as finding accommodation or employment.
2 While the treatment model involved 'an element of pressure', 'the help model obliges the client to make a series of moral and behavioural choices' (Bottoms and McWilliams,

1979: 178). In other words the client has to be an active agent in helping themselves, rather than a passive recipient of treatment.

3   Diverting appropriate offenders from going to prison where this seemed socially unnecessary had been 'a central part of the philosophy and practice of the Probation Service since its inception' (1979: 179). The Service should therefore be prepared to '"hold" many offenders as successfully in the community as in prison, and more cheaply' (1979: 182).

4   Because crime is predominantly social, crime reduction strategies must be social rather than individual. The Probation Service should therefore work with communities to satisfy a traditional expectation by the public that it help to reduce crime, by playing a full role in crime prevention measures (1979: 187).

While Bottoms and McWilliams' principles did offer some guidance, and were used as a basis for probation work in some settings, no overall paradigm or model of probation practice replaced the treatment paradigm. As previously noted, the Criminal Justice Act 1991 brought in a new sentencing framework based more on a 'just deserts' model than on reforming the offender. Hence there was to be progressive restriction of liberty ranging from discharges and financial penalties through community penalties to imprisonment, based first and foremost on the seriousness of the offence, with custody being reserved for the most serious cases. Consequently the sentences that involved the Probation Service – probation, community service orders and a new order enabling a combination of community service and probation – came to be presented as 'punishment in the community'. The Act marked a significant shift for the Probation Service, with less emphasis being placed on the offender's background and individual circumstances, and more on the offence and offending behaviour.

Peter Raynor and Maurice Vanstone, who played an important role in the development of the 'What Works?' programme in the UK (see Chapter 5), also recognised that the new sentencing framework required a re-appraisal of Bottoms and McWilliams' paradigm. They suggested a revised version based on the status of offenders 'as moral agents responsible for their actions' (Raynor and Vanstone, 1994: 399). 'Help' needed to take account of other people, not just the offender. Raynor and Vanstone proposed modifications which 'respect moral agency and individual choice, but recognise that the interests of communities and the needs of victims properly limit the extent to which we can support the freedom of offenders to choose continued offending' (1994: 402). A revised paradigm would therefore look like the final column of Table 3.1.

The approach adopted by Raynor and Vanstone was important because it was not just based on the consequentialist grounds of effectiveness, but sought to incorporate a rights-based approach, which recognised the rights and requirements of various parties: offenders, victims and communities alike. The principles espoused by Raynor and Vanstone were expressed in the STOP programme with which they were associated, which played an important role in the development of 'What Works?'

Table 3.1   Paradigms for probation

Treatment paradigm	Bottoms/McWilliams' non-treatment paradigm (1979)	Raynor/Vanstone's revised non-treatment paradigm (1994)
Treatment	Help	Help consistent with a commitment to the reduction of harm
Diagnosis	Shared assessment	Explicit dialogue and negotiation offering opportunities for informed consent to involvement in a process of change
Client's dependent need as the basis for social work action	Collaboratively defined task as the basis for social work action	Collaboratively defined task relevant to criminogenic needs, and potentially effective in meeting them

Source: derived from Raynor and Vanstone, 1994: 402

The Criminal Justice Act 1991 increased the tendency for probation work to become less welfare oriented and more a matter of supervision of punishment in the community. In this context the probation officer became less of a case worker and more of a case manager, and there were also changes in the nature of probation training. Until 1995 those entering the service trained for a Diploma in Social Work, which was replaced by a Diploma in Probation Studies following in-service training. This was seen by many in the service as turning it from a professional social work qualification to a less demanding vocational course (Home Office, 1995).

Behind these developments lay the belief that probation was a 'soft' option and that the courts and public needed to have 'confidence' in community penalties (Home Office, 1995: para 4.4). This assertion was contradicted by the findings of a MORI survey which concluded that 'Though some [members of the general public] see non-custodial sentences as an essentially "soft" option this view is not accepted by everyone. For the majority, non-custodial sentences have a part to play, mainly because of their rehabilitation potential' (MORI, 1998: 3). Nonetheless the 'soft option' belief prompted the development of initiatives to strengthen the appeal of community sentences to sentencers, within existing legislation. While sentencers responded favourably to the initiatives, they had only a limited impact on sentencing, and there was no evidence that the projects encouraged greater use of community sentences as an alternative to custody (Hedderman et al., 1999: xiv).

The 1990s also saw the rise of 'risk' in probation practice, which by the end of that decade was setting the context for all of the probation service's work (Kemshall, 1998; Robinson, 2003). This focus on risk – specifically the risks posed by offenders to the public – was initially encouraged by the emergence of a 'bifurcated' approach in criminal justice, which we touched upon at the end of Chapter 2, coupled with a growing preoccupation with 'public protection' as an overarching concern. The early 1990s saw the passing of a number of new legislative provisions which defined sex offenders and those convicted of serious violent offences as groups warranting increased levels of control and/or surveillance. These provisions placed new responsibilities on the probation service, in terms of assessing and effectively managing those individuals thought to pose a particular risk of harm to the public. It was in this context that the notion of 'risk management' – arguably a precursor of the term 'offender management' (see below) – first entered probation discourse (Robinson, 2002). But by the mid-1990s revised National Standards governing probation work introduced a new requirement to include a risk assessment in all pre-sentence reports, to include *both* an assessment of risk of harm *and* an assessment of risk (i.e. likelihood) of reoffending (see Chapter 7). By the end of the decade, an assessment of the risks posed by offenders had become the starting point for all of the service's work: including that falling under the general heading of 'rehabilitation'.

There was also discussion during the 1990s about re-organising the Probation Service. Eventually in 2001 what had been 54 relatively autonomous Probation Services run by Probation Committees were replaced by a National Probation Service whose remit was 'enforcement, rehabilitation and public protection'. The question was exactly how those three rather different goals would sit together. Would they each have equal status, or was there an order of priority, and where would rehabilitation end up? The answer to this was pre-empted by another re-organisation.

Rehabilitation in the context of 'corrections'

In 2002 Patrick Carter, a businessman who had chaired a number of Government reviews, was asked by the then Home Secretary to review correctional services in England and Wales. Reporting in 2003 Carter said that 'Despite recent improvements, a new approach is needed in order to break down the silos of prison and probation and ensure a better focus on managing offenders' (Carter, 2003: 1), and that there was a need for different parts of the criminal justice system to work more closely together. This reflected the view of an Audit Commission report in the previous year, *Route to Justice: improving the pathway of offenders through the criminal justice system* (Audit Commission, 2002) which had also highlighted the importance of taking a holistic view of offenders' routes through the criminal justice process. Carter recommended that a National Offender Management Service (NOMS) be established, combining the Prison and Probation Services. The Carter report was quickly accepted (Blunkett, 2004), and NOMS came into existence barely six months later in June 2004, with the intention of providing 'seamless' offender management, so that offenders would have a single 'offender manager' throughout their sentence.

Table 3.2 Criminal Justice Act 2003: requirements and main purposes

Requirement:	Punishment	Reparation	Rehabilitation	Protection
Unpaid work	✓	✓	✓	
Supervision			✓	
Accredited programme			✓	
Drug rehabilitation			✓	
Alcohol treatment			✓	
Mental health treatment			✓	
Residence			✓	✓
Specified activity		✓	✓	
Prohibited activity	✓			✓
Exclusion	✓			✓
Curfew	✓			✓
Attendance centre	✓			

Source: Home Office, 2005: 69

The NOMS reforms also centralised control of probation work with the creation of probation trusts, accountability for which passed from Probation Boards to the Home Secretary (and since 2007 to the Secretary for Justice). Thus, by the time of its centenary the Probation Service had experienced a transition from a voluntaristic, locally based service to being part of a wider, centralised service under the control of the Ministry of Justice. However, while there was increasing emphasis on *managing* offenders and the resources available to do so, research was also emerging which suggested that the personal relationship between offender and probation officer played a crucial role in rehabilitation (Raynor and Robinson, 2005: 155). We discuss this further in Chapter 9.

At around the time the Probation Service was being re-organised, it also had to take on board implementation of the Criminal Justice Act 2003, which defined the purposes of sentencing as 'to protect the public, punish the offender, reduce and deter crime, and reform and rehabilitate the offender'. This created a single community sentence under which twelve conditions would be available. The intention was to allow sentencers to put together community sentences tailored to the requirements of individual offenders. The purposes of the twelve components of the new generic order were specified such that some were explicitly about rehabilitation, while others were not, as is shown in Table 3.2.

A study of the early operation of the new Community Order indicated that it had not changed previous practice, with 'the Community Order appearing to mirror the old community sentences' (Mair et al., 2007: 31).

Assessing the potential for rehabilitation

The series of developments catalogued above raises the question of where rehabilitation fits into the work of what used to be the Probation Service, and how it is addressed. There are a number of considerations. One is that, whereas rehabilitation used to be at the forefront of probation work, it is now one of several tasks that 'offender management' is expected to address, and probably not the highest in the order of priorities. A second consideration is the effect that continual change has had on the service (Hough and Allen, 2006), and in particular on the morale of offender managers and their capacity to focus on rehabilitation. Moreover, as described in Chapter 5, the high hopes of the 'What Works?' initiative championed by many in the Probation Service have not been entirely fulfilled. The positive outlook when 'What Works?' was given governmental backing in 1998 has since been overshadowed by the emphasis on tough sentencing and public protection. At the same time the Probation Service has lost the identity which once characterised it as the organisation that sought to change offenders. On the positive side, the prospects for successful rehabilitation for those who have been in custody may have been enhanced by the concept of a 'seamless' sentence and a closer integration of prison and probation, which *should* mean better communication between the two, and more effective throughcare than in the past.

Rehabilitation in the Context of the Non-Statutory Sector

While dealing with offenders has been seen largely as the responsibility of the state in modern times, since the nineteenth century at least a role has also been played by non-statutory agencies. Some of these are also referred to as voluntary agencies (although they commonly have paid, full-time staff alongside any voluntary workers) and are often registered charities. As we explained in Chapter 2, the Probation Service itself started life as a voluntary organisation. Currently the preferred terminology is the voluntary and community sector (VCS).

Some organisations in this sector have concentrated on a particular area, such as the Apex Trust, which has been primarily concerned with the employment of offenders, and training for employment. Some have concentrated most on acting as a pressure group for penal reform, such as the Howard League, and the Prison Reform Trust. Others, such as the Rainer Foundation[3] and NACRO, have delivered services to offenders. It is also possible to find a mixture of functions being undertaken within a single organisation. For example, the Howard League has run projects for offenders on occasions, and NACRO has also done much to disseminate information to persuade the Government and public of the necessity of taking a positive approach towards offenders. Where such organisations have delivered services to offenders, these have usually been directed at assisting the rehabilitation of offenders.

It is not possible to consider the non-statutory sector in detail here, but the kind of contribution it makes can be illustrated by reference to NACRO, which is the main national non-statutory body concerned with offenders and criminal justice issues. NACRO was founded in 1966 at the time when the Probation Service took over the prison welfare and aftercare work which until then had been carried out by the National Association of Discharged Prisoners' Aid Societies (NADPAS, to which some reference was made in Chapter 2 in the context of the Gladstone Report). This addition to the work of the Probation Service had come about as a result of the recommendations of a report on *The Organisation of After-Care* (Advisory Council on the Treatment of Offenders, 1963). This report emphasised that it would be 'impossible for the probation and after-care service to undertake this formidable task unaided'. The Advisory Council recognised the potential of voluntary effort, and expressed the view that if such potential were to be tapped effectively then NADPAS might well have a part to play as 'a new national voluntary organisation to co-ordinate such effort and stimulate public interest'. Consequently NADPAS became NACRO. NACRO also had a brief to explore new ways of working with offenders and in the 1970s it began to develop pilot schemes in housing, training workshops and education as models which others could follow. During the 1980s, in addition to setting up pilot projects it began to work with other statutory and non-statutory agencies through development initiatives in areas such as juvenile offending, work with offenders from ethnic minority groups, and mentally disordered offenders. It also encouraged the initial development of victim support schemes, and played an early role in the growing field of crime prevention. Indeed, the sub-text under its title bore the inscription 'for the care of offenders and prevention of crime'. NACRO also addressed policy issues by developing research, setting up working parties and producing a wide range of briefing papers and publications.

For most of the twentieth century the work of the voluntary and community sector was seen as supplementing that of the statutory sector, working in areas not covered by statutory provision, and trying out new things that, if successful, could then be integrated into mainstream statutory provision. But over the years the emphasis changed somewhat, with the non-statutory sector becoming more likely to provide services that could be purchased in their own right. In 1990 the Government issued a paper, *Partnerships in Dealing with Offenders in the Community* (Home Office, 1990a), which reviewed the relationship between the Probation Service and what was referred to as the 'independent sector', and from 1991 probation services were expected to allocate up to five per cent (subsequently increased to seven per cent) of their revenue budget to services provided by the independent sector. With the implementation of the recommendations of the Carter review and the setting up of NOMS the situation changed significantly. This new approach to correctional services also envisaged the introduction of the idea of *contestability*, which meant that work with offenders would in future be opened up to market place competition, with the private and voluntary sectors competing alongside probation and prisons to deliver provision to regionally based managers who would become purchasers. Given the changes in probation work since the 1990s and the consequent constraints on their ability to focus on rehabilitation, the voluntary and community sector in many ways became the sector with probably the greatest rehabilitative potential. However, it is possible that in competing to deliver services alongside others, they too will be forced into having to meet criteria that place other priorities ahead of rehabilitation.

Rehabilitation in the Context of Therapeutic Communities

During and after the Second World War it was discovered that military personnel suffering from the trauma of battle could be helped to recover by working together in small groups in a community setting. This discovery gave rise to the final setting we will consider as a context for delivering rehabilitation: the 'therapeutic community'. In contrast to the individually centred psychoanalytic school of treatment, therapeutic communities are based on a social learning model of behaviour. They have several distinctive features, including an emphasis on self-help, usually with intensive group sessions, taking place over an extended period of time, and in circumstances where participants are isolated from outside influences. The aim is to transform the whole person, rather than deal with just a particular problem. Therapeutic communities were adopted as part of a new way of working with psychiatric patients in the 1960s at hospitals such as the Henderson in London, and have also been employed in the treatment of substance misuse. They are resource intensive, and tend to be selective in who goes to them because they require a high level of motivation on the part of the person concerned. For this reason they are not very widespread in the penal system, and are mainly found in relation to offenders with personality problems, or drug and alcohol problems. The two examples we mention below illustrate the rehabilitative work of therapeutic communities in a custodial and a community context.

Grendon Underwood

Grendon Underwood was opened in 1962, and is classified as a category B training prison with certified normal accommodation for 243 adult males. The prison has five therapeutic wings, each holding 40–46 prisoners and an induction wing holding 25 prisoners. Each wing operates as a separate therapeutic community, and the therapeutic environment requires prisoners to stay for a recommended two years. While Grendon has been unique within the prison system as a therapeutic prison, there are therapeutic wings at Wormwood Scrubs, and at Channings Wood and Lindholme for treating drug dependence.

The booklet, *Grendon: a therapeutic prison,* by HM Prison Service (undated) says there are three objectives to therapy at Grendon:

- to help each man improve his self-confidence and sense of worth
- to help each man create positive relationships with others, helping him to move towards greater consideration and concern for the feelings and property of others
- to help each man stop committing crimes.

Therapy at Grendon consists of core procedures, involving small group sessions of up to eight men meeting three times a week, that regularly take place in all the wings, and additional procedures, including psychodrama, life and social skills classes, cognitive skills training, and art therapy which take place from time to time, or only on some wings. There are also meetings to explore issues arising from groups and discuss general community matters.

Grendon receives about 200 referrals a year from other prisons, but by no means all are accepted as suitable. Indeed, there has been some resentment at Grendon's ability to select its inmates. At the time of an inspection in 2006 more than half (59 per cent) of the prisoners in Grendon were serving a life sentence, and the remainder sentences of four years or more. Almost half of the prisoners had committed an offence of violence against the person, 20 per cent sexual offences, and 17 per cent robbery (HM Chief Inspector of Prisons, 2007, Appendix II). In a study measuring psychopathy 26 per cent of the sample studied were classified as psychopaths, higher than previously found in UK prison samples, but 'consistent with the selection criteria for Grendon which emphasise the presence of "personality disorder" or "psychopathy" as a prerequisite' (Hobson and Shine, 1998).

Grendon Underwood has probably been subjected to more research than any other prison. Initial findings on reconviction rates were not encouraging (Newton, 1971; Gunn and Robertson, 1987). Genders and Player (1995) did not attempt to evaluate Grendon in terms of reconviction, arguing that the impact of a specific period of therapy such as Grendon had to be seen in the wider context of the men's careers. Nonetheless, later studies did produce more positive findings on reconviction. Cullen (1994) found that therapy at Grendon was significantly related to lower reconviction rates, that there was a relationship between time in therapy and rates of reconviction, with 18 months appearing to be the threshold for greatest improvement, and that the most positive effect was for those prisoners who left Grendon under parole supervision. Marshall (1997) found that Grendon had been selecting prisoners at higher risk of reconviction, which 'means that previous reconviction studies which have compared Grendon prisoners with the general prison population have not been comparing like with like'. When this was controlled for it was found that those admitted to Grendon had a significantly lower reconviction rate than a comparison group who were not admitted.

Cullen (1998) found that an important consideration was where men went to on leaving Grendon. If they were transferred back into other prisons before release their risk of reoffending rose, whereas Newton and Thornton[4] (1993) found that being released directly into the community from Grendon was related to the avoidance of further conviction. The implication is that the benefits of Grendon are lost when men are transferred to other prisons. As a result a report by HM Chief Inspector of Prisons recommended an expansion of direct release, allowing for 'a gradual weaning from therapy and a gradual resettlement into the community' (HM Chief Inspector of Prisons, 1997, Part A: para. 15).

Grendon sits rather uneasily within the prison system as a whole, and there is tension between its therapeutic needs and the demands of a system that is geared towards other objectives as well and is constrained by limited resources. The prison has undergone a number of reviews and re-appraisals of its role, but as one commentator has pointed out, 'the sole prison which can offer hard empirical proof of its efficacy is Grendon' (Cullen, 1998: 3). HM Chief Inspector of Prisons reports on Grendon, in 2004 and 2006, praised its high standards, but expressed some concern about the lack of attention to resettlement matters. In a report in 2007 HM Chief Inspector of Prisons said 'Grendon is an impressive prison which does remarkable work with some of the most challenging prisoners in the system. Perhaps inevitably the focus on therapy inhibits progress towards some other important resettlement outcomes, and this weakness still needs to be remedied, but the health – and importance – of the prison is not in doubt' (HMIP, 2007).

Phoenix House

The original therapeutic community for drug addicts was Synanon in California where, as with other therapeutic communities, the aim was to transform the whole person, rather than deal just with the drug use. The intention is to construct a new identity, leaving behind the old identity as a drug addict. Consequently, participants are isolated from outside influences as far as possible for a time, and focus on rebuilding their lives through a thorough re-appraisal of themselves, often using intensive group sessions. Following Synanon other communities developed, and during the 1970s Featherstone Lodge in South East London took the name of one from New York: Phoenix House. The early Synanon and Phoenix House regimes were very strict, with rule breaking being treated harshly. But since the 1970s they have become less autocratic, and have expanded their work to include the families of addicts, and have devoted more attention to preparing clients for re-integration into the outside community. The present Phoenix House programme consists of a series of stages. Phase One takes place at the main residential unit and lasts approximately six to eight months. It has three periods. The Induction Period lasts four to six weeks and allows entrants to break away from their previous lifestyle and adjust to Phoenix concepts and ways of working. Following this the 'Tribe Period' is an introspective period during which the resident develops his or her ability to deal with personal responsibilities and challenges. The Interphase Period is seen as a preparation for the final phase of the programme known as re-entry. The resident is encouraged to set an example for new entrants and to start moving towards the outside world again. Phase Two is the re-entry phase during which the person moves towards independent accommodation and practical workshops. This period normally lasts for about five to six months.

In April 1994 the Department of Health established a Task Force to review the effectiveness of services for drug misusers. It commissioned a National Treatment Outcome Research Study, which included residential rehabilitation provision such as Phoenix House. The results for residential rehabilitation showed substantial improvements in many areas of functioning, including reductions in, or abstinence from heroin, reduced levels of injecting behaviour, reductions in health problems, and reductions in criminal activity (Gossop et al., 1998; Gossop et al., 2000). A subsequent study of Phoenix House in Sheffield classified success or failure on the basis of reason for departure from the programme. While most (65%) completed drug detoxification, more than two-thirds (68%) left the programme early or were evicted for failure to comply with the programme's rules (Keen et al., 2001). However, this does not necessarily mean that the programme had no effect on them, and it is worth noting that the residents concerned had been drug dependent for an average of eight years, and the average length of time that they stayed in the programme was over eleven weeks. For those at the 'heavy end' of drug dependence this could represent something of an achievement.

Conclusion

At the start of this chapter we said that the underlying theme was the settings in which rehabilitation occurs, and the importance of the context in which rehabilitation takes place. What we have seen is a mixed picture. On the one hand the institutions of custody and community management have a commitment to rehabilitate offenders in principle, and much worthwhile work does go on in both settings, and with some success. On the other hand rehabilitation has to contend with forces which constantly constrain it. Prisons may not seem like the ideal places to rehabilitate people, but when the rehabilitative ideal was at its strongest they were considered to be almost quasi-medical facilities, and this found its greatest expression in Grendon and Holloway prisons. Rehabilitation clinics and therapeutic communities suggest that often withdrawal from the outside world, both voluntary and involuntary, can be an important stage in rehabilitation, but throughcare is vital. For those whose offences warrant imprisonment, prison may present an opportunity to re-assess and re-build their lives *if the conditions are right*. However, there is every indication that for some time conditions have been far from right. Not only has rehabilitation given way to other priorities, but the penal crisis (Cavadino and Dignan, 2007) has made the implementation of rehabilitative programmes and opportunities difficult.

Probation was once seen as the epitome of rehabilitation, but has increasingly given way to the need to be seen as an instrument of punishment in the community, and at the front line in protection of the public. Neither of these roles necessarily excludes rehabilitation, but they tend to make it something of an optional extra. The voluntary and community sector continue to present perhaps the greatest opportunities for rehabilitative work, but on a much smaller scale, and also need to compete to deliver other demands. In addition to those forces which have restricted opportunities for rehabilitation, the failure of the 'What Works?' initiative to deliver as much as originally hoped has also proved to be a setback. This is discussed further in Chapter 5. Rehabilitation therefore tends to have a marginal role within the statutory offender management services, and where it is more to the forefront, in therapeutic communities and the voluntary sector, they themselves are marginal to criminal justice policy.

Nonetheless rehabilitation does remain on all agendas, as we shall see in the chapter on social rehabilitation. The fact that it rides in the back seat of the criminal justice vehicle in the UK and certain other jurisdictions has been attributed to the neo-liberal penal ideology, which emanates largely from the US (Cavadino and Dignan, 2006), and it is perhaps significant that in the UK the American terminology of 'correctional services' has come increasingly into use. It is probably only with the repudiation of such an ideology that rehabilitation can again become a major force within criminal justice policy and provide the context in which the conditions will be right in the settings where rehabilitation can take place.

Questions to Consider

1 Should rehabilitation be part of the purpose of imprisonment, or should we just concentrate on making prison conditions as humane and positive as possible?
2 Does rehabilitation have a future in the work of 'offender managers'?
3 What role can the voluntary and community sector play in offender rehabilitation?

Suggested Further Reading

A good starting point regarding imprisonment is the chapter on this topic in successive editions of the *Oxford Handbook of Criminology*, the latest of which is by Rod Morgan and Alison Liebling (2007). Another key reference for both custodial and non-custodial penalties is Cavadino and Dignan's *The Penal System: An Introduction* (2007). On Grendon Underwood the book by Genders and Player (1995) is recommended, and the paper by Eric Cullen (1998) for the Prison Reform Trust is also worth reading.

Between 1983 and 1987 *The Howard Journal* published a series of four articles by Bill McWilliams, which cover the development of the Probation Service. The third of these, published in 1986, covers 'The English Probation System and the Diagnostic Ideal'. Peter Raynor's 'Community Penalties: probation, "What Works", and offender management' in the latest edition of *The Oxford Handbook of Criminology* (Raynor, 2007a) covers more recent developments, as does the *Handbook of Probation*, an edited collection by Gelsthorpe and Morgan (2007).

Notes

1 'Jails should offer remedial treatment, says Bingham', *The Daily Telegraph*, 28 January 2000.
2 'Ministers face legal challenge over jails crisis', *The Guardian*, 4 June 2007.
3 In fact the Foundation is the successor to the Church of England Temperance Society Mission. When the Home Office assumed full responsibility for the Probation Service in 1939 the Mission became known as the Rainer Foundation, after the Hertfordshire printer, Frederick Rainer, whose intervention prompted the Church of England Temperance Society into work in the Police Courts. It developed into an organisation providing residential care for young offenders.
4 This study by Newton and Thornton is unpublished. It is cited by Cullen (1998: 9), and the information has been confirmed by personal communication. The research is also cited in 'Grendon: a therapeutic prison', a guide published by HM Prison Service.

FOUR

The Evaluation Context

Introduction: Defining Evaluation

Research relevant to rehabilitation can take various forms. It might, for example, be concerned with investigating the nature of offending in order to understand what factors are most likely to bring about rehabilitation. Second, research might study criminal careers, particularly when and why people stop offending (e.g. Maruna, 2001) in order to understand how rehabilitation might be involved in this process of desistance. However, probably the most common form of rehabilitation related research is that which seeks to *evaluate* the effectiveness of interventions which attempt to reduce reoffending (which is a necessary part of rehabilitation, but as we have explained elsewhere, rehabilitation is more than the cessation of offending). It is this last, evaluation research, that we will be concerned with mainly in this chapter. We will look first at the principles that underlie evaluation, taking in some recent developments in evaluation in criminology generally. We will then focus more on the evaluation of attempts to reduce individual offending.

Evaluation can occur in various contexts (see Crow and Semmens, 2008, Chapter 4 for a fuller discussion of evaluation in criminology). An evaluation study might, for example, look at the effectiveness of crime prevention programmes in certain geographical areas (e.g. Ekblom et al.'s evaluation of the Safer Cities programme, 1996). Alternatively an evaluation might be carried out to look at the impact of a new piece of legislation (e.g. Crow et al., 1996). However, we will be looking at that kind of evaluation which looks at the impact of an intervention on offenders. Whatever form an evaluation takes, the underlying principles are largely the same (although these principles have been much discussed by criminologists in recent years, as we shall see).

We will start by considering what evaluation is. Put simply, *evaluation* is the process of examining whether interventions achieve their desired outcomes. However, the simplicity of this definition conceals much complexity. It is also important to define some other terms commonly used in association with evaluation (and not infrequently confused with it):

- **Aims** are the goals which an initiative or organisation is striving to achieve.
- **Monitoring** is the process of checking what is happening in relation to what an initiative or organisation planned to do.
- **Inputs** are what are put into an initiative, such as time, money, and activities.
- **Processes** are what happen in order to make an initiative occur (also referred to as implementation).
- **Outputs** are the direct results of inputs, such as the number of people who have been involved in the intervention.
- **Outcomes** are the desired and specific results, such as a reduction in offending, a reduction in the amount of burglary, reduced fear of crime, reduced incarceration, reduced costs, and so on. Outcomes should be directly related to aims, and should be based on measurable criteria.

Moreover, in this chapter we will be using terms like 'initiative', 'intervention', 'programme' and 'project'. Intervention and initiative are general terms indicating merely that something is being done. A programme tends to be structured, with specific components. Programmes, such as those based on cognitive behavioural therapy or a residential course of treatment, may involve key ingredients but take place in various locations (a bit like a meal from a McDonald's). A project, on the other hand, in the sense in which we use it is more likely to be specific to a particular location or agency, such as a sports project run by a local organisation. The term 'programme' is discussed further in Chapter 7.

The Experimental Model of Evaluation

The traditional, experimental model of evaluation is based on a simple causal model, as shown in Figure 4.1, and involves three variables:

1 The independent variable – this is the programme, such as cognitive behavioural therapy, or it might be an intervention aimed at improving someone's social circumstances.
2 The dependent variable – this is the outcome that the researcher is interested in, such as whether there is a reduction in offending.
3 Intervening, or extraneous variables – these are variables which might influence the effect of the independent variable upon the dependent variable; for example, something else creeps into the experiment such as the way the therapy is administered, or whether those involved in the intervention have a pre-disposition to be affected one way or the other.

This is a classic experimental model based on natural science methodology, and often used in evaluating new medical procedures. The important thing here is to

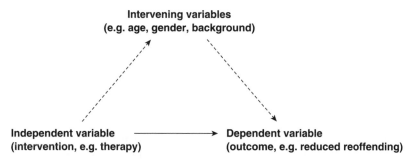

Figure 4.1 Causal analysis in evaluation

try to neutralise the effects of any intervening variables in some way, so that any change in the outcome variable could only have come about as a result of the influence of the intervention. Thus, in a clinical controlled trial some patients, the 'experimental' group, are given the treatment under investigation, such as a new drug, while others, a 'control' group, are not. Their conditions before and after treatment are then compared. It is essential to ensure that like is compared with like, so the experimental and control groups must differ *only* by one being given the treatment and the other not. Consequently, once it has been established who is eligible for treatment, patients are assigned to the experimental and control groups on a random basis – the random controlled trial (RCT). Those allocated to the non-intervention situation usually get something, such as an inert substance, known as a placebo, which mimics a situation where nothing happens. This is sometimes referred to as the OXO model of evaluation (see Figure 4.2).

Here observed measurements are made at time one, before intervention (O_1), and time two, after intervention (O_2), and X represents the intervention.

However, problems arise when it comes to applying such a model in the social realm. First, there can be practical difficulties in applying the model in its pure form. To some extent these can be overcome by what are referred to as quasi-experimental designs (Cook and Campbell, 1979), where statistical analysis is used to take account of possible intervening variables when comparing intervention with non-intervention situations, but this is not as effective as RCT. Where social interventions are concerned, such as programmes for offenders, one also has less control over what has happened in the non-intervention situation. Rarely will nothing be happening; individuals and groups who are not receiving an intervention are quite likely to be experiencing something, and researchers need to take account of what this is. There are also ethical concerns about the use of random allocation, which involves subjecting one group of people to something while denying it to another group. However, there have been exceptions to this. Some years ago a juvenile court in the north of England adopted a system whereby not all delinquents who had been truanting from school were dealt with by the court immediately, but had their cases adjourned for a number of months,

	Before intervention	Intervention	After intervention
Intervention group	O_1	X	O_2
Comparison group	O_1		O_2

Figure 4.2   The OXO Model

during which time their school attendance was monitored. What happened to them subsequently depended on their behaviour during the period of adjournment. This was nicknamed the Damocles experiment, and in order to test its efficacy juveniles were randomly allocated either to be given the Damocles treatment, or to be dealt with in the normal way (Hullin, 1978 and 1985). The procedure was controversial and was eventually discontinued.

During the 1990s American researchers produced a more highly developed version of the OXO model. As a result of reviewing evaluations of crime prevention projects Sherman et al. (1998) developed the Maryland Scale of Scientific Methods as a way of determining how strong the internal validity of each study was. Internal validity is defined as a study's ability to determine cause and effect, while external validity is the ability to generalise the findings of the study to analogous situations. The scale ranked each evaluation study on internal validity, from 1 (weakest) to 5 (strongest). Rating was based primarily on three factors:

1 **Control of other variables** in the analysis that might have been the true causes of any connection between a programme and crime prevention.
2 **Measurement error** from such things as subjects lost over time, or low response rates.
3 **Statistical capability** to detect programme effects (as a result of things like sample size, and the base rate of crime at the outset).

On this basis the researchers produced a five-point scale of evaluation techniques, ranging from simply measuring any change in reconviction for a single programme following intervention, through to the random assignment of groups to intervention and comparison conditions in a number of programmes. Harper and Chitty (2005: 7) produced a revised version of this adapted for reconviction studies, as follows:

Level 1   A relationship between intervention and reconviction
Level 2   Expected reconviction rates[1] compared to actual reconviction rates for the intervention group
Level 3   Comparison group present without demonstrated comparability to the intervention group
Level 4   Comparison group matched to intervention group on theoretically relevant factors, such as risk of reconviction
Level 5   Random assignment of offenders to the intervention and control condition (RCT).

The last is the most powerful way of evaluating impact, but is difficult to do in practice.

While the Maryland Scale refined the basic OXO model, it still considers the random controlled trial to be what is referred to as the 'gold standard' for programme evaluation. The OXO model and the Maryland Scale can be seen as essentially positivist in nature, in attempting to apply the methods of the physical sciences in a criminological context. However, this approach is predominantly outcome-oriented; it is primarily concerned with reconviction rates. To understand why this is a shortcoming we need to explore the relationship between evaluation and theory more fully.

One of the main criticisms of the traditional experimental model is that it is 'black box' research; that is, by being mainly interested in the end products, it pays too little attention to the processes that take place during the course of intervention which make the relationship between intervention and outcome comprehensible. In other words we need to know more than whether something 'works' or not. We also need to know *how* and *why*, and in what *circumstances* something has the effects that it does in order to generalise the results. The danger with the OXO model is that it becomes reduced to a purely technical exercise, forgetting that evaluation needs to be seen in a theoretical context (Crow, 2000). The OXO model represents only part of the total research process. What is missing is the fact that all interventions are essentially a test of a theory. For example, if one is evaluating an employment training programme for offenders with the aim of reducing their likelihood of reoffending then implicit within this is a theoretical proposition about the relationship between employment and criminality. Similarly, a project for drug users designed to reduce drug related offending is based on assumptions about the relationship between drug misuse and crime. A third example might be a project designed to provide sporting activities for young people at risk of getting into trouble, which is likely to encapsulate theories about youthful behaviour and offending.

In referring to theory we are not necessarily envisaging anything profound about the nature of crime and criminality; it is more a case of unravelling the thinking that is informing an intervention. Quite often such theories are not made explicit by the programme itself, or are poorly articulated, and part of the task of the researcher is to explore the theoretical assumptions implicit in any initiative. Seen in this context, therefore, an evaluation is an empirical test of a theoretical proposition, and the results of any evaluation should be seen not simply in terms of 'does it work?', but 'what does this tell us about the theory underpinning the initiative?' Thus:

Theory ⇒ Intervention ⇒ Outcome ⇒ Modified Theory

The OXO model referred to above should therefore really be located within this broader research process. Similar observations have been made by Carol Weiss, who refers to a programme's 'theories of change' (Weiss, 1998). She describes the theory of change as having two components: programme theory and implementation theory. Programme theory refers to 'the mechanisms that mediate between the delivery (and receipt) of the program and the emergence of the outcomes of interest' (1998: 57). It is a set of hypotheses on which people build their plans for a programme, and one of the jobs of the evaluator is to find out what these hypotheses are. Implementation theory refers to the fact that if the programme does the things it intends to do, then the desired outcomes should occur: 'Implementation implicitly incorporates a theory about what is required to translate objectives into ongoing service delivery and program operation' (1998: 58).

Two researchers in particular, Ray Pawson and Nick Tilley, have gone further and during the 1990s mounted a wholesale assault on the OXO model. This resulted in what became known as the 'paradigm wars', involving exchanges in academic journals between Pawson and Tilley on the one hand, and Trevor Bennett and David Farrington of the Institute of Criminology in Cambridge on the other. We will not recount this in detail here (a more detailed summary can be found in Crow and Semmens, 2008: Chapter 4), but in essence Pawson and Tilley suggested that it is necessary to understand a programme's *mechanisms* and the *context* in which it takes place. Pawson and Tilley's solution is based on what they term a 'scientific realist' model of evaluation. For a realist evaluator:

> Outcomes (O) are understood and investigated by bringing to the centre of investigation certain hypotheses about the mechanisms (M) through which the programme seeks to bring about change, as well as considering the contextual conditions (C), which are most conducive to that change. (Pawson and Tilley, 1994: 300)

One of the reasons for the debate between Pawson and Tilley on the one hand and Bennett and Farrington on the other is because it concerns different philosophical approaches to evaluation, hence the reference in one of the articles to the 'paradigm wars' (Pawson and Tilley, 1998: 73). Pawson and Tilley make a distinction between two modes of causative explanation:

(a) 'successionist' causal thinking (more frequently referred to as deterministic causality), which describes a constant conjunction between events ('the action of billiard balls is archetypally describable in these terms'. Pawson and Tilley, 1994: 293). This is the approach, they say, of quasi-experimentation.

(b) the 'generative' conception of causation, which they explain as describing the transformative potential of phenomena, rather like gunpowder whose potential to explode inheres in its chemical composition. This is the approach of the school of thought that they espouse, 'scientific realism'.

One feature that Pawson and Tilley and others have in common is their insistence on evaluation consisting of both process and outcome research, the

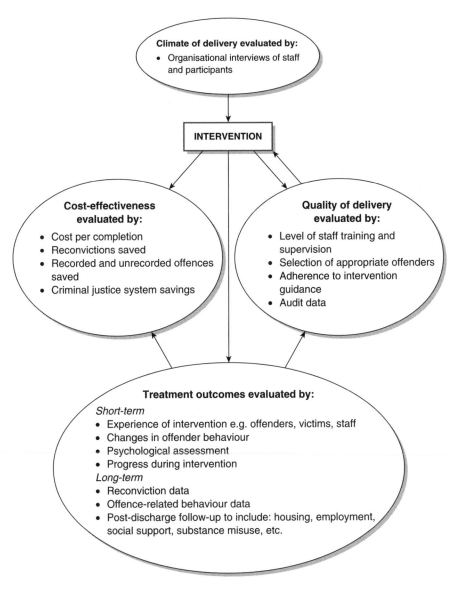

Climate of delivery evaluated by:
- Organisational interviews of staff and participants

INTERVENTION

Cost-effectiveness evaluated by:
- Cost per completion
- Reconvictions saved
- Recorded and unrecorded offences saved
- Criminal justice system savings

Quality of delivery evaluated by:
- Level of staff training and supervision
- Selection of appropriate offenders
- Adherence to intervention guidance
- Audit data

Treatment outcomes evaluated by:

Short-term
- Experience of intervention e.g. offenders, victims, staff
- Changes in offender behaviour
- Psychological assessment
- Progress during intervention

Long-term
- Reconviction data
- Offence-related behaviour data
- Post-discharge follow-up to include: housing, employment, social support, substance misuse, etc.

Figure 4.3 Friendship et al.'s integrated model to evaluate the impact of interventions (*Source*: Harper and Chitty (eds), 2005: 15)

process research being likely to incorporate qualitative components intended to explore programme theories and how programmes are implemented. In an attempt to bring together the various perspectives on evaluation that developed between 1994 and 2004 Home Office researchers produced what they considered to be an integrated model of evaluation for criminal justice interventions (Friendship et al., 2005), which is primarily concerned with the treatment of individual offenders (see Figure 4.3).

This model incorporates some quite specific suggestions for what needs to be done in relation to the various components of the model and, at this point, having looked at some of the issues underlying evaluation designs we go on to consider what these mean in practice for initiatives intended to reduce reoffending and contribute towards rehabilitation. It is hoped that this will help the reader to critically appraise studies evaluating such initiatives.

Evaluating Programmes for Offenders

Programme aims

The first thing to consider is what the aims of any intervention are. This is important because a programme's aims are likely to indicate, among other things, the programme's theoretical basis. What assumptions is it using about the nature of offending, drug addiction, or whatever is being addressed? It is important to emphasise that there always is a theory of some kind, even if it is not clearly set out as such by those who have initiated the programme. Attempting to clarify what the aims of a programme are will also indicate what the appropriate criteria are for assessing its effectiveness. When contemplating the aims of an initiative it is necessary to consider the perceptions of the various parties involved, including the participants themselves. It is not uncommon for officials and senior staff to have one idea of what a programme is about, while those who actually deliver it on the ground interpret the aims rather differently.

The aims of a programme or project are, however, liable to vary in the degree of clarity with which they are articulated. Some projects may set out their aims very precisely, while others refer in rather general terms to things like enabling offenders to lead 'a worthwhile and productive life'. Confusion or lack of clarity in specifying aims may be due to a failure on the part of those responsible for the initiative to articulate the aims clearly, or it could be that they are fudged and deliberately vague because they have to meet the needs and objectives of different groups. A mixture of aims is particularly likely to occur where more than one agency is involved, with one agency having one agenda, while another is more concerned with other goals. The eventual aims of a programme may be a compromise that has come about as a result of a series of negotiations. It is not uncommon to find that initiatives set up to do one thing (e.g. youth work, involving young people in drama workshops, promoting social or educational skills) claim to be reducing crime because that is how they can best get funding. Looked at more closely it may be found that the project is not necessarily doing things directed at reducing the likelihood of offending, or if it is, the connection is an indirect one.

An initiative may have several components (such as individual therapy, group sessions, vocational training and social skills training), or may be addressing several aims. This makes the task of evaluation more complex since it can be difficult to establish which component, if any, is having an impact on which participants. Projects may also accord different priorities to their activities and aims. Consequently it is important to look for hierarchies of objectives, with organisations perhaps having primary and secondary goals. Thus, if a programme of sporting activities has *as one of its aims* reducing the likelihood of young people getting into trouble, is this its primary aim, or something that depends on other things being achieved that are more important to the project? Similarly, training and education programmes for offenders may hope to reduce the chances of reoffending, but perhaps the first aim is to get people qualifications and jobs. Likewise, a project set up to work with drug addicts may have as its stated aim that of 'enabling people to lead a drug free and meaningful life as productive members of society'. When looked at more closely the reality may be that most of the people they deal with lead very chaotic lives, and simply turning up to an appointment is a major achievement. This is progress and needs to be recognised as such, but it reveals the gap that sometimes exists between stated aims and reality. A good evaluation should do more than tell the project that it has not rehabilitated anyone recently; it should look at what is happening or not happening in the intervention as a whole. It is, however, important to be wary of projects that have bland aims, or whose expressed aims amount to little more than trying to change the world.

Programme implementation and integrity

Another key element of any evaluation is to determine whether an initiative is in fact doing what it sets out to do. This is known as 'programme integrity', and is one of the key principles set out for effective intervention. It may sound obvious, but it is easy even for structured treatment programmes in institutional settings to drift and be drawn off course. A programme may end up doing something different from what was intended because the original intentions were found to be too ambitious, or could not be implemented in their original form. In this context it is relevant to consider how long the programme has been running. An evaluation may be set up at the outset of a new form of treatment or social initiative, but it may be some while before the programme 'settles down' and is running in the way intended.

Another kind of change in implementation can occur when an initiative has been going for some time, and there is 'programme drift'. New projects attract a lot of attention (not least from researchers), but after a while what the programme was originally supposed to do becomes lost. This can come about as a result of changes in the external environment in which the programme is operating, such as a shift in Government policy, or as one type of intervention goes out of fashion and another becomes more attractive. Programme drift may also occur because of changes in staff: key people who originally set up a project move on and new people want to bring in their own ideas.

Another aspect of evaluating programme implementation may be to consider whether the initiative was delivered to an appropriate target group. It is all too easy for a training project, for example, to take people who are most likely to boost its success rates rather than those most in need. Is a programme aimed at young people getting into trouble actually getting those most at risk, or is it getting young people who might not otherwise get into trouble anyway? This is likely to be particularly important if the initiative involves referrals being made by other agencies or individuals. It may be that those agencies are referring to the project those they don't want to deal with themselves, rather than the people at whom the initiative was aimed.

Outcome criteria

Identifying a programme's aims will also indicate the criteria by which it is appropriate to measure its success. In the case of programmes for offenders it is quite likely that the main measure of success will be reduced offending. However, it is always important to check whether this is in fact the case, and whether this is recognised by all the parties involved in an initiative. For example, at various times schemes have been established which were concerned with training offenders, and had as their *main* objective the obtaining of a qualification or a job, or going on to further training. It would be inappropriate to evaluate such schemes on the basis of whether or not participants are reconvicted if this was never explicitly acknowledged to be one of their main objectives (see Crow et al., 1989: 77–84, for a fuller discussion of this example). Similarly, in recent years a number of victim–offender mediation schemes have started. It may reasonably be argued that the principal concern of such schemes is mediation, rather than the rehabilitation of offenders as such, and that they should therefore be judged by criteria such as the satisfaction of the parties concerned with the mediation process, and any agreements reached during mediation. Before assuming that schemes should be evaluated on the basis of the reconviction rates of the offenders it is necessary to consider whether they are in fact designed to achieve such an objective. It is also important to look out for projects re-defining their criteria so that they are easier to achieve. Having failed to reduce reconviction there may be a temptation to revert to such things as increasing offenders' self-confidence or social skills as a fall-back to a 'softer' outcome measure.

Where the rehabilitation of offenders is concerned it may also be reasonable to consider criteria other than reconviction as legitimate measures. One may be the cost of the programme. If the programme has a high unit cost and the impact on reconviction rates is marginal, it may be worth considering whether the same effect might be achieved by alternative means. Other criteria of success may include whether the programme diverts people from custody, and whether there is some change in the attitudes of the offender. However, a word of warning is necessary when it comes to attitudinal measures, since it should not be assumed that these are related to changes in behaviour. It may also be important to consider whether a programme has adverse or unintended consequences, such as bringing people into contact with the criminal justice process and its agencies who might not otherwise have done so (referred to as 'net-widening').

Offending as an outcome

While the possible outcome criteria for an intervention should be considered with an open mind, reduced offending is likely to feature as one of the main measures. Reoffending is usually measured by reconviction information. This is often done by comparing actual reconvictions with the expected rate of reconviction for a given group of offenders using an instrument called the Offender Group Reconviction Scale (OGRS), which uses known predictors of reoffending to produce a predicted probability of reconviction (this is described in more detail in Chapter 6). The problems of measuring crime and reoffending are one of the most problematic topics in criminology. While we will not discuss the difficulties at length here, we will briefly highlight some of the main considerations as far as evaluating interventions is concerned (for more broadly based discussions see Lloyd et al., 1994; Friendship et al., 2005).

First, *reconviction is not the same as reoffending*. As a measure of outcome reconviction is affected by detection rates and enforcement policies. The use of OGRS for evaluating reconviction has its limitations because it depends on prediction data which may be unreliable or not appropriate for certain groups (Kershaw, 1998).

Another consideration is *the length of time used to follow up reconviction rates*. Where individual offenders are concerned, a two year follow-up period has traditionally been used. However, this may need to be adjusted to take account of particular circumstances. For example, young people in their teens tend to reoffend more rapidly than older people, so changes over six months or a year may need to be examined. Research on sex offenders has shown that such offenders need to be followed up for much longer periods than the usual two years (Ditchfield and Marshall, 1990; Marshall, 1994; Hedderman and Sugg, 1996). It may be that more than one follow-up is needed in order to see whether an initial reduction in reconviction has been maintained in the long term.

The presence or absence of reconviction may be too crude a measure on its own. Following intervention offenders who have frequently reoffended in the past may remain conviction free for a longer period than they have previously. This suggests that the intervention may have had some effect, even if its influence was only temporary. Someone may also be reconvicted for a less serious offence than previously, indicating at least a shift from, say, violent robbery to shoplifting.

It is also necessary when using reconvictions as a measure to take account of *'false positives'*: convictions for offences committed prior to intervention, which occur following the offence that led to intervention. In the same way, it is necessary to take account of the custodial and non-custodial periods 'at risk'. Periods when someone is in prison do not count for follow-up purposes.

Because of the difficulties posed by actual reconviction data some researchers have resorted to secondary *'offence-related' measures* to supplement crime data. This might include whether or not someone's general behaviour or attitudes change. Measures such as these are often referred to as 'non-reconviction benefits' (Friendship et al., 2005: 13). It might also include the use of unofficial sources of data such as police intelligence, offenders' self-reported offending, and information from probation, social and health services (e.g. Falshaw et al., 2003). The problem with such measures is that they may be unreliable indicators of potential behaviour, or based on the subjective judgements of others. Therefore the use of such measures can be controversial. On the one hand it might be argued that these are not true measures of outcome, and rely on subjective perceptions to obtain a less satisfactory (and perhaps more amenable) result than it is reasonable to expect. On the other hand they could be defended on the basis that more objective measures cannot be obtained, or are also likely to be unreliable, and that more qualitative measures do have value in their own right. Whether they are justified is likely to depend on the circumstances of a particular evaluation.

It is also important to consider *completion rates*. It is not unusual for participants in a programme to drop out before the end. To take one instance, this was found to be the case for Drug Treatment and Testing Orders (DTTOs) (Hough et al., 2003). What is important here is that those who drop out may be different from those who complete the programme in certain ways. For example, they may be the most recalcitrant individuals who are most likely to reoffend, and therefore the results are not a true test of the programme. The best that can be said is that the intervention works with the kind of people who complete it – which rather limits its applicability.

The Role of Evaluation in Rehabilitation

Evaluation studies have played an important role in the history and development of rehabilitation. We saw in Chapter 2 that studies by the Home Office

Research Unit paved the way for rejection of the treatment model and helped to bolster the conclusion (however misleadingly) that 'nothing works'. The IMPACT study, which appeared to support this conclusion in the UK, was a classic clinical trial type of research design, with experimental and control groups and random allocation (Folkard et al., 1976). The outcome criteria were predominantly reconviction rates. While some probation officers' ratings of offenders were also used, these were not accorded any great degree of importance, and the conclusion was that 'there was no solid evidence found to support the claim that experimental treatment produced more beneficial results than control treatment' (Folkard et al., 1976: 16–17).

It is interesting to contrast the IMPACT study with another evaluation of intensive probation (IP) conducted in the early 1990s (Mair, 1994). By this time the tenor of criminal justice policy had changed, with more emphasis on a managerial approach, and the study adopted different methods. The project itself had various aims. These included providing an alternative to custody for those likely to receive a custodial sentence, but the intentions were punitive rather than rehabilitative, and about making probation look 'rigorous and demanding'. It was about the management of offenders rather than their rehabilitation. The outcome criteria were five primary measures: reconviction rates, diversion from custody, financial costs, views of sentencers, and views of offenders (Mair, 1997a: 70). There were also some secondary measures, including employment, drug misuse and accommodation. However, the results of the study contained no data on reconviction rates, financial costs or the secondary measures. The study involved process as well as outcome evaluation, and there was much emphasis on how the programmes operated. The research was as much about the viability of such an initiative, whether it reached the target group of high risk offenders, whether it diverted people from custody (two-thirds of those referred who did not get IP received a custodial sentence), and the views and opinions of sentencers and offenders, more than on whether it did anything to reduce reoffending. Table 4.1 summarises the contrast between the two studies.

In fact during the 1980s and 1990s the UK Home Office was relatively uninterested in funding evaluation studies, and relatively little evaluation research took place. But in North America a technique for combining evaluation studies, known as meta-analysis (which we will refer to again in Chapter 5) was being deployed, and played an important role in the emergence of the 'What Works?' movement.

Meta-analysis

Following the rise of the 'nothing works' doctrine during the 1970s the studies that had given rise to the doctrine (especially Martinson's, 1974) were subjected to a certain amount of critical scrutiny. Several points were

Table 4.1   Comparing the IMPACT (1976) and Intensive Probation (1994) studies

	IMPACT	Intensive Probation
Aims	*Main aim*: to evaluate the effect of providing intensive practical intervention in the family, work and leisure situations of 'high risk probationers'	IP as an alternative to custody 'effective punishment' 'judicial confidence'
	Subsidiary aims: (i) to examine the type of treatment given to experimental cases to see whether this related to personality and situational characteristics of the offender	
	(ii) to investigate the possibility of interaction effects between types of offender, type of treatment (experimental versus control) and reconviction	
Criteria	Reconviction rates	Emphasis on viability
		Primary: diversion from custody; financial costs; reconviction rates*
		*Secondary**: employment; drug misuse; accommodation
Method	Clinical trial – experimental and control groups; random allocation	Process as much as outcomes: – views of sentencers – views of offenders
Results	'experimental treatment as opposed to control treatment made no difference', but some interaction effects – a differential treatment effect for different types of offender	Schemes varied considerably Organisation and management of schemes important Offenders felt positive about it Demonstrated that probation services could develop rigorous programmes that successfully targeted high risk offenders Some diversion from custody

* No data available on any of these

made about the satisfactoriness or otherwise of the studies, but one line of questioning was whether existing research methodology was adequate to detect treatment effects. It is possible that looking at studies of treatment programmes on a one by one basis obscures the overall impact that they are having. It is possible for positive and negative findings to cancel each other out, or to overlook the significance of positive findings amongst the negative ones (as probably happened in the case of Martinson), thus giving a negative impression of the state of knowledge. Meta-analysis is an attempt to produce a more powerful means of analysing outcome research by bringing together the results of different studies. Many reviews of research literature are 'narrative' in nature: the reviewer attempts a synthesis of the results of a number of studies using their own words. This was essentially the approach used by Martinson and others. Meta-analysis is a statistical technique for combining the results of sometimes quite large numbers of studies, taking account of the different methods used to evaluate the effects of intervention. It is claimed that meta-analyses are therefore more scientific than the narrative method. Furthermore, by combining studies it is claimed that the positive and negative findings of individual studies are less likely to cancel each other out because one is then able to examine aggregated statistical data.

Meta-analysis has been used in clinical and educational settings since at least the 1930s. Glass et al. (1981), amongst its main advocates in the social sciences, define meta-analysis as an approach to research integration that involves the combination of results from a number of studies: 'The essential character of meta-analysis is that it is the statistical analysis of the summary findings of many empirical studies' (Glass et al., 1981: 21).[2] Meta-analysis, they say, seeks general conclusions and does not prejudge research findings in terms of research quality.

Wolf (1986) identifies two types of meta-analytic approach:

1 **Combined results** – which focus on testing the statistical significance of the combined results across primary research studies
2 **Treatment effects** – which focus on the estimation of the magnitude of the experimental, i.e. treatment, effect across studies.

The *effect size* of the latter is what is most commonly used as the statistical basis for meta-analyses. Different researchers use different formulae for estimating the effect size of various studies, but they involve deriving a standardised measure of the magnitude of treatment effect that can be used across all the studies that comprise the meta-analysis. One method, for example, is to measure the mean difference in outcome between 'experimental' and 'control' cases in standard deviation units.[3]

Over the years there have been a number of large-scale meta-analytic reviews of the treatment of offenders, and it is claimed that these have on the whole shown positive results, confounding the 'nothing works' doctrine. In one review McGuire says:

Taking all of these meta-analyses together, it can be demonstrated that the net effect of 'treatment' in the many studies surveyed is, on average, a reduction in recidivism rates of between 10% and 12%. (McGuire and Priestley, 1995: 9)

There are, however, a number of concerns about the technique of meta-analysis. These are acknowledged by Glass et al. (1981: 218), and summarised as being of four main kinds:

1 What Glass, McGaw and Smith call the 'apples and oranges' problem. This is the obvious objection that it is dangerous to mix and attempt to integrate the findings of different studies. As outlined earlier, evaluation studies can have widely differing aims and samples, and take place in very different circumstances. Aggregating the data from them may not be valid.

2 In attempting to incorporate the findings of diverse studies, there is a likelihood that badly designed, poor quality research will be included. It has been suggested that meta-analysis advocates low standards of research quality (Eysenck, 1978).

3 Meta-analysis depends on using the findings that researchers report and publish. There are various reasons why the results of evaluations may not be incorporated in a meta-analysis. Much grant-aided research results in a final report submitted to the funding body. It may then be up to the funding body whether that report is ever published. For example, the Home Office in the UK is under no obligation to publish the results of research that it commissions. In addition, many small community-based projects involving offenders may result in reports that only appear in what is generally termed the 'grey' literature; that is, reports produced internally for an organisation (for example, the Probation Service). The meta-analyst may simply miss some studies that are relevant to the area of interest. Consequently there is likely to be selection bias in the results that are incorporated into a meta-analysis. There may well be systematic differences among the results of research that appear in journals, books and reports. For example, it is quite probable that successful interventions are more likely to be published than unsuccessful ones, and the results of any meta-analysis will therefore be biased.

4 Meta-analyses are conducted on large data sets in which multiple results are derived from the same study. This means that different sets of results may not be independent of each other, giving a mistaken impression of the reliability of the results. The main consequence of this non-independence is a reduction in the reliability of the estimation of averages and equations.

Mair and Copas (1996)[4] express several reservations about meta-analysis. They distinguish between *Level I* meta-analysis, a descriptive technique for reviewing a body of literature in a systematic and consistent way, which they believe is valid, and *Level II* meta-analysis, which draws inferences from the results using formal statistical procedures, about which they are much more dubious. In addition to the criticisms relating to publication bias, and the variable quality of design referred to above, Mair and Copas point out that meta-analyses quite often cover varying forms of treatment and a variety of outcome measures. In particular, they emphasise that what meta-analysis has *not* done is to establish precisely what works, to what extent, with whom, and in what settings and circumstances. As a cautionary note they cite the instance of a medical meta-analysis of small-scale studies of the use of magnesium in the treatment of heart disease, which concluded that intravenous magnesium was a safe, simple and effective form of intervention. However, when the opportunity arose to undertake a single large-scale study involving 58,000 people, it was found that magnesium had virtually no effect. Mair and Copas's conclusion is that on the one hand meta-analysis has successfully demolished the proposition that 'nothing works', but they point out that it only takes a moment's thought to realise that this is a fairly meaningless formulation anyway. They recommend caution, and encourage a critical approach to programme development, setting up carefully monitored programmes, and being prepared to find that some of them don't work.

In the light of these criticisms the kind of claim made above by McGuire needs to be viewed with caution. Meta-analyses helped researchers and practitioners to put the 'nothing works' nostrum behind them, but it soon became clear that much still needed to be done to understand what works with whom, how and why, and recent debates have indicated that there is a need to move towards a more interpretive, and less positivist approach to treatment evaluation.

By the end of the 1990s the wheel had come full circle. For the British Government's Crime Reduction Programme, focusing on 'What Works?', the emphasis was again firmly on the criterion of reducing reoffending, and the kind of methods that would ensure that like was compared with like, and that inferences could be made which would relate any impact to the intervention (see Chapter 5 for further discussion). While the Maryland Scale of Scientific Methods was recognised as valuable in this respect, the arguments of Pawson and Tilley were taken note of, and the result was the integrated model referred to earlier (Friendship et al., 2005).

One of the early 'What Works?' initiatives was not Government sponsored at all, however. The STOP (Straight Thinking On Probation) programme was a local initiative which sought to reduce offending by heavily convicted offenders (Raynor and Vanstone, 1997). This was based on the 'Reasoning and Rehabilitation' model pioneered by Ross and colleagues in Canada (also discussed in Chapter 7). Reconviction by programme participants was compared with similar local offenders who received sentences other than probation with STOP. In addition to looking at reconviction, the research also studied how well the local probation area delivered an unfamiliar programme, and what effect the programme had on the attitudes of offenders, using a recently developed attitude measure called CRIME-PICS. The reconviction study indicated that those who completed the programme did better than a custodial sentence for comparable offenders, but that the effect diminished between the first and second years of follow-up, and that this did have a positive effect on offender attitudes.

In due course an Accreditation Panel was established to ensure that prison and probation programmes were being adequately evaluated, and the Home

Office issued guidelines to evaluators setting out how programmes should be studied (Colledge et al., 1999). The result was a number of studies on CBT, and other 'Pathfinder' programmes on probation and resettlement, and Drug Treatment and Testing Orders (DTTOs). However, the Crime Reduction Programme ended prematurely in 2002 with mixed results (having originally been intended to run for another seven years) and disquiet was being voiced not only about some of the results of the evaluations, but also the way research was done. Gelsthorpe and Sharpe have been critical of the reification of the RCT as the 'gold standard' suggesting that it is 'indicative of a broad shift in penal policy in recent years – from offender rehabilitation to offender categorisation and management' (2006: 8), and arguing for a broader range of methods to be used. Maguire has also argued that evaluations were expected to deliver too much too quickly. They were hampered by poor implementation, and over-reliance on too narrow a methodology laid evaluations open to the risk that if insufficient reliable data were available 'the evaluator would be left without anything useful to say about the effectiveness of the programme' (Maguire, 2004: 230). The result, Maguire concludes, was that 'despite an unprecedented investment in evaluation, it left behind relatively little new learning about the effectiveness of particular interventions.' Instead the main lessons were about weaknesses in project planning and implementation.

An important element in the way that projects and their evaluation developed was the role played by the Treasury. HM Treasury requires that Government departments demonstrate the cost-effectiveness of their programmes, based on guidance issued by the Treasury in the form of the Green Book, which sets out a framework for project appraisal. This is supplemented in the context of Government social research by the Magenta Book of guidance for policy evaluation and analysis. It is not surprising that a Government should want to demonstrate value for the money it spends, but it can constrain research in terms of both scope and timescale. Raynor and Robinson have argued that 'The policy of recruiting as many offenders as possible to programmes to meet Treasury targets has probably tended to undermine the fit between offenders' needs and programmes and contributed to increasing attrition and non-completion, which in turn reduces the overall impact of the programmes if non-completers reconvict more' (2005: 116). Programmes claimed to have been affected in this way are the Basic Skills Pathfinder (McMahon et al., 2004), the Resettlement Pathfinder projects (Lewis et al., 2003), and the Drug Treatment and Testing Order (Hough et al., 2003). One of the most common complaints amongst researchers is that programmes which need careful planning and development are rushed in order to produce results before they have really had time to bed in. We have referred here to aspects of the Crime Reduction Programme relevant to the evaluation of programmes. The programme itself is discussed further in Chapter 5.

Conclusion

We have focused here on evaluation research because of the important role it has played in the development of offender rehabilitation. However, we would end by emphasising what was said at the beginning of the chapter: evaluation research is only one form of criminological research, and it has its limitations. Evaluations are a way of putting theories about the nature of offending to the test, and should therefore be seen as part of a wider process of inquiry. The 'Reasoning and Rehabilitation' approach tested by the STOP programme is a good example of this, and the theory underpinning this approach has been critically examined subsequently (Ward and Maruna, 2007). Continuing research opens up new possibilities for the future of rehabilitation, which in turn may lead to further evaluation of such possibilities.

Questions to Consider

1 Is the random controlled trial (RCT) the best way of evaluating a rehabilitation programme?
2 What needs to be considered when looking at whether a programme/intervention for offenders is working?
3 What are the advantages and disadvantages of meta-analysis?

Suggested Further Reading

There is much general literature on evaluative research. Chapter 4 of Crow and Semmens's *Researching Criminology* (2008) expands on some of the aspects considered here. Chapter 1 of Pawson and Tilley's book, *Realistic Evaluation* (1997), is entitled 'A History of Evaluation in 28½ Pages', and reflects their particular perspective. Carol Weiss's book, *Evaluation: Methods for Studying Programs and Policies* (1998), on theories of change is also recommended; Chapter 3 is a useful summary of her model. In the context of rehabilitation it is also worth reading Chapter 1 of the Home Office Research Study 291 (Harper and Chitty, 2005), *The Impact of Corrections on Re-Offending: A Review of 'What Works'*, which reflects a Home Office approach to such matters. There is also a good collection edited by George Mair (1997a) on *Evaluating the Effectiveness of Community Penalties*.

Notes

1 Expected reconviction rates are calculated using a risk prediction instrument developed by the Home Office called the Offender Group Reconviction Scale (OGRS) which assesses the likelihood of reconviction based on criminal history risk factors.

2 Other authors have also given definitions of the technique:

Wolf, 1986: 5 – 'the application of statistical procedures to collections of empirical findings from individual studies for the purpose of integrating, synthesizing, and making sense of them'.

McIvor, 1990: 11 – 'the pooling of data across a number of studies to compute the overall size of the effect achieved by a given method of intervention. Advocates argue that measuring size of effect, and not just whether it has occurred, is more accurate and realistic.'

Izzo and Ross, 1990: 135 – 'The procedure of meta-analysis involves collecting relevant studies, using the summary statistics from each study as units of analysis, and then analysing the aggregated data in a quantitative manner using statistical tests'.

McGuire and Priestley, 1995: 7–8 – '[Meta-analysis] involves the aggregation and side-by-side analysis of large numbers of experimental studies. ... Essentially, the procedure of meta-analysis requires recalculation of the data from different experiments in a new all-encompassing statistical analysis.'

3 This can be expressed as $ES = \dfrac{\overline{X}_{exptl} - \overline{X}_{Control}}{SD}$

4 Although unpublished, Vennard, Sugg and Hedderman (1997: 4, 10) make use of this paper in their review of cognitive-behavioural approaches.

FIVE

Reviving Rehabilitation: The 'What Works?' Movement

Introduction

This chapter covers the revival of rehabilitation in penal policy and practice, in the context of what has come to be known as the 'What Works?' movement. With roots spreading back as far as the 1970s, and reaching into a number of parts of the world, the quest to establish that some interventions *could* be effective in reducing reoffending gathered pace during the early 1990s and, in England and Wales, attracted considerable investment from an incoming Labour Government which was publicly committed to 'evidence-based' policy and practice in public services. In this chapter we consider the various strands and types of research which sought to question the 'nothing works' doctrine that had become entrenched in the 1970s, before moving on to consider its development in the context of the Government's *Crime Reduction Programme*. The chapter ends with an assessment of the success and implications of the 'What Works?' movement.

The Roots of 'What Works?'

> For an emperor which has been scantily clad, 'Nothing Works' has had a long reign. (Mair, 1991: 7)

The movement which came to be known in the academic context as 'new rehabilitationism' (Hudson, 1987), and in the practice and policy contexts as 'What Works?' has an interesting and quite complex history. This history has been detailed by a number of British commentators, including James McGuire

(McGuire and Priestley, 1995; McGuire, 2000); Peter Raynor (2004a; Raynor and Vanstone, 2002; Raynor and Robinson, 2005) and George Mair (1997b, 2004). As all of these accounts have made clear, the foundations of the 'What Works?' movement had more than one source, and were laid over a number of years, with significant contributions both in the UK and further afield. Nonetheless, once these foundations were laid, rehabilitation was set to enjoy a renewed legitimacy after more than a decade of relative neglect.

The research which laid the foundations of the 'What Works?' movement was of three main types. First, it included a number of research studies which involved *primary analysis*: that is, the collection and analysis of original data in the context of the evaluation of specific interventions. Second, *secondary analyses*, involving the re-analysis of existing data (either using better statistical techniques or posing new questions of existing data) played an important role in the quest to establish that some things work. Finally, the advanced statistical technique of *meta-analysis*, which involves analysing the results of a large number of primary outcome studies in order to integrate their findings, was very significant (see also Chapter 4). We shall encounter examples of each of these approaches in our discussion of the roots of 'What Works?'.

Starting with developments in the UK, one source of renewed optimism about rehabilitation came from the work of a small number of British academic researchers who, undeterred by the pessimistic 'nothing works' dogma instilled by the 1970s research (reviewed in Chapter 2), had in collaboration with local probation areas initiated small-scale *primary* studies of the effects of specific interventions with offenders. By the late 1980s, these had begun to yield some positive results (Raynor, 1988; Roberts, 1989). For example, Raynor's study, carried out in South Wales, showed a group of young adult male offenders on probation achieving a reconviction rate some 13% below comparable offenders sentenced to prison, as well as reporting a reduction in their social and personal problems. Roberts' study, carried out in Hereford and Worcester, also showed substantial reductions in offending by young adult probationers. These small-scale studies ran counter to the research agenda of the Home Office Research Unit which in the 1980s largely neglected questions of the effectiveness of probation (Raynor, 2004a). This apparent lack of 'official' interest in research was however less evident in Scotland, and the Scottish Office funded an early and extremely thorough *secondary analysis* of research findings by McIvor (1990), which played a significant role in bringing 'research news' both to other academics and to the probation service in particular.

Another significant British influence was the work of two psychologists, James McGuire and Philip Priestley, which also continued to challenge the idea that nothing could be done to alter patterns of offending behaviour. During the 1980s McGuire and Priestley developed a style of intervention based on analysing and modifying offending behaviour, and it has been argued that their book *Offending Behaviour*, published in 1985, marked the first stage of what came to be termed the 'What Works?' movement in the UK (Raynor and Vanstone, 1997). A parallel influence was the work of a group of Canadian psychologists (including Don Andrews, James Bonta, Paul Gendreau and Robert Ross), whose work centred on the development and testing of interventions, or 'programmes', informed by cognitive psychology and social learning theory. The idea of a 'programme' referred to the design and development of a series of carefully planned and sequenced activities or learning opportunities in which offenders could participate. Robert Ross, for example, developed a programme called *Reasoning and Rehabilitation* which was to prove extremely influential in respect of work with offenders both in prisons and in the community, in the UK and elsewhere. From the late 1980s, probation services were beginning to experiment with the *Reasoning and Rehabilitation* programme developed by Robert Ross and colleagues, and reports of its application were appearing in the *Probation Journal*. The subsequent spread of 'cognitive-behavioural programmes' in the UK was reinforced by the well-publicised implementation of the *Straight Thinking On Probation* (STOP) programme by the Mid-Glamorgan probation service in 1991 under the stewardship of academic researchers Peter Raynor and Maurice Vanstone at Swansea University in Wales. This initiative boasted a well-designed (primary) outcome evaluation, the results of which began to be published in the late 1990s. We shall return to the theme of cognitive-behavioural programmes in Chapter 7.

The work of Robert Ross and his colleagues was however just one of three main sources of momentum for the revival of rehabilitative optimism in Britain which is attributable to work overseas, and to North America in particular. Significantly, it was there that existing research had been re-examined in a more positive light (via *secondary* analyses) and new evidence was emerging about the effectiveness of certain types of intervention (e.g. Palmer, 1975; Gendreau and Ross, 1979). Ted Palmer (1975) had re-analysed the 82 studies cited in Martinson's (1974) article and concluded that of these, 39 studies had in fact yielded positive or partly positive results. Gendreau and Ross (1979) argued that interventions were often ineffective *not* because they were inherently flawed, but more often because they were poorly implemented, and lacked 'therapeutic integrity'. Meanwhile, in 1979 Robert Martinson both revised his original ('nothing works') conclusion and reported on a new survey of research studies. Raynor (1995) has speculated that, whilst this passed largely unnoticed in the UK, it may have been a factor in the continued quest for effective practice abroad (Martinson, 1979).

Arguably the most influential development, however, was the emergence of new reviews of research on the effectiveness of a variety of interventions using the statistical technique of *meta-analysis* (discussed in Chapter 4). Although meta-analysis has a long history in medical research, it was not until the late

1980s that it began to be used by correctional researchers, enabling them to aggregate the findings of large numbers of studies and identify not just whether interventions of various kinds could be said to 'work'; but more specifically to identify those components of interventions associated with positive outcomes (e.g. Andrews et al., 1990a; Lipsey, 1992). This powerful tool – which, unlike earlier methods of review, was able to cope with a wide variety of studies and to adjust for considerable variation in methodological rigour – had, it was claimed, begun to yield complex but positive findings beyond the 'mean effect size' which had been the focus of earlier, less sophisticated research reviews.

The Mid-1990s: The 'Principles of Effective Practice'

In an attempt to bring the latest research findings to practitioner audiences, a series of 'What Works?' conferences was organised by the Probation Service, starting in 1991. These conferences generated a series of publications, including an important book edited by James McGuire (1995) entitled *What Works: Reducing Reoffending.* This book, a compilation of twelve papers from the three conferences held to date, is widely considered to be the seminal British publication on the subject of effective practice. In their introduction, McGuire and Priestley were sufficiently confident to assert that 'the contention that "nothing works" is in need of radical revision' (1995: 5). Meanwhile, other summaries of the main findings of meta-analytic and narrative reviews were being published, each cautiously concurring that, whilst a *full* answer to the 'what works?' question had yet to be found, there was every reason to be optimistic. McGuire and Priestley expressed their own cautious optimism thus:

> It must be emphasized first that the meta-analytic reviews do not suggest that there is any single, outstanding approach that is by itself guaranteed to work as a means of reducing recidivism. There is no more a panacea in this area than in any other search for solutions to human ills ... [nonetheless] Within these studies *a number of principles* concerning the design and assembly of effective programmes can be identified. (McGuire and Priestley 1995: 14, emphasis added)

These emerging 'principles' were presented by McGuire and Priestley under six headings, and are summarised below.

Risk classification

According to the 'risk principle', or 'principle of risk classification', offenders most likely to benefit from more intensive interventions or programmes are those assessed as posing a high risk of reoffending. Summarising this principle, Andrews et al., (1990b: 20) explain that 'intensive service is reserved for higher risk cases because they respond better to intensive service than to less intensive service, while lower risk cases do as well or better with minimal as opposed to more intensive service.'

Criminogenic needs

According to the principle of 'criminogenic needs', interventions must target those offender problems or features that contribute to or are supportive of offending ('criminogenic' needs), rather than those that are most distantly related, or unrelated, to it ('non-criminogenic' needs). In other words, if the purpose of an intervention is to reduce reoffending, there should be a focus within it on criminogenic needs as goals of intervention.

Responsivity

The 'responsivity' principle indicated that interventions ought to be matched to, or take account of, the individual learning styles or abilities of offenders. According to Andrews et al., (1990b: 20), the type of intervention ought to be 'matched not only to criminogenic need but to those attributes and circum-stances of cases that render cases likely to profit from that particular type of service'. On balance, they argued, the learning styles of most offenders require active, participatory methods of working, rather than either a didactic mode on the one hand or a loose, unstructured, 'experiential' mode on the other.

Community base

To quote McGuire and Priestley, 'Programmes located in the community on balance yield more effective outcomes. This is not to dismiss institution-based work, but the findings do imply that proximity to individuals' home environ-ments has a greater prospect of facilitating real-life learning' (1995: 15).

Treatment modality

Summarising the findings of research examining the impact of interventions in a variety of settings, McGuire and Priestley explained that the more effective programmes tended to be (a) multimodal: i.e. they recognised a variety of offenders' problems; (b) skills-oriented: i.e. designed to teach practical, problem-solving, social interaction or coping skills; and (c) based on behavioural, cogni-tive or cognitive-behavioural approaches.

Programme integrity

A programme is said to have integrity when it 'is conducted in practice as intended in theory and design', and 'effectiveness' (in terms of reducing recidivism) was linked with high programme integrity (Hollin, 1995: 196). As Hollin explained, ideally this meant that staff delivering the programme were well trained and that the programme was well managed.

In the coming years, similar 'menus' of 'effective practice principles' would appear in the literature (e.g. Vennard et al., 1997; Vennard and Hedderman, 1998), all apparently pointing toward the same conclusion: namely, that if the effectiveness of 'rehabilitative' interventions was to be maximised in line with research findings, there was much work to do.

New Labour and the 'Effective Practice Initiative'

Although the publication of McGuire's edited collection was a milestone for the 'What Works?' movement, there were in the mid-1990s concerns about whether the book – and the 'new rehabilitation' agenda which it represented – would have the impact on practice that it merited. This concern reflected the very volatile political context of the early-mid 1990s, which saw the then Home Secretary Michael Howard announce (in 1993) that 'prison works'. This statement (though made with reference to prison's incapacitative effects) was in direct conflict with the conclusions of researchers, who were at pains to point to the failure of punitive strategies to reduce reoffending (e.g. McGuire and Priestley, 1995).

But despite ambivalence on the part of the Home Office, in 1996 HM Inspectorate of Probation launched its own 'What Works' project. Led by Andrew Underdown, a senior probation manager, the Inspectorate's project aimed to ascertain progress made by area probation services in achieving effective practice and to identify 'learning points' from their experiences to date. Central to the project was a national survey which sought to determine the extent and findings of evaluations (i.e. primary analyses) available for programmes operating in the Probation Service since 1992. This survey revealed a disappointing number of evaluated programmes; only 11 studies were identified as having 'some value' as case examples of good evaluation practice. One of the key conclusions of the Underdown report was that if the 'What Works?' movement was to achieve its potential then it would be necessary to nurture a more coordinated approach across the probation service, in the form of shared practices, standards and information. In other words, it made little sense for each of the then 54 probation areas to navigate its own way through the findings of the latest research: rather, some central direction was required (Underdown, 1998).

Meanwhile, the political landscape was shifting. In May 1997, a New Labour Government was elected, and declared publicly a commitment to the notion of evidence-based practice in public services. In parallel with the Comprehensive Spending Review launched shortly after taking office, the new government had established a series of major reviews relating to criminal justice, including a major cross-Departmental review of the entire criminal justice system which aimed 'to identify a set of "what works" principles, at the broadest level, that would provide the basis for a crime reduction strategy' (Goldblatt and Lewis, 1998: 1). The resulting publication included a chapter by Home Office researchers Julie Vennard and Carol Hedderman on 'effective interventions with offenders', which reinforced the six 'principles of effective practice' outlined previously by McGuire and Priestley.

As Cavadino et al. (1999) subsequently argued, the significance of the publication *Reducing Offending* related less to its findings, which were principally compiled from existing research, than to its reception by government:

> [The Home Secretary] published it with an official fanfare, including a statement to the House of Commons, praised it as 'a pivotal step towards developing an effective crime reduction strategy for the next decade' and announced a £250 million Crime Reduction Programme based on its findings. The Home Office's Director of Research and Statistics, Chris Nuttall (who directed the *Reducing Offending* review) confessed to being 'stunned' by this ministerial endorsement of the report and the government's shift towards an evidence-based approach. (Cavadino et al. 1999: 213–4)

This report, then, marked an apparent break with past, populist rhetoric under the Conservatives, and paved the way for an 'Effective Practice Initiative' (EPI) which was launched by the Home Office in 1998.

The launch of the EPI (as a successor to the Inspectorate's 'What Works' project) in the summer of 1998 marked a significant milestone, both for the 'What Works?' movement and for the Probation Service more generally. As a joint initiative of the Home Office, HM Inspectorate of Probation and the Association of Chief Probation Officers (ACOP), it wielded considerably greater 'clout' than its predecessor, and therefore marked the official appropriation of 'What Works?' by the 'centre' (Robinson, 2001). The EPI launched a *national implementation plan* for the effective supervision of offenders, setting out an expectation that area probation services 'should aim to ensure that every offender is supervised in accordance with those principles which have been shown to reduce expected rates of reoffending' (Home Office, 1998: 1). The document announcing the launch of the EPI contained a clear set of instructions to area probation services, but it also set out a number of tasks to be undertaken by the Home Office, HMIP and ACOP. These included the forthcoming publication of an 'Effective Practice Guide' (Chapman and Hough, 1998); the procurement of a risk/needs assessment instrument for use by all prisons and probation services (discussed further in Chapter 6); and the development of a national 'core curriculum' of supervision programmes called 'Pathfinders', modelled on the system of programme accreditation already established within the Prison Service.

The Crime Reduction Programme 'Pathfinders'

As Maguire (2004) has explained, the Crime Reduction Programme (CRP) was to be the biggest ever single investment in an evidence-based approach to crime reduction. It incorporated a wide range of interventions falling under the broad umbrella of 'crime reduction', delivered in many different settings and by many different agencies. It also attached great importance to the role of evaluations conducted by independent researchers to determine which interventions had a significant and cost-effective impact on crime and therefore warranted implementation on a national scale.

The development and evaluation of a number of 'Pathfinder' projects in the context of probation work was just one element of this major investment. As Raynor (2004a) has argued – and as this chapter has shown – in the probation context, the CRP was by no means the beginning of the movement to discover 'What Works?'; nonetheless, it did offer a valuable opportunity to increase the pace and scale of the project which was already underway. Indeed, the CRP would devote £21m over three years to the development and roll-out of a 'national curriculum' of interventions aimed at reducing reoffending.

By early 1999 the Home Office had identified the first three Pathfinder programmes, which had been chosen from 60 put forward by 25 probation areas. These were a general offending behaviour programme running in three probation areas; a sex offender programme developed in Thames Valley; and a 'Women's Offending' programme developed and running in Hereford and Worcester. The aim was to work with probation areas to make available nationally a number of 'core' programmes for community-based offender supervision which could demonstrate 'effectiveness criteria', and which would be approved by a panel of experts (in the form of a new joint prison/probation accreditation panel, which would replace the existing Prison Service Accreditation Panel). By mid-1999, new funding for 32 further Pathfinder projects had been announced. These projects fell into four main groups: offending behaviour programmes; community service projects; resettlement projects for short-term prisoners; and basic skills and employment projects (aimed at helping offenders gain elementary skills in literacy and numeracy, and getting offenders into employment). Each of these initiatives was launched in a number of probation areas and subject to independent research (by academic researchers based in British universities) to evaluate its impact.

Meanwhile, a Joint Prison/Probation Services Accreditation Panel (JAP) – subsequently re-named the Correctional Services Accreditation panel in 2002 – was set up in mid-1999. Charged with the key role of assessing the design and delivery of interventions aimed at reducing reoffending, the Panel comprised 12 independent experts and a further eight nominated members from the Home Office and other relevant organisations. In 2000 the first wave of approved or *accredited* Pathfinders – all general offending behaviour programmes based on cognitive-behavioural principles – began to be rolled out nationally across the probation service and it was announced that probation services would be expected to put 60,000 offenders through these programmes in the next three years (Home Office, 2000). Altogether, in its first two years, the Panel accredited 15 programmes: five general offending behaviour programmes; six programmes for sex offenders; two for violent offenders; one for drink impaired drivers; and one for substance misusing offenders (Rex et al., 2003b).

Doubts about the 'What Works?' Initiative

From fairly humble beginnings in the early 1990s, the 'What Works?' movement had, by the close of the decade, gathered a momentum and a level of central investment that few would have predicted. From one perspective, then, developments were extremely positive. However, at the same time a number of commentators were beginning to voice some concerns about the way the initiative was going.

Mair (1997b) expressed concerns about the quality of evidence derived from the major meta-analytic studies which, he argued, had been taken at face value and assumed by many to prove definitively 'What Works?'. Mair's doubts were based on the fact that the meta-analytic studies carried out to date had tended to concentrate on juvenile offenders in the USA, and continued to rely on studies carried out in the 1950s and 1960s. Their relevance to 1990s community penalties in respect of largely adult offenders in Britain, then, was potentially limited. Mair further argued that the claims made on behalf of meta-analysis tended to go too far: the so-called 'principles of effective practice' derived from meta-analytic studies, he explained, far from being 'proven facts', were speculative, and intended to guide the next generation of practitioners and researchers in their quest to find 'What Works?'. Mair (2004) subsequently likened 'What Works?' in England and Wales to an evangelical movement with 'strict commandments': an orthodoxy which it was becoming increasingly difficult to challenge.

Merrington and Stanley (2000) voiced similar concerns about the fact that probation areas were being asked to adopt accredited programmes in the absence of published evidence about their effectiveness. Ideally, they argued, it would have been preferable to delay large-scale implementation of interventions until *after* the experimental 'Pathfinder' phase, when evaluation results would be available.

Meanwhile, Robinson (2001) drew attention to what she called the *reification* of 'what works knowledge'. She noted that, where 'What Works?' had originally been formulated as a question, or set of hypotheses, it had increasingly come to be framed not so much as a question, but rather as *a question of implementation.* In this context Robinson referred in particular to the powerful over-confidence of some of the North American advocates of the 'new rehabilitation', which clearly afforded knowledge about 'What Works?' the status of 'scientific fact', and rejected any attempt to claim otherwise as an example of 'knowledge destruction'.

In the British context, Robinson observed, fears about the reification of 'What Works?' were being exacerbated by the appropriation of 'what works knowledge' by the Home Office. The Effective Practice Initiative was singled out as exemplifying this 'reifying' tendency, with its attempt to reduce effective interventions to a 'formula of ingredients', and its promotion of a *national implementation plan* for the effective supervision of offenders – the assumption being that knowledge of 'What Works?' had acquired the status of fact. She also considered the implications of this trend for the Probation Service and its staff, noting both positive and negative implications. On the positive side, 'What Works?' clearly promised to increase the credibility of the service and the professionalism of its staff; but on the other side of the coin, it could be argued that the increasing standardisation of probation practice associated with the 'implementation' of 'effective practice' (e.g. the introduction of accredited programmes) was *de-professionalising* to the extent that practitioners' scope to exercise discretion was being limited. The 'What Works?' movement was also identified by Robinson as having played a significant role in the decision to bring the 54 formerly relatively independent probation areas under the umbrella of a National Probation Service (in 2001) which, similarly, heralded less independence for individual probation areas in favour of a common approach.

Finally, Robinson was among a number of commentators who were concerned that, in the rush to promote what 'supposedly' would 'work', external expectations may have been raised excessively. This concern was reinforced when the Home Office announced that it was reinstating reconviction rates as a Key Performance Indicator for probation work, initially set at a 5% reduction by 2004.[1] It was further reinforced when the results of the Pathfinder evaluations began to be published, revealing a catalogue of implementation problems; weaknesses in evaluation design; few completed reconviction studies; and results that were 'mixed' and often difficult to interpret because of problems with evaluation methodologies (for summaries see Merrington and Stanley, 2004; Harper and Chitty, 2005; for critiques of the Home Office's approach to evaluation see Raynor, 2008 and Hollin, 2008).

High Hopes ... or Unrealistic Expectations?

In subsequent chapters we shall look in more detail at the legacy of the 'What Works?' movement, most notably in Chapter 6 which considers the development of methods for assessing offenders, and in Chapter 7 in which we examine in detail the development, spread and effectiveness of 'offending behaviour programmes', including the original Pathfinder programmes. We shall conclude the present chapter by considering the views of some of those who have sought to assess the overall success of 'What Works?' following the cessation of CRP funding for the initiative. Finally, we offer some thoughts about some of the implications of 'What Works?' in respect of offender rehabilitation.

In a reflective overview of the Crime Reduction Programme, Maguire (2004) has argued that it was something of a mixed blessing for criminal justice. In particular, he argues, it posed a number of daunting challenges. For example, it required the identification and coordination of large numbers of people and organisations with a range of skills in project design, oversight, management and evaluations that were in fact in limited supply. It also assumed a capacity for flexibility in criminal justice cultures: it was taken for granted that practitioners could easily be persuaded to work in new ways in the interests of 'effectiveness'. Further, Maguire argues, it assumed both that researchers would have no problems obtaining reliable data pertaining to the projects subject to evaluation, and that there would be sufficient numbers of cases for meaningful statistical analysis.

Equally problematic for Maguire was the fact that such a large-scale enterprise was bound to be accompanied by high expectations, and a degree of impatience for 'results' on the part of the Home Office and Treasury. Although initially conceived as a ten-year programme of pilot projects and research, the CRP was from the outset under pressure to demonstrate 'not only that it was progressing according to plan, but also – at the very least – to deliver some "quick wins" in terms of early demonstrations of effective crime reduction' (Maguire, 2004: 217–18). As a result, the CRP was expected to contribute significantly and quickly to the achievement of 'performance targets'. Maguire (2004: 218) cites the example of the 1999 Public Service Agreement between the Treasury and the Home Office, which included targets of a 30% reduction in vehicle crime by 2004 and a 25% reduction in burglary by 2005.

Maguire argues that this situation was exacerbated in the early months of the CRP, when there was an unexpected increase in recorded crime. This served to increase Home Office pressure to 'deliver tangible crime reductions, at the expense of longer-term pay-offs of research knowledge' (2004: 224). Under increasing pressure to produce quick results, in many cases new interventions were 'rolled out' nationally before research results were available. It was in this context that the Probation Service came under increasing pressure to process large numbers of offenders through accredited programmes, and a knock-on effect was that the Accreditation Panel lowered its standards for empirical evidence of effectiveness, introducing a system of 'provisional' accreditation, enabling programmes to be 'rolled out' before being fully accredited (Maguire, 2004: 225). Meanwhile, significant implementation problems were affecting a number of CRP projects and in turn hampering the ability of researchers to evaluate them. Maguire argues that this was perhaps the 'final straw' for the CRP: although some projects and evaluations did receive extended funding, what was originally planned as a ten-year programme officially ceased in March 2002 – just three years after it had commenced.

Reflecting specifically on the probation Pathfinders, Raynor (2004b) argues that the expectation of clear results in three years was not only unrealistic, but also led to some shortcuts which were ultimately damaging. Raynor cites the example of the targets for completions of accredited programmes set in 1999, which were negotiated with Treasury officials in the absence of evidence indicating that there would be sufficient numbers of eligible offenders to refer to such programmes. Although it was quickly realised that the targets were not feasible, much time and effort was expended attempting to meet them, causing many problems for staff and their managers. Moreover, as Raynor points out, in all of the Pathfinder studies, projects tended to start slowly and there were significant problems attracting sufficient – or the 'right' – referrals. For example, in the 'basic skills' and 'employment' Pathfinders, numbers of offenders were so small that the evaluations could not be conducted as planned (Haslewood-Pocsik et al., 2004; McMahon et al., 2004). Only 20 out of 1003 offenders assessed as having basic skills needs remained in the project long enough to be available for interview at the end of the project. Meanwhile, the 'offending behaviour programmes' Pathfinders encountered significant problems of attrition (i.e. large numbers of offenders dropping out of programmes), quite probably because unrealistic targets led to the inclusion of at least some 'inappropriate' offenders in programmes.

Ultimately, evaluators of the probation Pathfinders failed to deliver the clear answers hoped for by policymakers and the proponents of the 'What Works?' movement (Raynor, 2004b; Merrington and Stanley, 2004). Looking back at a decade of 'What Works?', Raynor and Robinson reflected that:

> The last ten years have seen a mixture of successes and failures, and an even larger volume of inconclusive outcomes: the process of judging what is working, what is promising and what would be better abandoned will continue for years. (2005: 132)

Conclusion: Putting 'What Works?' in Context

There can be little doubt that the 'What Works?' movement represents a significant milestone in the history of offender rehabilitation, albeit that future generations may regard it as a rather disappointing one. In a relatively short space of time, the 'cautious optimism' of the mid-1990s gave way to a set of expectations and goals which many regarded as unrealistic. So, was 'What Works?' a failure? We would argue that this is largely a matter of perspective. On the one hand, it is fair to say that the hopes associated with it were not – certainly in England and Wales – realised. On the other hand, and as we shall see in subsequent chapters, the impact of 'What Works?' has not been negligible.

In fact, it is no exaggeration to say that the 'principles of effective practice' (first outlined in England and Wales by McGuire and Priestley in 1995) have transformed many aspects of the practices associated with rehabilitation in several parts of the world – particularly within the 'correctional services' – albeit not without criticism (Ward and Maruna, 2007). In Chapter 7 we will examine in more detail the proliferation of structured rehabilitative 'programmes' focused on offending behaviour, which continue to be part of the rehabilitative armoury of the correctional services post-'What Works?'; and in Chapter 6 we will consider the impact of these principles on the practice of offender assessment, with a particular focus on how such practice has come to be heavily focused upon the twin concepts of risk and criminogenic need.

'What Works?' has also, as we shall see, played a significant role in the continuing evolution of rehabilitative approaches. In other words, criticisms and shortcomings of some of the approaches most closely associated with the 'What Works?' movement have in turn prompted researchers and practitioners to look for alternative ways of 'doing' rehabilitation. Thus for example critiques of the 'programmes' approach, with its emphasis on psychological correlates of offending and rehabilitation, have generated renewed interest in the social and relational contexts in which offending and rehabilitation take place. Developments in these areas are discussed in Chapters 8 and 9. By the same token, dissatisfaction with the 'risk/needs' paradigm has inspired an alternative paradigm for offender rehabilitation which goes by the name of the 'Good Lives' model. We shall encounter this model in Chapter 6 (see also Ward and Maruna, 2007). Thus, both directly and indirectly, the influence of 'What Works?' is still being felt.

Looked at through an historical lens, the 'What Works?' initiative also serves to reinforce the importance of the broader political context in determining the legitimacy of offender rehabilitation. Just as the political context of the 1970s provided 'fertile ground' in which the 'nothing works' doctrine could grow (Mair, 1991), so the shifting political sands which characterised the late 1990s offered the right climate for the so-called 'new rehabilitationism'. As we have seen in this chapter, the incoming Labour Government had publicly committed itself both to the promulgation of evidence-based policy and practice and to the goal of crime reduction, thereby rendering 'What Works?' a legitimate question and one worthy of substantial investment. But there were other ways in which the lessons of 'What Works?' meshed with political and policy priorities of the 1990s. For example, it did much to reinforce an approach towards decision-making in criminal justice which can be characterised as *risk-based*. As we noted in Chapter 3, such an approach was already in ascendance in the 1990s, thanks to a growing emphasis on public protection and the management of risk in penal policy, and 'bifurcation' in practice. By pointing to *risk of reoffending* as an appropriate basis for the rationing of 'rehabilitative' resources, 'What Works?' served to reinforce an approach toward offenders which was already increasingly preoccupied with questions of risk (Robinson, 2003a).

Questions to Consider

1 To what extent did the political context contribute to the revival of rehabilitative optimism in the 1990s?
2 George Mair (2004) likened 'What Works?' in England and Wales to 'a house built on sand'. What did he mean by this, and do you think he was right?
3 What is meant by the 'reification' of 'What Works?' To what extent was this a problem in England and Wales?
4 Was the 'What Works?' movement a success or a failure?
5 What lessons should be learned from 'What Works?'

Suggested Further Reading

McGuire and Priestley's (1995) edited collection *What Works? Reducing Reoffending* is the classic British text on this topic, summarising research to date and discussing the implications of those findings for practice. McGuire's (2002) subsequent book *Offender Rehabilitation and Treatment* seeks to update the earlier volume. George Mair's (1991) short essay 'what works: nothing or everything?' provides a very succinct exposition of the impact of the political context on questions about effectiveness. Mair's edited collection *What Matters in Probation* provides a critical perspective on the 'What Works?' movement with a probation focus.

Note

1 Solomon et al. (2007: 40–44) provide a detailed analysis of the Labour government's changing targets on reoffending, noting that all such targets (set since 2000) have been modified, missed or dropped – not least because of confusion and lack of clarity about definitions and targets.

SIX

Assessing Offenders: Risks, Needs, Responsivity and Strengths

Introduction

The assessment of offenders has long been appreciated as an essential function for those who work with offenders (Bonta, 1996). Before rehabilitative interventions can begin, it is necessary to make decisions about the type of intervention(s) relevant to and most likely to benefit the individual offender. As Hazel Kemshall has succinctly explained, assessment is a key part of the rehabilitative process because 'Not only does it frame problems, it defines their solutions' (1998: 173). Assessment then can be understood as a process which serves to classify the offender in relation to particular variables, setting out what the relevant issues or problems are in the case, and this serves as a starting point for making decisions about how to respond to or tackle the identified problems. However, assessment is not always or necessarily oriented toward the identification of 'problems'; it can also serve to identify more positive aspects of the individual or his circumstances, which can be harnessed to assist in the process of rehabilitation.

The history of assessment is as long as the history of rehabilitation, but the *methods* used to assess offenders, and the sorts of variables or factors which have been the focus of assessment practices have not remained the same. Bonta (1996) has usefully described three types or 'generations' of assessment. The 'first generation' of assessment in Bonta's typology is *clinical assessment*. Clinical assessment derives from the tradition of one-to-one casework in medical, social work and probation contexts, and refers to the practitioner's use of experience, interviewing skills, observation and professional judgement to arrive at an assessment of the individual. The 'second generation' in Bonta's typology is *actuarial assessment* which is derived from the methods used in the insurance industry, and is based upon statistical calculations of probability. The 'third generation', and the most recent development, is *risk/needs assessment*, which tends to blur the traditional distinction between clinical and actuarial methods. We shall be encountering and evaluating all three of these models in this chapter.

In recent years, and in the context of developing knowledge about the so-called 'principles of effective practice' which were discussed in the previous chapter, assessment practice has assumed increasing importance as a precursor of effective rehabilitative interventions and, reflecting these 'principles', the assessments carried out by probation officers, prison officers and others have come to focus in particular on the related concepts of risk and (criminogenic) need.

Assessing Risks

Risk assessment involves making judgements or predictions about the likely future behaviour of an individual and this involves thinking about future behaviour on a number of levels. Hazel Kemshall, a leading authority on the subject, defines risk assessment as:

> a probability calculation that a harmful behaviour or event will occur, [which] involves an assessment about the frequency of the behaviour/event, its likely impact and who it will affect. (1996: v)

A thorough risk assessment, then, should consider both the *gravity or seriousness* of any future offending behaviour and the *probability or likelihood* of such a behaviour occurring. These two dimensions of risk are commonly referred to as *risk of harm* and *risk of reoffending* respectively. A further important dimension of risk assessment concerns the likely target(s) or victim(s) of the individual's offending (or other harmful) behaviour. Thus, the practitioner should take into account both the risk(s) posed by the offender to him or her self (i.e. risk of self-harming behaviour), as well as the likely risks to others: that is, to the public at large, to particular communities (e.g. children; ethnic minority groups), and/or to specific individuals (e.g. a former partner; a known associate).

Whilst risk assessment on both of these dimensions has assumed increasing importance since the mid-1990s (see Robinson, 2003a and Chapter 3, this volume), it is the assessment of *risk of reoffending* which has come to be a key task for those professionals whose practice is oriented toward offender rehabilitation. In the context of the 'What Works?' movement discussed in Chapter 5, the importance of assessing risk of recidivism was highlighted by the *principle of risk classification*. As we saw in that chapter, the 'risk principle' was derived from Canadian research which indicated not only that intensive programmes tended to be most effective for higher-risk offenders, but also that subjecting lower risk offenders to intensive programmes could actually be counter-productive (Andrews et al., 1990b). The risk principle thus dictated that, in order to maximise the rehabilitative potential of the service's work, there should be:

> a matching between offender risk level and degree of service intervention, such that higher-risk individuals receive more intensive services, while those at lower risk receive lower or minimal intervention. (McGuire and Priestley, 1995: 14)

The ability of penal practitioners to *routinely* assess risk of reoffending has subsequently come to be an accepted prerequisite of effective rehabilitative practice, and in the last decade or so the pursuit of accurate assessments of risk has been accompanied by a move toward more 'formalised' risk assessment methods.

Predicting recidivism: actuarial risk assessment

Derived from the methods used in the insurance industry, *actuarial* risk assessment is based upon statistical calculations of probability. It takes into account a set of identified factors or items, each of which has been empirically demonstrated to correlate with reconviction. Although the development of actuarial risk assessment has a long history in penal contexts, Home Office statistical researchers began to develop a 'reconviction predictor scale' for use by probation staff in the early 1990s (Humphrey et al., 1992; Copas et al., 1994). This scale underwent a number of revisions and refinements prior to being launched as the 'Offender Group Reconviction Scale' (OGRS), a windows-based computer programme for use by probation personnel (Copas and Marshall, 1998; Taylor, 1999).

OGRS was developed on the basis of a national Home Office database consisting of information about the demographic characteristics and offending histories of a large sample of offenders, and was designed for the assessment of male and female offenders aged 17 and over. The instrument provides an estimate, expressed as a percentage, of the statistical likelihood of one or more reconvictions within two years of release from custody or from the beginning of a community sentence. The key variables which OGRS considers in calculating the statistical likelihood of reconviction are:

- age
- sex
- offence
- number of custodial sentences while aged under 21
- number of previous convictions
- age at first conviction.

The main strength of actuarial methods (such as the OGRS) lies in their reliance on clearly articulated risk factors or indicators which are grounded in empirical data. This means that they can offer high levels of predictive validity or accuracy. In other words, tools such as OGRS undoubtedly improve the ability of practitioners to classify offenders into 'high' and 'low' risk groups. Actuarially-based assessment tools can also aid in the evaluation of the effectiveness of 'rehabilitative' interventions. Using an actuarial tool such as OGRS as an evaluation instrument involves calculating an *expected reconviction rate* for each of a group of offenders (i.e. an OGRS score) and then calculating an average, which may be compared to the *actual reconviction rate* for the same group of offenders when the two-year follow-up period has elapsed. A lower observed or actual rate of reconviction than that which was expected indicates, in principle, that the intervention has been effective in reducing the risk of reconviction.

However, despite their proven predictive validity, actuarial methods suffer from a number of limitations. One important limitation derives from the fact that they are both based on and designed for use with groups or *populations* of offenders. This means that they cannot provide accurate predictions of risk in respect of *individuals*. For example, OGRS can do no more than provide an estimate of the probability that *an* offender with a particular set of characteristics will be reconvicted within two years; it does not purport to make an accurate prediction for a specific individual. Thus, if an offender has an OGRS score of 75%, this indicates that three-quarters of offenders of this age and sex and with a comparable criminal record are likely to be reconvicted within two years. The score cannot tell the assessor whether this particular individual will be one of the 75% of offenders with this profile who *will* be reconvicted, or one of the 25% who *will not*.

Another limitation of actuarial tools concerns the fact that they predict the probability of *reconviction*, which is not synonymous with the probability of *reoffending*. In general terms, the probability of reoffending is likely to exceed the probability of reconviction, since a great deal of offending goes undetected. This disparity between rates of reoffending and reconviction is greater for some types of offending than for others, due to differential rates of reporting, detection and prosecution for different types of crime. For example, offenders who are convicted of burglary are likely to be reconvicted more quickly than those who commit a sexual offence (Taylor, 1999).[1] A related point is that actuarially based tools can increase the likelihood of 'consistently discriminatory assessments' (Bhui, 1999) because the data on which such assessments are based may to a large extent be a reflection of discriminatory processes in the criminal justice system, such as the over-policing of black communities.

A further limitation of tools such as OGRS is that they tend to rely on a particular type of information about offenders: namely *static factors*. These factors are static in the sense that they cannot be altered or modified: for example, an offender can do nothing to change his or her age, sex or offending history. Whilst these static factors are strongly predictive of reconviction, they provide little direction for the practitioner who wishes to know what kind of intervention might *reduce* the individual's risk of reoffending. For this *dynamic* risk factors need to be assessed (these are discussed below). The reliance on static factors also makes actuarial tools relatively ineffective when it comes to assessing changes in levels of risk over time, because they take no account of changes in the offender's personal circumstances, behaviour or attitudes. To the extent that rehabilitation is understood as a process oriented toward the reduction of risk, such tools are of limited value for evaluative purposes.

Assessing Needs

Whilst risk assessment is a relatively new concern of those practitioners engaged in rehabilitative practices, the assessment of offenders' needs has a much longer history. This is not, however, to imply that the practice of assessing offenders' needs has not changed in recent years. On the contrary, there have been significant developments in respect of both *how* needs are assessed (with a move towards much more structured assessments) and *which* needs are considered important or legitimate as targets for intervention. Central to assessment practice today – certainly in the penal realm – is a key distinction between so-called 'criminogenic' and 'non-criminogenic' needs, and it is the identification of the former which is today considered to be at the heart of effective rehabilitative practice.

Until relatively recently, needs assessments conducted by probation officers and other penal professionals tended to rely upon the clinical approach (Bonta's 'first generation' of assessment practice). However, the mid-1990s witnessed a growing critique of the clinical approach, which centred on the lack of consistency between assessments conducted by different practitioners, and on the questionable accuracy of such assessments, which were not necessarily being guided by the latest research on factors known to be associated with offending (e.g. Burnett, 1996). As Bonta (1996) has argued, the most serious weakness of the clinical approach is that the rules for collecting and interpreting information about the individual are subject to considerable personal discretion: for example, the practitioner is free to ask questions that he or she considers important or interesting, which renders objectivity problematic. The subjectivity of a purely clinical approach was illustrated in Burnett's (1996) research on assessment practice. In the course of this research over one hundred probation officers and senior probation officers in ten probation areas were interviewed, and it was found that over half thought that the assessment of the offender and/or the proposal in a Pre-Sentence Report was likely to differ according to the particular experience or skills of the report writer.

As we saw in Chapter 5, 'What Works?' research had, by the mid-1990s, begun to identify a number of factors pertaining to the lifestyles and attributes of offenders which could be shown to be linked with offending behaviour (e.g. Andrews et al., 1990b; Andrews, 1995). These factors have come to be known as *criminogenic needs*, or *dynamic risk factors*. As Bonta has explained:

> Criminogenic needs are linked to criminal behaviour. If we alter these needs, then we change the likelihood of criminal behaviour. Thus criminogenic needs are actually risk pre-dictors, but they are *dynamic* in nature rather than static. (Bonta, 1996: 23)

In other words, in assessing criminogenic needs, we are also assessing the individual's risk of reoffending. It therefore follows that if we intervene to try to ameliorate or do something positive in respect of the offender's criminogenic needs, we can in principle lower his or her risk of reoffending. So-called criminogenic needs are therefore a crucial 'discovery' in that they can usefully point to the areas of the offender's life – such as his or her accommodation or employment situation, drug or alcohol use, or attitudes – which, if subject to intervention and help, are likely to reduce his or her risk of further offending.

Risk/needs assessment instruments

Since the mid-1990s, a number of assessment instruments incorporating dynamic risk factors or criminogenic needs have been available to penal practitioners. These are commonly referred to as 'risk/needs' assessment instruments and have been described by Bonta (1996) as the 'third generation' of offender assessment.[2]

The first combined risk/needs instrument to be used by probation staff in England, Wales and Scotland was the *Level of Service Inventory – Revised* (LSI-R) (Andrews and Bonta, 1995). Designed and developed in Canada, the LSI-R combines both static and dynamic factors which are organised into ten sub-components. The ten sub-components cover both static and dynamic areas such as criminal history, education/employment, accommodation and alcohol/drug use, all of which have been statistically proven to be related to risk of reconviction (for an overview of the use of LSI-R in Britain, see Raynor, 2007b).

In the light of the popularity of instruments like LSI-R, and with a view to standardising assessment practice across the 'correctional services', the Home Office announced plans to develop a new 'Offender Assessment System' (OASys) in 1999 (Home Office, 1999). OASys was to replace LSI-R and other assessment instruments which had been taken up and/or developed by probation areas in the 1990s. Meanwhile, the Youth Justice Board funded the development of the 'Asset' system for the assessment of young offenders, which is now the standard tool used by all Youth Offending Teams in England and Wales (Baker, 2004).

OASys was rolled out nationally in probation areas and prisons in England and Wales between 2001–2004 (Howard, 2006). OASys started life as a paper-based system, but work soon started to develop an electronic, on-screen version called e-OASys. It was designed to meet a comprehensive specification, such that it included both an assessment of reconviction (incorporating both static and dynamic factors) and a structured format for the assessment of risk of harm. The criminogenic need areas covered by OASys are as follows:

- accommodation
- education, training and employability
- financial management and income
- relationships
- lifestyle and associates
- drug misuse
- alcohol misuse
- emotional well-being
- thinking and behaviour
- attitudes.

Each 'criminogenic need' section in OASys is similar in format. Each section begins with a number of questions about the individual's current status in respect of the relevant criminogenic need, and these questions are 'scored' by the practitioner. There is also an 'evidence box' in which details or evidence can be written to explain the scores assigned. Finally, the practitioner is required to indicate whether the particular issue under examination (accommodation, relationships, etc) is linked with risk (of harm and/or reoffending) in this particular case. It is here then that the distinction is drawn between which needs are 'criminogenic' and which are 'non-criminogenic' for the individual offender being assessed.

Having completed the main sections of OASys, scores in the individual sections are added up to produce a total score. Each section or 'need area' is differentially 'weighted' to reflect the relative strength of their relationship with reconviction. The total weighted score is then classified as low (scores 0–40), medium (scores 41–99) or high (scores 100–168) (Howard, 2006).

OASys also triggers other, more specialist assessments in relevant cases (e.g. basic skills; sexual and violent offender assessments). It also provides a system for translating the OASys assessment(s) into a supervision or sentence plan, which summarises the interventions necessary to address the criminogenic needs identified in the assessment. Finally, OASys (in common with the Asset system for young offenders) includes a Self Assessment Questionnaire for the offender to complete. This invites the offender to assess themselves in relation to a range of social and personal problems and to estimate their own risk of reoffending (Moore, 2007; Baker, 2004).

Problems and potential   Risk/needs assessment instruments boast a number of useful applications (see also Merrington, 2004; Bonta and Wormith, 2007). Not only have they been shown to be effective in predicting risk of reconviction (e.g. Raynor et al., 2000; Howard, 2006), but their inclusion of dynamic variables also

Table 6.1   Criminogenic needs in a sample of 10,000 OASys assessments

	% of offenders assessed as having a problem	
	Community sample	Custodial sample
Accommodation	31%	43%
Education, training and employment	53%	65%
Financial management and income	22%	29%
Relationships	36%	42%
Lifestyle and associates	35%	52%
Drug misuse	27%	39%
Alcohol misuse	34%	33%
Emotional well-being	40%	38%
Thinking and behaviour	50%	59%
Attitudes	21%	32%
Average no. of criminogenic needs	3.50	4.31

Source: adapted from Harper et al., 2005: 19; Table 2.1

enables users to identify the areas of an offender's life which, if tackled in probation supervision, are likely to lead to a reduction in the level of risk posed. These two key functions combine to render such instruments potentially useful in determining which offenders are most likely to benefit from specific 'rehabilitative' interventions.

Risk/needs assessment instruments can also provide a measure of the effectiveness of probation intervention. This is achieved by repeating the assessment process after the offender has completed an intervention or period of supervision. A lower score at the point of re-assessment indicates some amelioration of the individual's criminogenic needs, which is clearly a positive result (though of course without a comparison or control, it is difficult to be sure that the observed changes are in fact attributable to the intervention – see further Chapter 4).

Thanks to their inclusion of dynamic variables, risk/needs assessment instruments – in contrast to 'pure' actuarial instruments such as OGRS – are as valid for gauging the progress of individual offenders as they are for measuring effectiveness at the level of aggregates (i.e. groups of offenders). Risk/needs assessment data can also be used to inform managers of rehabilitative services about the spread or 'profile' of criminogenic needs in local and/or national offender populations. For example, Harper et al. (2005) have reported that among a (non-random) sample of 10,000 OASys assessments, the incidence of criminogenic needs was as shown in Table 6.1.

Data such as these can be extremely useful in informing service managers about the need for particular resources or types of intervention in a particular geographical area. For example it might recommend increased provision of services to help offenders find accommodation, or access education, training or employment. There are also obvious advantages which flow from a common approach to offender assessment among practitioners working in different contexts. Both OASys (for adults) and Asset (for young offenders) are playing a key role in bringing practitioners with different professional backgrounds and training in line in terms of both their approach to assessing risk and to the 'seamless' management of offenders in, and between, custodial and community settings (e.g. Baker, 2004; Home Office, 1999). The Prison Service began using OASys in mid-2003 and the intention is that OASys assessments conducted by probation staff should be following offenders into prisons. Work is also in progress in developing compatible electronic versions of OASys (e-OASys) in prison and probation contexts offering the possibility of 'area to area data exchange and also data exchange with the Prison Service' (National Probation Service, 2003).

This brings us to the issue of practitioners' perceptions of such instruments. It is worth remembering that the effectiveness of any assessment system is reliant upon the skills and support of its users. Tools like OASys do not complete themselves: the information must be gathered, interpreted and recorded by a practitioner in each case. Research on users' views conducted to date has revealed a broad consensus among practitioners, who have particularly welcomed the move toward greater consistency in assessment practice which instruments like OASys promote (Robinson, 2003b; Mair et al., 2006). However, research has also revealed a number of problems in respect of the implementation of risk/needs assessment instruments. For users, the incorporation of these instruments into everyday practice has entailed considerable demands, both in terms of the time required to gather the relevant information (by interviewing the offender and consulting other sources) and to physically complete the assessment, whether on paper or in electronic form (e-OASys). In a survey of 180 OASys users conducted by Mair et al. (2006), the most common complaint among users was that it was time-consuming to complete. Asked how long it took them to complete, a fifth said it took up to an hour; almost a quarter said it took between 60–90 minutes; another fifth took between 91–120 minutes; and the remainder took longer than two hours. And, whilst the majority (60%) said that it was easy to use, almost a quarter (22%) said it was a bit or very difficult. One of the main problems in the design of risk/needs assessment instruments, then, has been achieving a balance between comprehensiveness and user-friendliness.

A further problem has been achieving a balance between, on the one hand, the pursuit of consistency and standardisation in the assessment process; and, on the other, the discretion or professional judgement of the user. There are two paradoxical aspects to this. First, because risk/needs assessment instruments rely on the assessor's ability to elicit and interpret a range of information, some have questioned the 'inter-rater reliability' of instruments like OASys.[3] Second, research has revealed that at least some practitioners feel ambivalent about the introduction of such instruments because they are associated with conflicting implications for 'professionalism'. On the one hand, they herald a more standardised approach to assessment, which is associated with enhanced consistency, fairness, accuracy and effectiveness. On the other hand, they tend to de-emphasise the role of professional judgement and consequently generate fears about de-professionalisation (Robinson, 2003b). In the words of one LSI-R using practitioner, 'I feel it *enhances* [professional credibility] because it's a standardized, verified tool, that you can say you're basing decisions on. But at the same time I think people feel there's a danger that a trained chimp could do it' (quoted in Robinson, 2003b: 34).

Whilst it is difficult to entirely remove practitioners' fears about increasing standardisation, which of course affects not just assessment but most other areas of practice, it has been argued that greater attention to implementation issues could minimise genuine concerns. If practitioners are to engage positively with instruments like OASys in both the short and longer term, they need to be persuaded that the benefits of such instruments outweigh the costs. Practitioners are likely to be encouraged by tangible evidence that the rich data which such instruments generate is being used to improve the quality of services which offenders receive, and not simply as a means of exerting ever greater control over professional discretion (Robinson, 2003b).

Finally, some researchers have questioned the degree to which actuarially based risk/needs assessment instruments, designed with reference to (largely white) male offender populations, are applicable to women and other minority groups of offenders. Shaw and Hannah-Moffat (2000), among others, have argued that the notion of 'criminogenic' (i.e. offending related) need is not necessarily the same for minority groups as it is for white men (see also Hollin and Palmer, 2006a; Hedderman, 2004; Kemshall et al., 2004; Gelsthorpe, 2001). For example, Gelsthorpe (2001) discusses evidence that women offenders show higher levels of poverty, victimisation, mental health problems, self-harm and problems linked to family relationships than male offenders. It has also been argued that anti-social beliefs and attitudes play a smaller role in explaining women's offending than in explaining offending by men. Questions therefore arise about whether the specific needs of women and other minority groups are being overlooked in assessments. Indeed, in the survey of OASys users by Mair et al. (2006) referred to above, about half of the respondents felt that the assessment did not deal adequately with 'diversity issues' (race, gender, sexual orientation and disability).

It has also been argued that there is a danger that the blurring of 'needs' and 'risks' could potentially result in inflated estimates of risk in respect of women and other minority and/or disadvantaged groups and justify greater than necessary levels of intervention and control (Hannah-Moffat, 1999; Hudson, 2001). Indeed there is some evidence that risk/needs assessment tools *do* over-predict the risk of reconviction for female offenders. Presenting an analysis of LSI-R assessments on offenders in Jersey (1170 men and 210 women), Raynor (2007b: 130–1) explains that whilst the women had slightly lower scores than the men, their reconviction rates were dramatically lower. For example, of those offenders with the highest LSI-R scores (23 or over), the proportions reconvicted within one year were 44.6% for men but just half that – 22.2% – for the women. For Hudson (2001), risk/needs assessment instruments pose a threat to racial equality because some of the data which they take into account reflects discriminatory processes in wider society (e.g. employment status) and/or measures of 'lifestyle' which treat patterns among white populations as the 'norm' (e.g. family relationship/residency patterns).

So, does this mean that risk/needs instruments should not be used to assess non-white and non-male populations of offenders? Raynor (2007b: 131) argues that it does not. Rather, he argues, careful use of such instruments 'can make a useful contribution to the evidence-based exploration of [gender] differences'. In other words, risk/needs assessment data can generate knowledge about the *relevance, weight* and *incidence* of particular risk factors/criminogenic needs in different populations of offenders. On the basis of his own analysis of data from several hundred LSI-R assessments, Raynor suggests that:

(a) a similar range of factors is *relevant* to assessing reconviction risk for men and women; but
(b) their *weights* (i.e. the levels of reconviction with which they are associated) are consistently lower for women; and
(c) the *incidence* of particular risk factors differs between male and female samples, with women assessed as having *more* problems around employment, finances, drug misuse and family relationships than men, but *less* serious criminal histories.

Assessing Responsivity

Throughout this chapter we have referred to the impact of 'What Works?' findings on assessment practice, and the intimate association between notions of effective rehabilitation and effective assessment incorporating a structured analysis of risks and needs. We have explained that risk/needs assessments now play a major role in informing decisions about the type and/or intensity of supervision appropriate to individual offenders. It is increasingly the case in the correctional services that 'resources follow risk': that is, the higher the risk, the more resources (including rehabilitative resources) the offender is likely to attract.

However, whilst developments in assessment technology and practice have clearly reflected the principles of 'risk' and '(criminogenic) need' derived from research, there has arguably been a corresponding neglect of a third principle: namely, that of 'responsivity'. It will be recalled (see Chapter 5) that the responsivity principle concerns individual differences between offenders in respect of a variety of issues which have the potential to impact on their ability to benefit from 'rehabilitative' interventions. To recap, Andrews et al. (1990b: 20) described this principle as follows:

> Styles and modes of service are matched to the learning styles and abilities of offenders. A professional offers a type of service that is matched not only to criminogenic need but to those attributes and circumstances of cases that render cases likely to profit from that particular type of service.

Andrews et al. clearly leave the issue of just what the relevant 'attributes and circumstances' of offenders are open to interpretation, and these may well differ from individual to individual. However, Ogloff and Davis (2004) have helpfully distinguished two general groups of factors which are likely to affect responsivity. These are referred to as *idiographic* and *nomothetic* factors. Idiographic factors, they explain, are internal to the individual (e.g. intellectual functioning, self-esteem and motivation); whilst nomothetic factors are external (e.g. staff characteristics, therapeutic relationships, environmental support, and the content and delivery of programmes). Some of these factors are discussed elsewhere in this book, but in the context of the present discussion, we think that the idiographic factor of an offender's motivation to change merits particular attention.

In thinking about motivation as a 'responsivity' factor, it is well worth reminding ourselves that penal practitioners are, to a large extent, dealing with *involuntary* clients, and it cannot be assumed that individuals subject to penal sanctions will be ready or willing to 'change' or desist. As McGuire (2000: 68–9) has observed, levels of motivation can vary substantially, even among those who appear to be in urgent need of help: some may be highly motivated to engage with rehabilitative interventions, whilst others may be disinterested in or even resistant to any notion of change (see also Chapter 1).

Prochaska and DiClemente's 'cycle of change'

With this in mind, probation practitioners have experimented with a 'model of change' developed by researchers in the field of addictive behaviours. This model, developed by American psychologists Prochaska and DiClemente (see Prochaska et al., 1992), represents change as a cycle or process, featuring five stages or 'motivational states', as follows:

Pre-contemplation Individuals at this stage are likely to have only limited awareness of their problems and/or may refuse to acknowledge that problems exist. They therefore see no reason to change.

Contemplation   At the contemplation stage, individuals have recognised a problem or problems and are considering taking action but are likely to need help to determine an appropriate 'change strategy'.

Determination   At this stage the individual has resolved to take action in respect of their problem(s) but needs help to choose from among a range of strategies.

Action   The individual has embarked on a course of action but is likely to need help to maintain good progress.

Maintenance   At this stage the individual is making good progress but is not yet 'problem-free' and needs support to avoid relapse into 'old habits'.

As Fleet and Annison have explained, 'if we can identify which point on the cycle most closely reflects the offender's position in relation to offending, it can provide useful guidance as to what we need to be doing' (2003: 133). In other words, an assessment of the offender's motivation to change is arguably vital in respect of informing decisions about appropriate interventions.

It is therefore encouraging that risk/needs assessment tools like OASys and Asset *do* require practitioners to consider the offender's motivation.[4] OASys, for example, invites the assessor to consider the offender's motivation to address offending in its section on attitudes. However, it is not clear how much weight is given in practice to issues of motivation in informing decisions about appropriate interventions; nor is there consensus on just how important a role motivation ought to play in such decisions. On the one hand, and in the light of research which has revealed a key role for personal motivation in processes of desistance (i.e. self-directed rehabilitation), it has been suggested that correctional services might more fruitfully focus their limited resources on those offenders who demonstrate a desire and willingness to desist (Maruna, 2001; Farrall, 2002). In other words, there is an argument that motivation ought to be prioritised over risk and needs assessment in identifying offenders 'worthy' of rehabilitative interventions. On the other hand, it has been pointed out that some interventions *can* be effective even when they are coerced (e.g. see Day et al., 2004). From this perspective, motivation may be less important.

Bonta (1996: 31–2) has suggested that whilst the assessment of risk and criminogenic needs are an essential prerequisite to effective rehabilitation, attention to 'responsivity factors' (including motivation, personality and emotional and cognitive abilities) is also important. Responsivity, he argues, is the 'third aspect of assessment' which is understood less well but may nonetheless play an important role in maximising the effectiveness of rehabilitative interventions. Indeed, he concludes, the assessment of possible responsivity factors may well constitute a *fourth generation* of assessment.

Assessing Strengths

A key criticism of the risk/needs approach to offender assessment is its tendency to focus on the negative aspects of individual offenders' lives and experiences. For example, discussing the use of Asset by youth offending teams (YOTs), Smith (2003: 192) has warned that the emphasis of such instruments on assessing risk may serve to 'generate a pre-disposition to "seeing the worst in people"'. Even among proponents of 'What Works?' concerns have been raised about what has been described as a *deficit model* 'which sees offenders as characterised primarily by deficiencies to be corrected and needs to be met by others' (Raynor, 2004a: 212).

Drawing on developments in what they call 'positive psychology', Tony Ward and others have argued for the development of 'strengths-based' rehabilitation (see also Maruna and LeBel, 2003; Ward and Maruna, 2007). Ward and Brown have argued that whilst the dominant risk/needs model undoubtedly has merit, it tends toward 'negative' treatment goals:

> The focus is on the *reduction* of maladaptive behaviours, the *elimination* of distorted beliefs, the *removal* of problematic desires, and the *modification* of offence supportive emotions and attitudes. In other words, the goals are essentially negative in nature and concerned with eradicating factors rather than promoting prosocial and personally more satisfying goals. (2004: 245)

In contrast, they propose a *Good Lives Model* of offender rehabilitation. This model adopts a more positive perspective: it seeks to equip offenders with the capabilities to secure 'primary human goods' (defined as valued aspects of human functioning and living) in socially acceptable and personally meaningful ways (2004: 246). Although Ward and Brown do not specifically discuss processes of offender assessment, implicit in their model is an assumption that assessment ought to focus on 'an offender's preferences, strengths, primary goods, and relevant environments' and specify 'exactly what competencies and resources are required to achieve those goods' (2004: 248).

The *Good Lives Model* is proposed as an alternative to the dominant risk/needs model of offending behaviour.[5] However, even within a risk/needs model it is – theoretically at least – possible to generate an assessment which is not entirely predicated on negatives. This can be achieved by taking into account so-called *protective factors*, which are sometimes referred to as 'positive risk factors'. Protective factors are those attributes of a person or aspects of his or her life which moderate the effects of exposure to risk: in other words, factors which reduce rather than increase risk. Current knowledge about protective factors is limited and emanates from research on children and young people, but known protective factors among these groups include *individual factors* (female gender; resilient temperament;

sense of self-efficacy; positive, outgoing disposition; high intelligence) and *social bonding* factors (stable, warm, affectionate relationship with one or both parents; link with adults and peers who hold positive attitudes) (Youth Justice Board, 2005a).

Asset is one assessment instrument which does in fact contain a section on 'positive' or 'protective' factors to encourage the identification of aspects of a young person's life which could be strengthened to reduce the risk of reoffending. These are divided in the assessment instrument into (a) 'social and family circumstances' (which include living arrangements and neighbourhood; family/personal relationships; education/employment; professional help/support; other) and (b) 'personal factors' (which include lifestyle; resilience; attitudes and thinking; actions and behaviour; motivation). In a study of over 3000 completed Asset assessments, the highest number of positive factors identified were in the areas of living arrangements and family and personal relationships (Baker et al., 2003: 48–9). Researchers involved in the development of the Asset instrument have recently argued that further research on risk and protective factors might open up the possibility of *scoring* protective factors in tools like Asset when calculating an overall risk score, thereby giving 'credit' to a young person for the presence of such factors (Youth Justice Board, 2005b).

Conclusion

In this chapter we have reviewed the purposes of offender assessment and the ways in which assessment can inform decisions about the rehabilitation of offenders. We focused on the main ways in which assessment practice has evolved in recent years, particularly in the context of the 'What Works?' movement discussed in the previous chapter. In the space of just a decade, assessment practice has moved from being a largely unstructured activity informed by experience and discretion, to one which tends to be characterised by uniformity, structure and a rather more systematic approach. But it is not just the format of assessments which has evolved: of particular note has been the move toward assessments which are multi-purpose or multi-functional. In the early twenty-first century, offender assessment systems continue to reflect traditional concerns with offenders' needs and problems, but in addition they are increasingly concerned with the assessment of the risks posed by the offender. As we have seen, this dual contemporary focus on risks and needs is directly attributable to the lessons of the 'What Works?' movement discussed in the previous chapter. And reflecting this focus, decisions about appropriate interventions are increasingly driven by risk/needs assessments, with such decisions about the allocation of resources reflecting a general rule that resources should follow risk.

Questions remain, however – both among proponents and critics of 'What Works?' – about whether too much emphasis is being placed on risks (and the criminogenic needs on which they are based) at the expense of other factors which could be at least as important to processes of rehabilitation. Of particular note in this regard are responsivity factors (not least motivation to change) and potentially protective factors (the presence of which may increase an individual's likelihood of successful rehabilitation).

Questions to Consider

1 'Risk assessment is a necessary but not a sufficient basis for decisions about appropriate rehabilitative intervention.' Do you agree?
2 What are the key limitations of (a) clinical, (b) actuarial, and (c) risk/needs assessment methods from the perspective of rehabilitation?
3 Can assessment ever be entirely objective?
4 What are 'responsivity factors' and how much weight should be given to them in assessment?
5 To what extent can structured assessment tools contribute to effective offender rehabilitation?

Suggested Further Reading

Bonta (1996) provides a very useful review of the development of approaches to offender assessment. The debate between proponents of the risk/needs model (Andrews and others) and the 'Good Lives' model (Ward and others) is one which is likely to continue, and makes very interesting reading.

Notes

1 There are a number of specialist assessment instruments for the assessment of sexual and violent offenders. For a review of some of these see Kemshall (2001).
2 Actuarial instruments represent the 'second generation', whilst the relatively unstructured 'clinical' method constitutes Bonta's 'first generation'.
3 One study of inter-rater reliability in relation to assessments using LSI-R and another tool reported satisfactory findings, but the sample was small (Raynor et. al., 2000).
4 Further, as already noted, both tools include a Self-assessment Questionnaire for offenders, which provides an insight into which problems or needs the offender recognises for him or herself.
5 The 'Good Lives' model has been criticised for lacking empirical support (see Bonta and Andrews, 2003; Ogloff and Davis, 2004).

SEVEN

Offending Behaviour Programmes

Introduction

In Chapter 5 we explored the revival and re-legitimation of rehabilitation in the context of an international 'What Works?' movement which began to have a significant impact on penal policy and practice from the 1990s. In that chapter we noted that a key element of 'What Works?' was the development and proliferation of programmes of intervention, known collectively as offending behaviour programmes (OBPs). Our task in this chapter is to consider the rise of such programmes in more detail and to examine whether they have in fact lived up to their considerable promise. We begin by defining what is meant by a 'programme' in this context, and go on to examine how the development of programmes to tackle offending behaviour has seen the adoption and application of psychological explanations of deviant behaviour. We then move on to examine some specific offending behaviour programmes and consider their effectiveness in custodial and community contexts. In the final part of the chapter we debate whether offending behaviour programmes signal a return to a 'treatment model' in offender rehabilitation, as some critics have asserted.

What is a Programme?

Defining what is meant by a 'programme' in the context of offender rehabilitation is not as straightforward as one might expect. McGuire (2001) has distinguished three possible definitions. The first, and narrowest, definition of a programme is 'a planned sequence of learning opportunities'. In this respect,

McGuire argues, a rehabilitative programme shared much in common with the notion of a *curriculum* in educational settings: it constitutes a circumscribed set of activities; it has a specific objective; and it consists of a number of inter-connected elements. More broadly, however, in criminal justice settings the term 'programme' can be used to describe initiatives like mentoring schemes for young offenders, or therapeutic communities for drug-misusers. Third, and more broadly still, all criminal justice interventions can be (and have been) described as 'programmes' (McGuire, 2001).

In this chapter, we shall be dealing with those programmes which meet the first of McGuire's definitions. It is worth noting that in much of the literature, there is an assumption that 'programmes' denote interventions delivered to groups of offenders, and Hollin and Palmer (2006b) review some of the main benefits associated with groupwork provision. However, it is worth noting that the notion of a programme is not in fact synonymous with groupwork. In principle, a programme can be delivered to a single offender or to a group of individuals.

Theoretical Background

In earlier chapters we have argued that approaches to offender rehabilitation are never 'theory-free'. Offending behaviour programmes are no exception. Whilst there is much potential for variation in terms of the content of OBPs, the theoretical roots of the kind of programmes that we are referring to here lie in the discipline of psychology: specifically, two 'schools' of psychology – behavioural and cognitive. These schools of psychology have separate origins but have in recent decades tended to converge under the umbrella of 'cognitive-behavioural' approaches. It is for this reason that the terms 'offending behaviour programmes' and 'cognitive-behavioural programmes' are often used in the literature interchangeably. However, it is important to recognise that the history of cognitive-behavioural approaches is rather longer than the history of OBPs: that is, such approaches were principally developed in experimental and clinical contexts to deal with a range of emotional and behavioural disorders, including depression, anxiety and phobias. Indeed, cognitive-behavioural theory underpins one of the most popular current approaches to psychotherapy, and is used by a wide range of practitioners in clinical settings (e.g. psychologists, psychiatrists, mental health nurses, social workers and counsellors). It is not possible in the space available here to do justice to the theoretical development of cognitive-behavioural psychology (see McGuire, 2000 for a detailed introduction), but what follows is a brief introduction to the two main theoretical approaches which underpin cognitive-behavioural interventions: namely, behavioural and cognitive psychology.

Derived from the work of psychologists including Ivan Pavlov, John Watson and B.F. Skinner, *behavioural theory* emphasises how behaviour is shaped or influenced by external factors, namely the person's environment. Behaviourism stresses the role of external, environmental factors in shaping behaviour: in other words, it attempts to explain behaviour in its social context. It tends to ignore internal, 'mediating' processes like thinking about and interpreting events because these are not observable processes. It suggests that we learn to behave in particular ways via reinforcement – namely receiving rewards and disincentives. Thus, behaviour which is followed by something which is perceived as positive is likely to be repeated, whereas behaviour which is followed by consequences which are perceived to be negative is less likely to be repeated. Through experimentation, behavioural psychologists have shown how behaviour can be manipulated by positive or negative reinforcement.

Social learning theory (or *cognitive social learning theory*) is a variant of behavioural theory which represents a synthesis of or bridge between ideas from the behavioural and cognitive traditions (McGuire, 2006). Research by Albert Bandura (1975) and his colleagues showed that learning could take place in the absence of direct experience of rewards and punishments (reinforcement): that is, animals could learn indirectly, by observing the behaviours of others and the outcomes of those behaviours. Bandura's research revealed three key types of 'model' which proved particularly powerful in the context of human learning: these were family members; peer group members; and 'symbolic models', as observed via the media. This idea of *observational learning* saw a departure from traditional behavioural theory in that it implied a reliance on internal (cognitive) mechanisms, and it is in this sense that social learning theory provides a conceptual bridge between behavioural and cognitive theories.

Cognitive theory derives from the work of another group of psychologists, among them Aaron Beck (e.g. Beck, 1976), and it emphasises the way our behaviour is influenced by our thoughts or thinking patterns, which are also known as cognitive processes. Cognitive theory sees behaviour as more than the product of environmental or external forces, and points to the ways in which our behaviour is mediated by internal processes: thoughts, judgements, interpretations, beliefs and so on. Cognitive theory goes a long way towards explaining why different people do not necessarily respond in the same way to the same situation or external event. In the course of treating people with neurotic conditions like depression and anxiety, Beck discovered that these conditions were often accompanied by negative 'self-talk', which served to reinforce a person's illness. So for example a depressed person might say to himself 'The future is hopeless and I am powerless to change things' or 'I deserve to be unhappy because I am a worthless person'. Similarly, an anorexic might repeat: 'I am fat and unattractive', or 'I am a bad person and therefore do not deserve to eat' and these beliefs reinforce the behaviour associated with the eating disorder. Beck found that challenging these negative thoughts (or *cognitive distortions*) and replacing them with positive and more realistic ones could be an effective form of therapy for these conditions.

The term 'Cognitive-Behavioural Therapy' (CBT) is variously used to refer to behaviour therapy, cognitive therapy, and to therapy based on the pragmatic combination of principles of behavioural and cognitive theories. CBT takes as its focus *not* the 'whole person' or 'personality', but rather specific (negative) behaviours and the thought processes which support or maintain them. It tends to focus on problems and situations affecting the individual in the here-and-now, and whilst it may involve analysis of specific instances of the problem behaviour in depth, its focus (unlike Freudian-inspired 'psychodynamic' therapies) is not usually the person's early child-hood or unconscious motivations.

Cognitive-Behavioural Theory and Offending Behaviour

During the 1980s, cognitive, behavioural and social learning theories came to be applied by criminological psychologists to explain both the onset and main-tenance of offending behaviour (McGuire, 2006). Particularly influential were the so-called 'Canadian school' of clinical and correctional psychologists, who led the way in the development, delivery and evaluation of a new breed of interventions or 'programmes' based on cognitive and behavioural principles. This was made possible because these individuals were working within correctional and government jurisdictions which continued to be supportive of rehabilitative policies (Goggin and Gendreau, 2006).

In 1985, Ross and Fabiano proposed a *cognitive model of offender rehabilitation*; a variant of social learning theory with a particular focus on what they called 'cognitive skills'. On the basis of a review of the psychological literature (specifically the 'cognitive correlates' of criminal behaviour), Ross and Fabiano found evidence to support a hypothesis that persistent offenders differed from non-offending populations in that they were more rigid in their thinking styles, more impulsive, less likely to think before acting, and less likely to consider the potential consequences of alternative courses of action (Ross and Fabiano, 1985). In short, it was hypothesised that many offenders had *cognitive deficits*. This review seemed to suggest that targeting these deficits, and building offenders' 'cognitive skills' could be a fruitful strategy for reducing their propensity to offend.

And thus, the first of many programmes designed specifically to tackle offending behaviour was born (e.g. Ross et al., 1988). Developed by Robert Ross and his colleagues for use with Canadian offender populations, *Reasoning and Rehabilitation* (R and R) focused specifically on the thinking skills thought to guide (or fail to guide) the behaviour of offenders. As Robinson and Porporino have explained, R and R emphasised:

> teaching offenders to become more reflective rather than reactive, more anticipatory and planful in their responses to potential problems, and more generally flexible, open-minded, reasoned, and deliberate in their thinking. (2000: 179–80)

Delivered in a series of 36 two-hour sessions to small groups of offenders, the R and R programme was *multi-modal*: that is, it utilised a variety of techniques to help offenders acquire the requisite skills. These techniques included role-playing; dilemma games; cognitive 'puzzles'; and board games aimed at examining offenders' values (Robinson and Porporino, 2000).

In 1988, Ross and his colleagues published the first evaluation of the R and R programme. This study, known as the 'Pickering Experiment', compared the outcomes of probationers who had completed the R and R programme with the outcomes of two other groups of offenders: one exposed to 'regular' probation, and the other a group who had completed a 'life skills' course. In total, 62 offenders were randomly allocated to one of the three groups. In terms of recidivism, the R and R completers showed superior outcomes: after nine months only 18.1% had been reconvicted, compared with 69.5% of those on 'ordinary' probation and 47.5% of those in the 'life skills' group. Not surprisingly, the R and R programme was subsequently adopted throughout Canadian corrections and adapted for use in many other countries.

In the UK, the R and R programme was adapted by academics in collaboration with probation practitioners and managers in the Mid-Glamorgan Probation Service in South Wales. The adapted version of R and R was called 'Straight Thinking on Probation' (STOP). It was not, however, the first instance of a new focus on 'offending behaviour' in the UK. As Vanstone (2000) has argued, R and R was prefaced by two other important developments, both led by British psychologists James McGuire and Philip Priestley. The first of these, *Social Skills and Personal Problem Solving*, grew out of a project funded in the late 1970s by the Home Office and focused on the setting up of a pre-release programme in two prisons and one in a community setting (Sheffield Day Training Centre). This involved the use of cognitive-behavioural methods, and encouraging evaluation results led to the setting up of short courses for offenders on a range of topics, including employment, alcohol and drug dependence (Priestley et al., 1984). The second stemmed from an acknowledgement that the offence had tended to be neglected as a legitimate focus for work with offenders (McGuire and Priestley, 1985). The delivery of 'offending behaviour' programmes developed by McGuire and Priestley began in the early 1980s, spreading quickly from the juvenile arena to probation practice with adult offenders (Vanstone, 2000).

Cognitive-behavioural approaches had also been gaining popularity in the context of work with sex offenders, in both custodial and community contexts (see also Chapter 3). The *Sex Offender Treatment Programme* (SOTP), developed by psychologists in the English and Welsh Prison Service, began to be used in prisons from the early 1990s (Grubin and Thornton, 1994) and at around the same time probation areas began to develop specialist programmes for sex offenders in the community (Beckett et al., 1994).

Not to be confused with the SOTP, the STOP programme in Mid-Glamorgan consisted of 35 intensive sessions, and ran from 1991. Its implementation was accompanied by a carefully designed evaluation which compared STOP completers with a variety of comparison groups, including standard probation orders; community service orders; custody; and suspended sentences (Raynor and Vanstone, 1996; 1997). Raynor and colleagues compared the actual reconviction rates for treatment and control groups with predicted rates, calculated using a reconviction predictor scale (see Chapter 6). The reconviction study was based on 107 offenders sentenced to the STOP programme and 548 offenders in the various comparison groups. After twelve months, the reconviction rate for STOP completers was less than the predicted rate (35% were reconvicted; the predicted rate was 42%). Those offenders in comparison groups who received custodial sentences also had a combined predicted reconviction rate of 42%, but their actual reconviction rate was 49%. Further, of those who were reconvicted after twelve months, the STOP group tended to be reconvicted of less serious offences: only 8% of STOP completers had been reconvicted of a serious offence (defined as a violent or sexual offence or burglary) compared with 21% of those given custody. However, the positive impact of the programme in terms of reconviction was not sustained at twenty-four months: 63% of STOP completers had been reconvicted, against a predicted rate of 61%. Raynor and Vanstone (1997) nonetheless concluded that, overall, the results of the reconviction study were consistent with the view that the programme could have 'a reductive impact on people's offending' (1997: 39).

Meanwhile, as we saw in Chapter 4, new secondary and meta-analytic reviews of research were singling out cognitive-behavioural methods as the most promising in terms of reducing recidivism, such that by the mid-1990s, summaries of contemporary knowledge of 'what works' were favouring skills-oriented interventions based on behavioural, cognitive or cognitive-behavioural approaches (e.g. McGuire and Priestley, 1995; Vennard et al., 1997; Vennard and Hedderman, 1998). For example, summarising contemporary knowledge about effective rehabilitation in 1997, Home Office researchers concluded that 'Cognitive-behavioural methods are generally more successful in modifying patterns of thinking and behaviour than more traditional counselling and therapy' (Vennard et al., 1997: 1).

Elsewhere, however, the same 'encouraging' evidence was being presented in a rather more positive – some would say 'evangelical' – light. Writing in 1995, Canadian criminological psychologist Don Andrews proclaimed: 'The psychology of crime is back!' (Andrews, 1995: 40). He continued:

> there now exists a psychology of criminal conduct (PCC) that is empirically defensible and whose applications are promising for the design and delivery of effective direct service programmes. This rational empirical psychology of crime ... provides an intellectually serious and practical base for the prediction of criminal behaviour and the modification of criminal propensity (Andrews, 1995: 35).

General Offending Behaviour Programmes

As we saw in Chapter 5, offending behaviour programmes quickly came to constitute a central focus for proponents of effective rehabilitation. For those keen to capitalise as quickly as possible on the positive findings of research, the 'programmes' approach appeared to offer a relatively straightforward and quick route to the implementation of effective practice in the short to medium term. As both prisons and probation areas were already delivering a range of programmes, the focus was on identifying the most effective from among these, with a view to the development of a 'core curriculum' of effective programmes from which prisons and probation areas would ultimately choose. This was to be overseen by a Joint Prison/Probation Services Accreditation Panel (JAP), the role of which would be to set the 'gold standards by which offending behaviour programmes could be judged' (Hollin and Palmer, 2006c: 11).

In 2000 the first wave of accredited programmes began to be rolled out nationally across the Probation Service. All bearing titles reflecting cognitive-behavioural credentials, these were *Reasoning and Rehabilitation* (R and R); *Enhanced Thinking Skills* (ETS) – both of which had previously been accredited (in 1996–7) for use in prisons – and *Think First*, initially piloted in three English probation areas in the mid-1990s but, in common with the other two programmes, already accredited for use in prisons (McGuire, 2006). All were *general offending behaviour programmes* based on cognitive-behavioural principles. 'General' offending behaviour programmes are those designed for use with individuals who have been convicted a number of times, and usually for a variety of offences – typically including property and violent offences.[1] Their roll-out was accompanied by a clear expectation that general offending behaviour programmes would become a standard ingredient of provision for a significant proportion of offenders serving both custodial and community sentences.

Reflecting the smaller-scale use of offending behaviour programmes to date, R and R, ETS and Think First were all designed for delivery in a *groupwork* context – whether in prison or in the community. An additional programme, designed by Philip Priestley, was also accredited for use with offenders on a one-to-one basis.

For illustrative purposes, we draw here on James McGuire's (2006: 87–9) useful description of the methods and contents of one of these programmes: Think First. In common with offending behaviour programmes of all kinds, whether delivered in custodial or community settings, the Think First programme is highly structured, such that its content and the sequencing of specific exercises is set out in a detailed manual. McGuire explains that the programme has two main elements. The first of these is a 'cognitive-social-learning model of change', which is common to all three programmes. This element involves applying specific methods of problem-solving, self-management and social skills training. In practical terms, programme tutors teach offenders to:

- identify and articulate personal difficulties or problems
- generate ideas for alternative courses of action that might constitute possible solutions to the problem ('alternative thinking')
- identify the steps required to put the solution into practice ('means-end thinking')
- anticipate the possible outcomes or consequences of different courses of action ('consequential thinking')
- make rational, well-informed choices between the various options ('decision-making').

In conjunction with this process, and to facilitate programme participants' ability to put this into action, offenders receive self-control training (which involves learning to control impulsiveness and manage the problem-solving process without becoming overwhelmed) and social skills training (which involves improving social interaction). They also learn to consider the perspectives of others who may be affected by the problem.

The second element involves a more specific focus on offending behaviour (as a 'problem') and includes the detailed analysis of specific offences, with a view to helping offenders develop and practice strategies to change their behaviour. Participants select a specific offence and are encouraged to analyse it in detail, using an exercise called '5-WH' (which involves the what, who, when, where and why of the incident). Subsequently they are encouraged to look for patterns in their offending behaviour. In the final part of the programme, problem-solving and skills training methods are applied by offenders to enable them to develop strategies to avoid offending in the future.

Evaluations of General Offending Behaviour Programmes

Evaluative research on offending behaviour programmes has been developing and expanding over a number of years, with evidence about their effectiveness accruing from primary, secondary and meta-analytic studies (see also Chapter 4). Within the scope of this chapter, it is not possible to review this growing body of international research in depth (see McGuire, 2006 for a review): instead, we summarise the findings of the larger-scale primary evaluations of offending behaviour programmes which have been conducted in England and Wales since the early 1990s; the latter of these under the auspices of the Crime Reduction Programme discussed in Chapter 5.

Evaluating prison-based programmes

We noted above that the year 2000 saw the first wave of accredited programmes 'rolled out' nationally across the Probation Service. We also noted that the three general offending behaviour programmes (*Reasoning and Rehabilitation, Enhanced Thinking Skills* and *Think First*) had been used for some time in a number of English and Welsh prisons. It is for this reason that in this jurisdiction the evaluation of prison-based programmes has the longest history. Indeed, R and R and ETS have been evaluated in the Prison Service in a series of four studies, which span several years' delivery.

The first of these (Friendship et al., 2002b) reported recidivism outcomes after two years for a large sample of adult males (n = 670) who had participated in either R and R or ETS between 1992 and 1996 – prior to the programme's accreditation. The study utilised a quasi-experimental design, such that programme completers were compared with a group of prisoners (n = 1801) matched on relevant variables. OGRS scores (see Chapter 6) were comparable in treatment and control groups. Two years after release from custody, a statistically significant treatment effect was found for prisoners of medium-low risk of reconviction, and for those of medium-high risk. The low and high risk groups also showed a treatment effect, but this was not statistically significant. The overall treatment effect was highly significant.

The second study (Falshaw at al., 2003b) examined reconviction outcomes for a later cohort who had completed one of the two programmes post-accreditation: between 1996 and 1998. This study, which used the same research design as described above, found no difference between the two-year reconviction rates for treatment and control groups of male prisoners. In this study 649 adult male programme participants were compared to a sample of 1947 other prisoners, matched on OGRS, who had not participated in the programme. Overall, 40% of the treatment sample was reconvicted, compared with 39% of the control group. When the treatment and control samples were compared in the four OGRS risk bands (high, medium-high, medium-low, low), no significant differences were found in reconviction rates between treatment and control groups.

In the third study (Cann et al., 2003), which included both young and adult prisoners attending programmes between 1998–2000, no significant differences were found between treatment and (matched) comparison groups *per se* (i.e. using an 'intention to treat' design). However, for programme *completers*, one-year reconviction rates *were* significantly lower than for the comparison group; albeit that these differences were not maintained after two years.

In the fourth study, Cann (2006) examined the impact of programmes on 180 female offenders who had started either ETS or R and R between 1996 and 2000. The comparison sample comprised 540 female offenders who had not participated in either programme. The control group was retrospectively constructed by selecting females who matched the programme participants on the following variables: ethnicity; offence type; sentence length; year of discharge and OGRS scores. There were no statistically significant differences between programme participants and control groups either overall or in any of the risk (OGRS) categories.

Evaluating community-based programmes

Under the auspices of the Crime Reduction Programme, teams of academic researchers at the Universities of Leicester and Liverpool were contracted to conduct a national evaluation of the effectiveness of ten accredited probation Pathfinder programmes. These included four general offending behaviour programmes (R and R; ETS; Think First and a further programme developed for use with offenders on a one-to-one basis) and six 'specialist' programmes (two aggression programmes; one substance misuse and one drink-drive programme; and two sex offender programmes). This evaluation has produced an interim report on programme implementation (Hollin et al., 2002) and two outcome evaluations, and is the largest evaluation of community-based interventions conducted to date (McGuire, 2006). The first of the outcome evaluations (Hollin et al., 2004) collected data from 16 Probation Service areas. This was a retrospective study in which the 'treatment' group comprised offenders whose community sentence (passed between 2000–2001) included a requirement to attend an OBP. The second (reported in McGuire, 2006) was a retrospective study in which the treatment group was composed of offenders sentenced during 2002 with a requirement to attend one of seven Pathfinder programmes. This part of the study collected data from 15 Probation Service areas. The comparison group for the first study comprised a random sample of 2630 offenders serving community sentences *without* a programme requirement in seven probation areas. In the second study the comparison group included several hundred additional offenders; a total of 3305.

One of the key findings of this study (and other smaller-scale studies of community-based programmes – for example, Roberts, 2004) was that only relatively small proportions of offenders who were required to complete a programme as part of their sentence actually managed to complete one.[2] In other words, attrition rates were very high. Not only did significant proportions of offenders start and drop out of a programme, but large numbers failed to start a programme at all. For example, in the retrospective study by Hollin et al., completion rates for the three programmes ranged from just 18–33%, whilst around 50% failed to start programmes and drop-out rates for those who did start ranged from 41–61% (McGuire, 2006).

Summarising the results of the two outcome studies, McGuire (2006) explains that with respect to recidivism, findings were similar for all three programmes in both studies. Firstly, the researchers found that offenders who completed the programme had the lowest reconviction rates, and non-completers the highest, with the comparison group falling in between. This finding was statistically significant for all three programmes. For example, in the retrospective study, completing a programme made participants 33.9% less likely to be reconvicted than non-completers and the comparison group, whilst being a non-completer made an individual 57.2% more likely to be reconvicted than the completers or comparison group.

Explaining the results

Taken together, the findings of these larger-scale outcome studies are rather difficult to summarise, and are arguably even more difficult to explain. Indeed, it is probably fair to say that these rather mixed findings have prompted more questions than they have answered. Far from confirming in any straightforward sense 'what works', they have gone some way toward reinstating the question mark in this well-worn phrase. Researchers and commentators have however sought to make sense of these results, producing a variety of (often compatible) explanations. For example, as we have seen, a chronological reading of the four prison-based evaluations indicates a decline in the effectiveness of the programmes being evaluated. This reveals a sense of puzzlement among the researchers, whereby they try to account for the disappointing results which confront them with a series of tentative explanations. Raynor (2004b), in a thoughtful discussion of the community-based evaluations published to date, considers whether the results are best explained with reference to failures of theory, implementation or research (see also Goggin and Gendreau, 2006). Raynor asks: is the theoretical backbone of programmes faulty? Have programmes been put into practice badly? Or has the design of evaluations been flawed, such that we can neither properly test the effectiveness of programmes, nor make sense of our findings?

One possible framework within which to think about the mixed findings of evaluative research in respect of offending behaviour programmes is that suggested by the 'principles of effective practice' identified by meta-analytic research, and discussed in Chapter 5. It will be recalled that these, as originally outlined by McGuire and Priestley (1995), included principles of risk, criminogenic need, responsivity and programme integrity. Andrews and Dowden (2005) have argued that interventions which adhere to fewer than two of the risk, need and responsivity principles should be considered 'inappropriate'.

According to the 'risk principle', offenders most likely to benefit from more intensive interventions or programmes are those assessed as posing a high risk of reoffending. In other words, in order to maximize their effectiveness, programmes ought to be reserved for and targeted at higher risk offenders. However, a number of researchers have drawn attention to the failure to abide strictly by this principle in practice. As we have seen, evaluations have tended to include offenders with a wide range of OGRS scores – not just those posing medium-high risk who are, theoretically, best suited to programmes (see also Hollin et al., 2002; 2004; Turner, 2006). For example, Falshaw et al. (2003b) noted a shift in programme targeting toward lower risk offenders: in this study a quarter of programme participants had OGRS scores below 25. Cann (2006) also pointed to the low risk levels of participants in her evaluation as a possible explanation for disappointing findings. In respect of community-based programmes, Raynor (2007b) has drawn attention to the likely pernicious effect of unrealistically high government targets for programme commencements, which put a great deal of pressure on probation areas to get 'bums on seats'. He points out that initial targets were based on 'negotiations with the Treasury in 1999 rather than on any measurement of the need for them or the numbers of offenders likely to benefit' (2007b: 136).

According to the principle of 'criminogenic needs', interventions must target those offender problems or features that contribute to or are supportive of their offending. As we have seen, offending behaviour programmes tend to focus on cognitive deficits and antisocial attitudes as the main focus of intervention. For this reason they have met with criticism on the grounds that they 'abrogate responsibility for treating the offender as a "whole person" in a social context' (Worrall and Hoy, 2005: 141). Whilst this does not necessarily mean that offenders' other criminogenic needs are wholly ignored, it does mean that offending behaviour programmes *on their own* are unlikely to be sufficient to reduce reoffending for individuals with multiple criminogenic needs (see Table 5.1). It is also possible that for at least some offenders, other criminogenic needs (for example, drug misuse or alcohol problems; basic skills deficits) will get in the way of programme attendance or completion. Without additional interventions to tackle problems like these, offending behaviour programmes arguably stand little chance of success.

Questions also remain about the extent to which different populations of offenders share similar criminogenic needs. As we noted in Chapter 6, it has been argued that criminogenic needs are not necessarily the same for minority groups as they are for white men (Shaw and Hannah-Moffat, 2000;

Gelsthorpe, 2001; Hedderman, 2004; Kemshall et al., 2004; Hollin and Palmer, 2006a). For example, it has been argued that anti-social beliefs and attitudes play a smaller role in explaining women's offending than in explaining offending by men. Cann (2006) points out that although evidence suggests that female offenders do have cognitive skills deficits, those deficits may not be criminogenic in nature. Recent evidence from OASys assessments also suggests that female offenders have markedly higher levels of criminogenic need in areas of relationships and emotional well-being (Harper et al., 2005). It is possible then that offending behaviour programmes are less beneficial to minority groups than to groups of white male offenders; an explanation considered in relation to the prison-based study of OBPs for female offenders by Cann (2006).

Diversity in offender populations is also relevant in respect of the 'responsivity principle', which indicates that interventions ought to be matched to, or take account of, the individual learning styles and abilities of offenders. As we have noted elsewhere (see Chapter 6), responsivity can be a rather vague concept, but it is useful to distinguish between *idiographic* and *nomothetic* responsivity factors (Ogloff and Davis, 2004). Idiographic factors are internal to the individual and include factors such as intellectual functioning and motivation. We have already noted the literacy and verbal skills demands of programmes, which are likely to inhibit the responsivity of some offenders. Indeed, research by Davies et al. (2004) suggests that for many offenders, the literacy and verbal communication demands of programmes exceed their skills. Doubts have also been voiced about the suitability of programmes designed with young, white males in mind to female and non-white offenders. Motivation is also likely to be a key factor, and is one which has been discussed at some length as a variable likely to have impacted on the findings of some of the studies we have reviewed. Particularly noteworthy is the contrast between the findings of the first and subsequent prison-based studies. As we have seen the first study yielded by far the most positive results, and it has been noted that this was an evaluation of programmes *pre-accreditation*. The relevance of this is that whilst participation in programmes both pre- and post-accreditation was voluntary for prisoners, post-accreditation attendance was more likely to be specified as part of a sentence plan and more likely to influence release decisions (Falshaw et al., 2003b). Research by Clarke et al. (2004a; 2004b), which involved interviews with 77 offenders who had completed programmes in six English prisons, noted that some prisoners reported that prison staff had given them the impression that programme participation was mandatory and/or likely to improve their chances of achieving re-categorisation or securing parole. More generally, it has been noted that motivation may be a key factor differentiating programme completers from non-completers, and it may be this factor – rather than the content of the programme itself – which accounts for any observed reductions in reoffending (Chitty, 2005).

Nomothetic responsivity factors are external to the individual, and in this context include variables such as programme characteristics and environmental support (Ogloff and Davis, 2004). Some light is shed on nomothetic factors by those studies which have included a process evaluation: that is, which have sought to capture data pertaining to the implementation of programmes and, in particular offenders' views about the programmes in which they have participated (e.g. Raynor and Vanstone, 1997; Clarke et al., 2004a; 2004b; Hollin et al., 2002). Generally, the feedback of offenders who have completed programmes has been positive. For example, the majority of STOP programme completers (n = 63) reported that they found the programme useful and enjoyable, but a smaller group (16%) said they found elements of the programme boring (Raynor and Vanstone, 1997). In the study by Clarke et al. (2004a; 2004b) referred to above, most of the graduates of R and R and ETS who were interviewed said they had benefited from the programme, and the delivery of the programme (through groupwork and participatory methods) was generally regarded as effective and enjoyable. However, interviewees thought that the policy of selecting participants on the basis of parole eligibility date disadvantaged some highly motivated prisoners who were at an earlier stage of their sentence. Further, most said that they would have preferred to have been able to access programmes mid-sentence to enable them to practice new skills prior to release, and that they would have benefited from some post-programme support to facilitate the consolidation of learning.

A number of small-scale studies which have sought to understand the phenomenon of *non-completion* also offer useful insights. For example, a study conducted in West Yorkshire probation area revealed that attrition (specifically, failure to start programmes) was often due to organisational factors, such as no programme being available at the required time, and a number of other issues (e.g. problems around travel to programme sites; offenders being in breach of their community sentence; missed communications) were also important in explaining attrition (Briggs and Turner, 2003). A subsequent study, also in West Yorkshire, compared 168 programme completers and 122 non-completers across four accredited programmes (Turner, 2006). This study found that most offenders faced barriers to attendance, but non-completers tended to encounter more problems, and earlier on, than completers. These problems included drink/drug relapses and communication (e.g. postal) problems. A further important finding was that higher levels of case management support, including discussion of barriers to attendance, were linked with completion. Finally, offenders who started their programme within four months were more likely to complete than those who had to wait four months or more.

Programme integrity is the final 'effectiveness principle' which is of relevance here. It will be recalled from Chapter 5 that a programme is said to have integrity when it 'is conducted in practice as intended in theory and design'

(Hollin, 1995: 196). Ideally this means that programme staff are well trained and that the programme is well managed. In general terms, programme integrity has received relatively little attention as a possible explanation for poorer outcomes. As we have explained, a manual is generally the vehicle for the delivery of offending behaviour programmes, and this sets out the practical aspects of the programme: the aims and objectives of individual sessions; the recommended methods of delivery and the sequencing of exercises and topics (Hollin, 2006). Programme sessions are also routinely subject to video recording, such that programme integrity can be monitored relatively easily. However, there remains some conflict between the need for integrity in delivery and what Hollin (2006a) (following Wilson, 1996) calls *clinical artistry*. As Hollin explains, offending behaviour programmes allow little scope for practitioners to exercise clinical judgement with respect to delivery. Programme staff interviewed by Clarke et al. (2004a; 2004b) recognised the importance of programme integrity but also felt that there ought to be some degree of flexibility in the delivery of programmes: for example, scope to amend some of the material and/or language specified in the manual.

More broadly, questions have been raised about the possible impact on the quality of programmes in the context of the rapid expansion which took place in the late 1990s. Lipsey (1999) has drawn an important distinction between what he calls *demonstration* and *practical projects*. The former are the smaller scale pilot studies (e.g. of R and R and STOP, reviewed above) which are often included in meta-analyses and other secondary analyses. Practical projects, in contrast, refer to those programmes which have 'gone to scale': i.e. which have been implemented across a number of sites. As Hollin and Palmer (2006b) explain, research comparing the results of practical and demonstration projects has consistently shown that the latter out-perform the former, and the studies referred to in the present chapter are no exception. For example, Falshaw et al. (2003b) speculate that their null findings (in the second prison study) might be at least in part explicable with reference to this large-scale expansion, which saw a fourfold increase in programme completions between 1995–1996 (when the first study was undertaken) and 1998–1999 (when their own study was conducted).

Offending Behaviour Programmes in Context

As we have seen, since the late 1980s, offending behaviour programmes have developed and spread at an exponential rate, coming to be presented as something of a panacea or 'magic bullet' targeting the problem of recidivism, as well as the new, 'modernised' face of offender rehabilitation. But to what extent do offending behaviour programmes really represent a *new* approach to offender rehabilitation?

In recent years, offending behaviour programmes have attracted criticism on the grounds that they appear to some to revive a 'treatment model' in offender rehabilitation. For example, Kendall (2002; 2004) has argued that OBPs, by virtue of locating the causes of crime in the individual, do indeed revive such a model:

> During the heyday of rehabilitation various abuses were carried out on offenders on treatment grounds. This was perhaps best illustrated by experiments designed to alter the criminal mind. Arguably, the methods employed at this time were mostly rooted in a medical-somatic approach modelled closely upon physical medicine. In contrast, it might be suggested that new rehabilitative models pose less harm since they rely on a social-psychological approach which acknowledges environmental influences and involves [offenders] in their own treatment. However [...] the root problem is still ultimately regarded to be lying within the individual and they become the focus of intervention rather than the social structure. As in the past, rehabilitation is focused upon altering the criminal mind. (2002: 193)

As we have seen, Kendall is right when she points out that OBPs proceed on the basis that offending has certain psychological correlates: it is assumed that offenders exhibit cognitive deficits and/or distortions and therefore need to be taught 'how to think' (Robinson and Porporino, 2000: 180). However, proponents of cognitive-behavioural approaches take issue with other aspects of her critique. For example, James McGuire (2006) maintains that a focus on psychological mechanisms or individual-level explanations is *not* an attempt to 'pathologise' offenders, since (i) cognitive-social-learning deficits are not assumed to be specific to offenders, and (ii) there is no attempt to deny the importance of environmental factors in giving rise to offending.

Clive Hollin agrees that we are not witnessing a return to a treatment model, whilst acknowledging a discursive turn in that direction:

> Within the medical and broader clinical literatures the terms 'therapy', 'treatment', and 'patient' are in common usage. The use of these terms within the context of offending behaviour programmes could be seen as implying a medical model of offending, in which criminal behaviour is understood by recourse to a psychopathological position. It is not the intention here to use this approach and, in the context of offending behaviour programmes, terms such as therapy and patient are inappropriate. The difficulty arises in deciding which terms are appropriate to describe the process and interactions implicit within an offending behaviour programme. (Hollin, 2006: 34)

Hollin tries to resolve this dilemma by concluding that whilst the approach adopted by OBPs might be termed 'psychoeducational', it is in his view appropriate to refer to OBPs as 'treatment' – but only in the general sense that they imply 'the application of a process ... to achieve a specified outcome' (2006: 34).

Others have pointed to the ways in which offending behaviour programmes seek to engage the offender as an active agent in the rehabilitation process, rather than as a passive recipient of 'treatment'. In other words, far from being a form of treatment which is imposed upon and thought to work independently of the will of the offender, OBPs can arguably be understood as *appealing to* the offender's free will (Cavadino and Dignan, 2007: 43). An example of this is to be found in Robinson and Porporino's (2000) statement that R and R's 'underlying philosophy is that offenders should be given "choice" to apply the skills they learn' (Robinson and Porporino, 2000: 180). In this formulation, offenders are, through participation in programmes, 'empowered' to act differently, but there are no guarantees that they will choose to do so.

From the purview of cognitive-behavioural interventions, then, the offender is not viewed as a *passive recipient* of treatment, but rather as an *active agent* who must engage fully in order to benefit from treatment. Further, such interventions seek to engage offenders not just as active subjects, but also as *moral* actors with the capacity both to re-evaluate past (anti-social) choices and to make superior, pro-social choices in the future (e.g. Palmer, 2003). In this context the emphasis is on what Duff (2001) has referred to as the enterprise of 'transparent persuasion'. This involves, first, the communication of censure: the new programmes, as we have seen, are 'offence focused' and proceed on the basis that the offender has done wrong. They then proceed by encouraging offenders to 'think ethically' and in particular to develop a capacity for 'victim empathy' which, it is hoped, will serve to dissuade them from future offending:

> In censuring someone for a wrong she has done, we hope to bring her to recognizing the fact and implications of that wrong; and in recognizing that she has done wrong, she will also recognize that she needs to amend her behaviour and the attitudes that informed it to avoid committing such wrongs in the future. (Duff, 2001: 101)

Thus whilst offending behaviour programmes do not exactly re-invent the 'sinner' of pre-modern reformative efforts, they do arguably reprise themes of personal responsibility, choice and recognition of the moral implications of those choices.

Indeed, for a number of commentators it is precisely this engagement with the offender as a moral actor, and the emphasis on offending as an active choice on the part of the individual offender, which explains the rapid rise of cognitive-behavioural approaches, in England and Wales and other parts of the Western world. Whereas some have explained the rise of cognitive-behaviourism with reference to its superior effectiveness, at least some of the success of contemporary programmes has been attributed to their resonance with 'advanced liberal' forms of governance, which emphasise personal responsibility for wrongdoing and rely upon strategies of 'responsibilisation' as the dominant response to anti-social behaviour (Rose, 2000; Garland, 1996; Kemshall, 2002; Crawford, 2003; Kendall, 2004). In Rose's terms, such programmes fit with an emerging 'ethopolitics' which seeks to 'regenerate and reactivate the ethical values that are now believed to regulate individual conduct and that help maintain order and obedience to the law by binding individuals into shared moral norms and values' (2000: 324).

In this context it is possible to discern a resonance between the new orthodoxy in offender rehabilitation (i.e. offending behaviour programmes) and the new enthusiasm for approaches to dealing with offending which fall under the broad heading of restorative justice (see also Hutchinson, 2006 and Chapter 9, this volume). Restorative justice is an international phenomenon which, in England and Wales, has been manifest in particular in the late 1990s reform of the youth justice system, which now features a raft of new 'restorative' initiatives designed to responsibilise young offenders (Dignan, 2005; Crawford and Newburn, 2003; cf Braithwaite, 1989). Whilst there is clearly much more to restorative justice than the rehabilitation or 'responsibilisation' of offenders (not least the possibility of significant benefits for participating victims), offending behaviour programmes and restorative approaches nonetheless converge in their attempts to engage offenders in a 'moral discourse' which encourages the acknowledgement of wrongdoing and seeks to instil in offenders a new consciousness of their behaviour, including an awareness of its impact on others (Dignan, 2005).

Conclusion

Reflecting on their rapid spread in the Probation Service, Smith (2005: 627) has argued that offending behaviour programmes came by the late 1990s to be regarded by probation managers as the only form of practice that was sufficiently evidence-based to be defensible. Indeed, by 2003 the then Chief Inspector of Probation was voicing concerns about 'programme fetishism' in the Probation Service (Morgan, 2003):

> The message to practitioners therefore became: 'Do this, because this is what is supported by the evidence, and do nothing else; nothing else matters'. (Smith 2005: 627)

Whilst this is a somewhat exaggerated account of the mood in probation in the late 1990s, few in the service at the time would deny that programmes received the lion's share of attention and resources, or that programmes were 'rolled out' in prisons and across the Probation Service with every expectation that they would prove an effective route to the rehabilitation of significant numbers of offenders and a sound investment.

Perhaps not surprisingly, offending behaviour programmes have struggled to meet the high expectations placed on them, and questions remain about whether those expectations were ever realistic. Certainly some are of the opinion that they were not. In the words of one programme graduate:

> people have to understand that groups are stepping stones, I don't believe that any one group, is going to be the remedy to any one prisoner's ills. (quoted in Clarke et al., 2004a: 9)

In the following two chapters we move on to consider two approaches to rehabilitation which have tended to be neglected in the context of the 'programme fetishism' to which Morgan (2003) referred.

Questions to Consider

1 How would you characterise the 'criminological subject' of offending behaviour programmes?
2 Offending behaviour programmes: 'authoritarian' or 'anthropocentric'? (Rotman, 1990).
3 To what extent would you agree that offending behaviour programmes 'abrogate responsibility for treating the offender as a "whole person" in a social context'? (Worrall and Hoy, 2005: 141).
4 To what extent are offending behaviour programmes suitable for female offenders?
5 Do offending behaviour programmes have a future? Why/why not?

Suggested Further Reading

The edited collection *Offending Behaviour Programmes* by Clive Hollin and Emma Palmer (2006) is an excellent source of information about the history, theory and evaluation of programmes, with contributions from a number of authoritative sources. The qualitative Home Office study *Delivering Cognitive Skills Programmes in Prison* provides an informative account of programme implementation which includes feedback from participating offenders (Clarke et al., 2004a; 2004b). In a number of articles Peter Raynor (2004b; 2008) provides a detailed account of the development and evaluation of programmes in the probation context. For a critical perspective on offending behaviour programmes, see Kendall (2002; 2004).

Notes

1 In contrast, 'specialist' programmes cater to offenders with a history of particular offences, such as sexual offences, domestic violence, or alcohol/drug related offending.
2 In the earlier STOP evaluation, 62% completed the programme in the first full year, or 75% if those who dropped out for legitimate reasons (like illness or employment) were discounted (Raynor and Vanstone, 1997: 34).

EIGHT

Social Rehabilitation

Introduction

In this chapter we consider what is meant by social rehabilitation. We then go on to look at some of the main social sectors (housing, employment, training and support) that affect the possibility of social rehabilitation. The chapter concludes by reviewing what efforts have been made in recent years to try to improve the prospects for social rehabilitation, and with what success.

What is Social Rehabilitation?

For much of this book the focus has been on the individual offender and the agencies that deal with him or her. However, having examined the treatment of individual offenders and its limitations, it is equally important to consider the social context of rehabilitation. Indeed studies of treatment programmes often emphasise that they can only be effective if they operate in the context of favourable social opportunities (see for example McIvor, 1990; Lipsey, 1992). This is not surprising, since offending dealt with by the courts is associated with various forms of economic and social deprivation, such as poor housing, low income, and lack of job opportunities, and tends to be most prevalent in deprived areas. Programmes for offenders are usually of limited duration, and unless individual treatment is accompanied by social rehabilitation then, at the end of a programme, participants are likely to remain in, or return to, the same conditions in which they committed their offences.

We can define social rehabilitation as a process by which the offender takes his or her place in society. Implicit in this is some notion of acceptance on the part of 'society', or at least the parts of society that are significant for the offender. As we have already noted regarding words starting with 're-', it also raises the question of what place the offender had in society previously. Social rehabilitation is both a backwards and forwards looking concept for offenders: just as the social context is important to an understanding of offending, so it is important to understanding the processes of desistance and rehabilitation.

A related term used in the past, that has come into fashion again in this century, is the notion of 'resettlement'.[1] Resettlement has mainly been applied in relation to offenders released from custody (although recent policy initiatives have also been regarded as applying to those serving sentences in the community). It usually describes a largely practical activity by which offenders regain contact with the various aspects of the social world that constitute normal living: housing, work, education and training, health, family life and friendships. To illustrate this, data from the offender assessment system known as OASys (see Chapter 6) showed that education, training and employment were assessed as factors associated with offending for 53 per cent of those serving community sentences, and 65 per cent of those serving custodial sentences. Accommodation was assessed as a factor in the offending of three out of ten (31%) offenders on community sentences and four out of ten (43%) of those with custodial sentences (Harper and Chitty, 2005: x, Table 1). In the context of social policy in England and Wales such factors are referred to as the resettlement 'pathways' (Home Office, 2004), and these pathways are also amongst the main dimensions of social rehabilitation. However, rehabilitation involves more than resettlement. It could be said that resettlement is a necessary, but not a sufficient basis for rehabilitation. We will describe and comment on the recent focus on resettlement later in this chapter. However, before considering such matters of criminal justice and social policy we will consider the various dimensions of social rehabilitation mentioned above.

The Problems

Housing

We start with housing because it is one of the most basic of human needs. Research over many years has shown that unsatisfactory accommodation and homelessness are related to the development of offending and contribute to its continuance.[2] A study of a Reception Centre for homeless men in South London carried out in the early seventies said:

> It is doubtful if any other group in the community has comparable conviction rates. The many prison sentences must be partly due to the lack of alternative sentences available for homeless criminals. The fact that the men in residence, who had on average spent three months in the centre in the year before their attendance, had spent far less time in prison

during that year in spite of longer previous records, suggests that the provision of more adequate accommodation for these men would prevent a certain amount of crime and committal to prison. (Tidmarsh et al., 1972: 15)

The relationship also operates in the opposite direction. A review of research on single homelessness in Britain said, 'There are clear links between homelessness, particularly rough sleeping, and experience of the criminal justice system' (Fitzpatrick and Klinker, 2000). The review also pointed out that homelessness often follows release from prison. Finding satisfactory accommodation is a particular problem for ex-prisoners who for one reason or another have no family home they can go to. In a national survey of the prison population in the early 1990s, 12 per cent of convicted prisoners and 16 per cent of remand prisoners said they had no permanent residence just before their imprisonment. Half of the respondents who were near their release date did not expect to return to where they had been living before imprisonment (Walmsley et al., 1992). In a later survey it was reported that one third of prisoners did not have accommodation arranged on release (Niven and Olagundaye, 2002).

Studies have shown that people are more likely to reoffend if they do not have satisfactory, settled accommodation. Research funded by the Joseph Rowntree Foundation (1996) covering four prisons found that two-thirds of ex-prisoners who had no satisfactory accommodation to go to on release reoffended within 12 months, whereas only a quarter of those with good accommodation did so.

Getting people with no home to return to into some form of accommodation has been one of the traditional concerns of both the Probation Service and non-statutory agencies. However, research over many years has suggested that the help that offenders have received in this regard has been variable. Research in the 1960s found that probation officers were not sufficiently active in addressing the housing needs of their clients (Davies, 1969). But a later review noted a change in the situation, and commented in the mid-1990s that 'housing issues are well on the way to becoming a central concern for practitioners in today's Probation Service' (Stewart, 1996: 77). More recently still, however, Niven and Olagundaye (2002) in their survey found that less than a fifth (18%) of all respondents received help looking for accommodation on release (23% of all females). Of those with no accommodation arranged on release, 71 per cent had not received any help in finding somewhere to live. For those who did receive help, the most frequent sources of help and advice were: Probation Service (49%); Prison officer/resettlement officer (24%); and Voluntary Organisations (11%). Of those who had an address on release, 31 per cent had paid work arranged compared with only 9 per cent of those who did not have somewhere to live on release.

The problems are two-fold. First, accommodation on release has often taken the form of a hostel or other temporary accommodation. There has sometimes been a problem in ensuring an adequate supply of such accommodation in the right location at the time when it is needed, and agencies such as NACRO have argued the case for more provision (NACRO, 1998). Commenting on the Joseph Rowntree Foundation research referred to above, Carlisle (1997: 13) said that housing provision for ex-prisoners who had lost their homes did not meet the need in many cases. It was difficult to arrange accommodation prior to release other than to a hostel, and places in statutory approved probation hostels were restricted to those on a statutory supervision order. The second problem is not just getting people into short-term accommodation, but meeting the objective of settling them into longer term housing. Carlisle (1997: 13) reported that some long-term ex-prisoners who had stayed in approved hostels acquired local authority or housing association housing as a result of having their names on a waiting list while in a hostel. However, not all the ex-prisoners in need of such housing are in a position to acquire it.

While research has consistently pointed to the relationship between lack of stable accommodation and offending, it is harder to find studies showing that providing satisfactory housing reduces recidivism. In their review of what is effective in resettling ex-prisoners Seiter and Kadela (2003) looked at the results of four studies of halfway house programmes, and concluded that the evidence from these suggested that halfway house programmes do work in easing the transition from prison to the community. But Elliott-Marshall et al. (2005: 63) say, 'There is very little evidence on the impact of different forms of help in finding accommodation/types of accommodation in reducing reconvictions [...] Studies examining the statistical effectiveness of interventions to address accommodation needs were lacking'. Nonetheless they suggest that, first, the majority of offenders want access to normal, rather than special housing provision. Next, they point out that since accommodation needs change during the course of people's lives, different kinds of assistance are needed at different stages of their lives. Third, they say that housing needs should be considered in the context of being one of several needs. They also note that some groups, such as sex offenders and mentally disordered offenders, pose special issues. Finally, they say that services for offenders tend to be time-limited, but there may be a need for ongoing support. In relation to this, there is a shortage of appropriate move-on accommodation.

While the problems that exist in terms of housing offenders without anywhere to live are well known, the solutions are less obvious. Short-term and social housing is under pressure from many quarters. Maguire et al. in a study of accommodation for ex-prisoners in the Southwest Region of the UK, have indicated that the private sector might be expected to provide some assistance but 'this will be successful only if ways are devised of, on the one hand, helping them to overcome the financial obstacles they face in accessing it and, on the other, encouraging good landlords with decent properties to take on the extra risks of accepting offenders as tenants' (2007: 8).

Housing problems are not peculiar to offenders. There are many without an offending background who lack satisfactory accommodation, and given that the housing needs of offenders are unlikely to be satisfied completely in the near future the question arises of whether it is possible to be 'rehabilitated' whilst not having secure long-term accommodation. Many would argue that a satisfactory place to live is a defining characteristic of rehabilitation, in physical terms at least, and if this is so then there is a long way to go in reaching this goal.

Employment

Similar issues to those mentioned above in relation to housing apply where the employment of offenders is concerned.[3] In other words, to briefly summarise:

- Offenders are disproportionately likely to be unemployed, to be particularly susceptible to long-term unemployment, and to lack the skills and training that enable them to compete in the job market.
- Unemployed offenders are more likely to be re-convicted.
- Having no job affects the way offenders are dealt with by the criminal justice system.
- Getting offenders into jobs has been problematic and training and employment programmes have not always been successful in reducing offending.

A national survey of the prison population in the early 1990s found that a third of prisoners were unemployed prior to their imprisonment, and prior to their release only one sixth had a job to go to. Forty per cent of convicted prisoners felt that having no job was what led them to get into trouble with the police for the first time (Walmsley et al., 1992). Another survey of the prison population a decade later (Niven and Olagundaye, 2002) reported that just under a quarter (24%) of all prisoners interviewed said they had a paid job arranged after release. Those who had a job to go to were significantly less likely to say they thought they would go back to crime at some point in the future (11%) compared with those without any employment arranged (34%).

Studies going back many years have found that historically offenders received little assistance with obtaining jobs. Silberman and Chapman (1971) found that less than 15 per cent of probation clients were given direct help with employment problems, and in a study of parolees Morris and Beverley (1975) found that, of those who found work on release, most did so through their own efforts and none through the help of a probation officer. Similarly, a more recent study concluded that 'the findings suggest that ex-offenders seeking work can count on very little help from the criminal justice system and that both employers and ex-offenders are ignorant about the risks and opportunities which exist' (Gill, 1997: 337). However, another study of probation cases in eleven Probation Service areas found that where employment interventions took place, the proportion of offenders who started employment doubled, and it was concluded that more intervention would lead to more job starts. Despite the fact that employment intervention could be shown to have had some success, the report noted that 'in the majority of cases, no such interventions were made [...] Hence the evidence in this research strongly suggests that probation services can increase offender employability' (Bridges, 1998). Another study of two probation schemes in Inner London and Surrey reported that in their first year they were able to find employment for 12 and 25 per cent of their caseloads respectively, although there was no indication as to whether this was better than might have been expected if the schemes had not been operating (Sarno et al., 1999). Although these studies suggest that some progress could have been achieved by the Probation Service, another study of the best way to improve employment and training prospects for ex-offenders concluded that provision needed to be concerned not just with the needs of individual offenders, but had to have a strategic approach to maximising the use of resources for unemployed offenders. Existing provision tended to be fragmented and short term in nature. Services therefore needed to employ holistic approaches to deal with the multiple disadvantages of the group, to integrate them into mainstream provision, and to address the relationship between labour supply and demand in a systematic and integrated manner (Fletcher et al., 1998). Niven and Olagundaye (2002) found that over half of those prisoners with jobs or training arranged on release had achieved this because of pre-existing contacts through friends or family (39%), or a former employer (16%), highlighting the importance of sustaining such links during imprisonment. Just over one-eighth (13%) had managed to make their arrangements through prison job clubs, pre-release programmes, prison education departments, a Probation Officer, or the employment service. Of those who had been involved in prison employment and resettlement programmes, those participating in prison job clubs were most likely to have jobs or training arranged on release, but this was almost matched by those attending pre-release and victim awareness programmes. Webster et al. (2001: 19) found that 'help is rarely targeted at those at higher risk of offending, although there is some evidence to suggest that, as with other interventions, these are the ones who benefit most.'

Many studies have shown that probationers, ex-prisoners and other groups of offenders are more likely to reoffend at a later date if they are unemployed (Evans, 1968; Davies, 1969; Martin and Webster, 1971; McLintock, 1976; Home Office, 1978; Softley, 1978; Phillpotts and Lancucki, 1979; Gormally et al., 1981; Farrington and Morris, 1983; Harraway et al., 1985). This is true even when one takes into consideration the possibility that those who are most likely to be reconvicted are also those who are least likely to get jobs (Evans, 1968; Gormally et al., 1981). Of course, reconviction is not an infallible measure of reoffending, let alone rehabilitation. However, in the past an association between unemployment and recidivism seems to carry a high level of probability.

If offenders without jobs are more likely to reoffend than those with jobs, does it follow that employment and training programmes for offenders reduce offending or aid rehabilitation? There have been numerous programmes designed to improve the employment prospects of offenders over the years (Crow et al., 1989, Chapter 4). Unfortunately, relatively few have been the subject of adequate research. Of those that have, most have been in the USA, and few in the UK. In a review of the literature on prison and community-based employment programmes in the UK, Webster et al. (2001: 18) concluded that 'Good quality research into the impact of employment initiatives in prison and in the community is scarce [...] The current evidence base is simply too poor to yield firm conclusions about the value of different employment interventions with offenders.' In relation to whether work in prison improves offenders' prospects of employment on release, Colbourne (2001) asks, 'If, as American research has indicated, finding employment is the most significant factor in preventing re-offending, why have there been no controlled studies of the impact of prison work on re-offending rates in the UK?'

Despite these comments, there have been studies of attempts to improve the employment prospects for offenders. In the USA Taggart (1972) reviewed attempts in the 1960s to improve employment and reoffending rates for offenders, and concluded that this work left little room for more than the most restrained optimism, and that there was no evidence that manpower programmes had had more than a marginal impact on their recipients. Around the same time a study in the UK suggested that attempts to improve the employment prospects of prisoners prior to release showed no improvement in terms of reduced reconviction rates (Davies, 1974: 107). Moreover, in the UK a study of an employment placement service run by the charity the Apex Trust showed that relatively few ex-prisoners were helped into employment for any significant length of time and 'There is not really any indication that the Apex service has any definite effect in reducing the proportion of men who are reconvicted within one year after release (Soothill, 1974: 119–20). However, in subsequent analyses it was found that those who got jobs by their own efforts, having rejected the offer of help from Apex, were less likely to be reconvicted than those accepting Apex's services. A study of a workshop for ex-offenders run by the South Yorkshire Probation Service found little evidence of any effect on offending (Manpower Services Commission, 1976).

More recently, Harper and Chitty's review of 'What Works?' in reducing reoffending cites a number of studies (2005: 21) and suggests that they show that it is not merely the fact of having a job that is associated with reduced reoffending, but the stability and quality of that employment along with the level of satisfaction expressed towards it (Motiuk and Brown, 1993; Farrington, 1989). It is also suggested that since the employment status of fathers was predictive of the onset of delinquency in their children (Farrington, 1989), interventions to assist offenders into stable and satisfying employment may have an effect in reducing offending for subsequent generations. Whilst the reductive and rehabilitative potential of employment schemes is uncertain, Webster et al. say that the literature does suggest that two types of employment related work are *un*helpful:

> Raising job expectations through training without any serious prospect of a job on release may be actively damaging rather than just ineffective. This makes tailoring interventions to the local job market and/or employer involvement in programmes key success factors. Also, employment in prison workshops does not appear to increase the chances of employment on release (2001: 19, which also addresses Colbourne's point, above).

However, other studies have been more promising. In a study of the Post-Release Employment Project (PREP) in the USA, Saylor and Gaes (1997) evaluated the impact of prison work experience and vocational and apprenticeship training on post-prison rates of employment and offending. Eight to twelve years after release it was found that men employed in prison industries had survival times (measured by the number of days before re-commitment to prison) that were 20 per cent longer than comparison group members, and men completing vocational or apprenticeship training had a 28 per cent longer survival time than comparison members. The researchers concluded that 'Despite the stigma of imprisonment and the lowered expectations of an ex-offender, it appears that prison programs can have an effect on post-release employment and post-release arrest in the short run and recommitment in the long run'. Seiter and Kadela (2003) reviewed the findings from seven vocational and work programmes in the USA and concluded that vocational training and work release programmes are effective in reducing recidivism, and in improving job readiness skills for ex-offenders.

So, just as with housing, we find a long-standing relationship between offending and the problem of achieving stable employment which has not been successfully resolved. Where there have been interventions there have been mixed results, but the indications are that for successful rehabilitation much depends on such things as the job market and quality of jobs available.

Learning and skills

The ability to obtain and sustain a worthwhile job depends in large measure on having a good education and qualifications. While unemployment has declined in absolute terms in recent years, good jobs are increasingly likely to require some kind of training and qualifications.

Not only do many offenders have low levels of educational attainment and qualifications, but quite a high proportion do not have good levels of literacy and numeracy. The Social Exclusion Unit reported that 80 per cent of prisoners have writing skills that are at or below the level of an 11-year-old child. When it comes to numeracy it is 65 per cent, and 50 per cent have the reading skills of an eleven-year-old or younger (Social Exclusion Unit, 2002: 6). However, Harper and Chitty (2005: x) noted that there is currently no evidence to suggest that a lack of basic skills is related directly to offending. Nonetheless, basic skills are related to other factors associated with offending, such as poor school experience, unemployment, social exclusion and various psychological or cognitive factors linked to self-concept and attitudes to offending (Porporino and Robinson, 1992). Niven and Olagundaye found that, for those assessed as being at level 1 or below in literacy and numeracy on reception, 34% of those achieving level 2 in either literacy or numeracy during custody had work or training arranged on release compared with 27% of those who had not achieved a level 2 qualification during custody. More prisoners who achieved educational qualifications while in prison (such as GCSEs or NVQs) were likely to have a paid job on release (26%) compared with those not achieving any qualifications (23%).[4]

The duration of involvement in training activities may be more important than enrolment in programmes *per se*. Adams et al. (1994) found that prisoners who spent more time in academic and vocational programmes were less likely to be re-imprisoned after release than those with less intensive involvement. The benefits of greater participation were most evident among prisoners with the lowest level of academic achievement. Seiter and Kadela's review (2003) included two education programmes, providing mixed results. They concluded that educational programmes increased educational achievement scores, but did not decrease recidivism. This may be because the effectiveness of educational improvement depends on linking it with suitable employment.

An evaluation of Community Service Pathfinders in England and Wales covered seven projects in ten probation areas, including a skills accreditation approach, to enable offenders performing community service to acquire skills and qualifications, with the aim of improving their employability. The authors said the outcomes suggested that the projects focusing on skills accreditation produced the best results (Rex et al., 2003a). McMahon et al. (2004) evaluated basic skills Pathfinder programmes in the Probation Service. This was affected by problems of attrition (drop-out) and was unable to offer much in the way of conclusions about outcomes, although it did produce some learning points for running such programmes in future. Hurry and Moriarty (2004) evaluated 42 education, training and employment (ETE) projects for the Youth Justice Board which provided education, training or work experience, projects of a career-oriented service type, and projects providing diversionary activities. Most of these young people had no previous qualifications, and there were some significant improvements in literacy and numeracy levels. For projects providing education, around half the students achieved some kind of qualification, usually a 'Word Power' or 'Number Power' certificate. A reduction of around 25% was observed in 12-month offending rates after enrolment on an ETE project compared with before, but there was no comparison group.

In an effort to tackle the employment and skills issue, in 2005 the Department for Education and Skills issued a Green Paper, *Reducing Re-Offending Through Skills and Employment* (2005). An important feature of this was to focus strongly on jobs, with employers driving the design and delivery of programmes so that offenders would gain skills and experience which would meet employers' needs. This was followed by a plan to implement the proposals which would engage employers, increase the effectiveness of learning and skills delivered to offenders, and promote the development of skills and jobs in prisons and probation (DFES, 2006).

Social support

Apart from individual capabilities the possibilities for offender rehabilitation can be affected by what is often referred to as 'social capital': the networks and resources available for people to achieve success.[5] Offenders do not necessarily lack social capital, but they may have experience of the kinds of 'negative' social capital that are conducive to offending behaviour. Putnam (2000), for example, distinguishes between bridging social capital, which is outward looking and inclusive, and bonding social capital, which is inward looking and exclusive, and more likely to be 'criminogenic'. American researchers in particular have noted that offenders often come from geographical areas and social backgrounds where there is poverty and disadvantage, where neighbourhoods have few social resources (Travis and Petersilia, 2001; Rose et al., 1999).

One way of gaining non-offending social support may be through a mentor (discussed in more detail in Chapter 9). However, Elliott-Marshall et al. (2005: 68) note that reviews of findings from the USA and the UK show that while some American studies point to mentoring having relatively modest effects on deviant behaviour, the British evidence base is 'very poor', largely because the topic is under-researched (Hall, 2003; Lewis et al., 2003). An evaluation of ten 'Mentoring Plus' programmes, which targeted disaffected young people (Shiner et al., 2004), showed that in general mentoring does not reduce offending and drug misuse.

The literature has often noted the important role that families and friends can play in the rehabilitation process. For example, Visher and Travis concluded that 'existing research provides strong empirical evidence that the family of a former prisoner has a significant impact on post release success or failure' (2003: 102). This can range from practical advantages such as providing a place to live or a job to go to, to giving the support that will help to avoid future offending. As with other aspects of rehabilitation, the role of families and friends can be a complex one, since an offender's family background or peers may have been part of their offending behaviour previously. Generally, however, the indications are that having supportive family and friends increases the chances of successful rehabilitation (Harper et al., 2005: 24).

A survey of the resettlement prospects of just over 2000 prisoners which took place in 2001 noted that there was a relationship between the prospects of employment on release and having family relationships (Niven and Olagundaye, 2002). Those without jobs to go to were less likely to receive visits from partners or family during their sentence (66% compared with 84% for those with jobs on release), and those who had jobs on release were more likely to be married or living with a partner on release than those who had no jobs on release (40% compared with 22%). Harper et al. (2005) report that in a follow-up survey in 2003 almost two-thirds (62%) of prisoners who were not employed or in training before they entered custody but had one of these arranged on release, had relied on family and friends or other personal contacts to arrange this before they were released. In the same survey, nearly four-fifths (79%) of those who had received at least one visit from a family member or partner had accommodation arranged on release compared with only half (51%) of those who did not receive a visit (Niven and Stewart, 2005).

We have considered here just a few of the 'pathways' relevant to social rehabilitation. We could go on to consider other matters, such as physical and mental health. In addition it is also relevant to note that such social problems are seldom found in isolation. Not all, but many individuals experience some combination of homelessness, joblessness, mental disorder, lack of social networks, lack of skills, and so on, resulting in a cycle of deterioration which it is hard to break out of.

We have included references to research going back almost half a century because this illustrates how intractable the social rehabilitation of offenders is. Of course there are those who would say that poor housing, job opportunities, education, health and leisure opportunities are problems for many in society, not just offenders and that these problems need to be confronted on a society wide basis, not solely in terms of improving the prospects for offenders. There may well be some truth in this argument, but for the time being we have elected to restrict our considerations to the offender sphere of activity.

What is Needed

The research that has been done on social aspects of roffending and rehabilitation highlights some of the main issues that need to be addressed. The first is the importance of what is referred to as multi-modal action. As noted above, offenders often have several criminogenic needs, and it is therefore important to address the full range of interventions that offenders require, and not simply to address each need in isolation (Gaes et al., 1999), and this means integrated programmes (Webster et al., 2001). This holistic approach to offender rehabilitation requires co-ordinated services, which the National Offender Management Service was designed to achieve (see below).

A second theme apparent from the research is that, important though practical interventions are, successful rehabilitation is not *just* about professional workers providing practical support. It needs to be combined with improving offenders' motivation and personal capacities (Lewis et al., 2003) in order to address their own needs (as discussed in Chapter 6). Several studies refer to the importance of personal determination and resilience in resisting reoffending on release from prison (O'Brien, 2001; Harman and Paylor, 2005; Visher and Travis, 2003). This reinforces the arguments of the desistance theorists such as Maruna (2001) that one of the things the criminal justice system needs to concentrate on is supporting ex-prisoners' own efforts. Unfortunately it also raises the question of what should be done about those who lack such determination and capacity. But this at least suggests a twin-track strategy of supporting those who have the capacity to help themselves, while targeting resources more effectively on those who are less capable.

A third suggestion to emerge from the literature points to the importance of not only addressing the needs of the offender, but also paying attention to the communities from which they come. Researchers point to the fact that commonly the communities to which prisoners return are deprived and disadvantaged, and ill-equipped for resettling returning prisoners to any great extent (Travis and Petersilia, 2001; Women Prisoners Association, 2004; Richie, 2001; Visher and Travis, 2003). While much of this research is of American origin, it is not unlikely that similar conditions apply in the UK.

This leads to the further suggestion of recognising the importance of wider social conditions in facilitating (or obstructing) resettlement. For example, with regard to employment, much depends on economic conditions. Niven and Olagundaye (2002) refer to the fact that the proportion of prisoners expecting to take up employment soon after release was approximately double the proportion found in a previous survey a decade before (NACRO, unpublished; 24% compared with 11%). This probably reflects in part the lower level of unemployment in 2001, 5% compared with 10% in 1992 (Office of National Statistics website, 2002). While unemployment has declined, there has also been a decline in the availability of social housing. The number of households in the social sector declined by 1.6 million between 1981 and 2003–04 (Office of the Deputy Prime Minister, 2004). So a resettlement strategy conducive to successful rehabilitation needs to consider not only individual rehabilitation, but the social context in which it takes place.

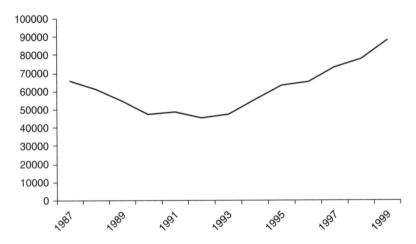

Figure 8.1 No. of discharges from Prison Service establishments, 1987–99, all prisoners (*Prison Statistics, England and Wales, 1992–2002*)

The Responses: Social Rehabilitation and Social Policy

We have shown that the lack of economic and social opportunities faced by offenders has often been inadequately addressed. However, since the late 1990s there have been various developments directed at remedying this, but only in the particular context of resettlement aimed at reducing reoffending. This owes much to developments in the USA. There, a growing awareness of the need to do something about resettling released prisoners came about, in part at least, as a by-product of the rising prisoner population over the previous decade or so, since more prisoners meant more ex-prisoners re-entering the community on release, and ill prepared to lead a crime-free life. In 2000 the US based Urban Institute, an economic and social policy research organisation, convened a Re-Entry Roundtable to explore various aspects of the re-entry issue, whose 'aim is to sharpen the nation's thinking on the issues of sentencing and prisoner reintegration, and to foster policy innovations that will improve outcomes for individuals, families, and communities'. This resulted in a series of reports and publications on the issue (e.g. Travis and Petersilia, 2001; Seiter and Kadela, 2003).

Criminal justice policy in the UK has often been influenced by what happens in the USA and, as there, throughout the 1990s a rising prisoner population resulted in a rising number of prisoners returning to the community on release (see Figure 8.1).

In 2001 HM Inspectors of Prison and Probation produced a joint report, *Through the Prison Gate*, which said, 'the recent focus of prisons on security, and of the probation service on risk of harm, has allowed resettlement needs to be under-prioritised' (HM Inspectorates of Prisons and Probation, 2001: 4). The report made recommendations for improved joint work between the Prison and Probation Services. Subsequently the Social Exclusion Unit report *Reducing Re-offending by Ex-Prisoners* (2002) recommended that 'the Government should develop and implement a National Rehabilitation strategy ... involving all relevant Departments, and led by the Home Office.' In the same year the Audit Commission report *Route to Justice: improving the pathway of offenders through the criminal justice system* highlighted the importance of taking a holistic view of offenders' routes through the criminal justice process, including the management of release into the community and ensuring successful resettlement. The *Reducing Re-offending National Action Plan* (Home Office, 2004) was published in July 2004, to be implemented through regional plans developed around the country. Meanwhile, the Criminal Justice Act 2003 provided sentencing options such as Custody Plus, intended to ensure better supervision on release, and better management of the transition from custody to the community – which has not been implemented.

The regional plans involved a variety of statutory and independent organisations, recognising the need for multiple interventions, and addressed seven 'resettlement pathways': accommodation, employment, learning and skills, drug use, family and social support, financial management, and physical and mental health. However, unlike the Crime Reduction Programme referred to in an earlier chapter, the Reducing Re-offending Action Plan was not accompanied by the funding of research to assess its effectiveness. Research has therefore been limited, and has depended on individual initiatives at regional level, where there has been very little funding available,[6] and it is difficult to get an overall picture of how successful the initiatives have been.

What can be said is that the Action Plan did take note of the lessons to have emerged from previous research, including that which has come from the USA in recent years. The policy took account of the need for multiple interventions to address multiple needs, it adopted a holistic approach to offender rehabilitation, and it attempted to address the problem *in principle* at both national and regional level. What is not known is the extent to which these things have happened in practice.

What remains is the need to address social exclusion in society as a whole. If social rehabilitation is to bring about reintegration then something more than the provision of accommodation, drug treatment, training and employment is needed, no matter how desirable they may be. This opens up several issues. One of these is the need for communities to play their part in rehabilitation: a community which feels there has been some restoration by the offender, and that there is the potential for the offender to make further contributions towards the well-being of the community is more likely to play a positive role in offender rehabilitation (Maruna and LeBel, 2003).

The other point to make about the policy developments of the early twenty-first century is that, although the term rehabilitation is used at times in various documents and reports, it does refer specifically to resettlement. As we pointed out in Chapter 1, the term rehabilitation can be used in a variety of contexts. For example, does it imply a particular type of punishment or sanction? Is it best understood as a type of punishment or an alternative to punishment? Or is it perhaps better summed up as a process which *follows* punishment? Not only that, but what started out as a resettlement initiative became transmuted by 2004 into a 'reducing reoffending' initiative, where resettlement became a means to a utilitarian end, rather than addressing rehabilitation in its own terms. This raises questions about whether rehabilitation can ever be justified without recourse to other objectives. This is something to which we turn our attention in the final chapter.

Questions to Consider

1 Would offending behaviour programmes still be needed if more attention was paid to the social causes of crime?
2 What resources should be devoted to social rehabilitation compared with other approaches to dealing with offending?
3 Of the various social 'pathways', which do you think is the most important?
4 What are the prospects for the future of social rehabilitation?

Suggested Further Reading

The social rehabilitation of offenders is a topic where the literature is rather piecemeal, and there are few sources about the topic as a whole. The chapter by Robin Elliot-Marshall and colleagues in Home Office Research Study 291, edited by Gemma Harper and Chloë Chitty (2005), reviews 'Alternative approaches to integrating offenders into the community'. Aspects of social rehabilitation relating to resettlement have been brought together in a review done by one of us for the Yorkshire and Humberside Resettlement Committee of NOMS (Crow, 2006). Apart from that the best resources are the texts mentioned already in this chapter, which can be found on the Home Office website, and as far as US developments are concerned on the Re-Entry Roundtable website (at http://www.urban.org/projects/reentry-roundtable/), and in two special issues of the journal *Crime and Delinquency* (Vol. 47, Issue 3, 2001 and Vol. 49, Issue 3, 2003).

Notes

1 The term used in the USA is 're-entry'.
2 A useful summary of research on the links between homelessness and offending can be found in a paper by NACRO (1998), *Going Straight Home?*
3 Earlier reviews of unemployment and offending can be found in Crow et al., 1989, and Crow, 1996.
4 However, the difference was not statistically significant for either of these comparisons.
5 Bourdieu identified four forms of capital: economic, cultural, social and symbolic. He defined social capital as the resources that individuals gain by possessing a network of institutional relationships (1992). Giddens defines social capital as 'the social knowledge and connections that enable people to accomplish their goals and extend their influence' (2006: 674).
6 The research by Maguire et al. (2007) in the South West of England has been one of the few exceptions.

NINE

Emerging Approaches: Rehabilitation and the Relational Context

Introduction

In the last chapter we moved on from the structured rehabilitative programmes which occupied us in Chapter 7 and, more generally, from what we might loosely call 'treatment-oriented' approaches. We introduced the notion of social rehabilitation which, we argued, encompasses those approaches which emphasise the ex-offender's place in society, access to social resources, and return to citizenship. We noted that recent years have witnessed a revival of social rehabilitation, particularly in respect of attempts to resettle or reintegrate ex-prisoners, and that this revival owes much to the disappointing outcomes of the more programmatic, psychological approaches which rose to prominence in the 1990s. In this chapter we continue our exploration of rehabilitation in its social context, but here we focus less on the importance of offenders' access to concrete resources like accommodation, employment and so on in moving toward rehabilitation. Instead we consider a variety of contemporary and emerging approaches which share in common a focus on what we might call the *relational* dimension of, or context for, rehabilitation.[1] In this chapter we explore the argument – put forward by Gordon Bazemore and others (e.g. Bazemore, 1999; Bazemore and O'Brien, 2002; Maruna, 2001) – that rehabilitation is not best understood as something which happens to or is 'done to' offenders in a social vacuum: rather, it is a process which takes place in the context of – and indeed seeks to build – *relationships* of various kinds.

As we shall see, this basic idea – in common with the notion of 'social rehabilitation' discussed in the last chapter – is far from new: indeed, both can be traced back at least as far as the origins of probation work. However, we shall also see that the notion of relational rehabilitation is an idea which is attracting increasing interest in a number of contexts in and around criminal justice. This, we think, is partly because of the acknowledged limitations of psychological interventions; but also reflects, we think, a developing interest in what offenders themselves have had to say about the sorts of approaches and interventions that are effective from their perspective.

The chapter begins by examining the rehabilitative potential of relationships between offenders and those professionals responsible for supervising them in the context of court orders. We then move on to consider the less formal sphere of mentoring, which is an approach which has been used most often in respect of young people (including young offenders). Third, we consider the more recent emergence of a group of approaches which have been described under the umbrella of 'therapeutic jurisprudence', focusing in particular on the notion that the court and its personnel might have therapeutic functions which have not always been understood or exploited. Our fourth topic – and one we are only able to scratch the surface of – is the rapidly expanding arena of 'restorative justice', which we touched upon at the end of Chapter 7. Finally we consider the emergence of 'circles of support and accountability' in respect of sexual offenders in the community.

The Supervisory Relationship: a Therapeutic Alliance?

The idea that the relationship between an offender and his or her supervising probation officer or other 'helper' plays an important role in the success of treatment or rehabilitation is not a new one. For most of its substantial history, probation supervision has been delivered in the context of a one-to-one relationship between a practitioner and an offender. In the course of the twentieth century, whilst the style and theoretical approach underpinning probation supervision did not remain constant it was generally accepted that the 'relational basis' of supervision was the key to its effectiveness. Indeed, the key point of continuity in probation's well-documented transition from the 'penal philanthropy' to 'social casework' was a focus on the personal relationship between probation officers and individual offenders, and a belief in the personal influence of the worker (e.g. Bochel, 1976). In the late 1960s, Davies referred to the casework relationship as 'the probation officer's main instrument' (1969: 21). This view reflected the then dominance of psychological theories, and in particular the influence of Freudian psychoanalytic theory (see Chapter 2).

However, by the 1990s the traditional casework model, based on a one-to-one relationship between supervising officer and offender, was no longer the solid 'bedrock' of probation as it had been for so long. This was due to a number of developments, including the increasing use of specialist, inter-sectoral 'partnerships' whereby voluntary and other agencies took on some specific responsibilities for delivering interventions (see Chapter 3) and the spread of specialist programmes (including OBPs), the introduction of which set in motion a process of separating the *management* and *delivery* of community supervision. This meant it was increasingly the case that an offender would have to see more than one person as part of his or her community sentence: a *case manager* would retain overall responsibility for the order but the offender may have to attend appointments with other specialist service providers, and may go several weeks without seeing their case manager whilst (for example) attending a treatment programme. So the experience of supervision came – for many offenders subject to community sentences – to be a rather fragmented one (Partridge, 2004; Robinson, 2005).

This development was however somewhat in conflict with one of the messages which had emerged from the early 'What Works?' literature: namely, that a consistent relationship between case manager and offender was likely to be important to the offender's experience of participation in specialist interventions and also likely to impact on outcomes (e.g. Underdown, 1998). For example, drawing on the work of some of the better known Canadian researchers, Underdown highlighted the crucial role of the probation officer or case manager as 'change agent' in the context of offending behaviour programmes (Gendreau et al., 1999). Underdown argued that by providing preparatory and motivational work prior to programme commencement, supportive work during a programme and opportunities for rehearsal following completion, the case manager would be uniquely placed to support the learning processes which offending behaviour programmes were seeking to promote. It is now generally accepted, however, that in the rush to implement programmes and achieve referral targets, this aspect of 'effective practice' was neglected. Indeed, it has been argued that poor case management may well have been responsible for some of the disappointing results from programme evaluations (e.g. Raynor, 2004a).

The importance of quality and consistency

But is there more to effective supervision or case management than the facilitation and reinforcement of learning acquired on programmes? There is in fact a growing body of research which indicates that this is indeed the case. Specifically, it indicates that from the perspective of offenders, both the *quality* and the *consistency* of their relationships with supervisors are central to effective practice, and this appears to be the case both in terms of promoting motivation and compliance in the short term, and encouraging desistance from offending in the longer term.

For example, Sue Rex (1999) conducted a study in which she interviewed 21 probation officers and 60 offenders under their supervision. She found that those offenders who attributed positive changes in their behaviour to proba- tion supervision conveyed a sense of being committed to and engaged by their supervising officer. As many as half of the probationers she interviewed revealed feelings of personal loyalty and accountability toward their supervi- sor, and probationers said they were more willing to accept advice or guidance in the context of a genuine, engaging relationship.

In another study, this time of 105 offenders on community orders, Beaumont et al. (2001) found that those who reported the most positive experiences had enjoyed a substantial period working with a specific supervisor and described one-to-one contact in positive terms. Meanwhile, those who felt that supervi- sion had been poor pointed to unsatisfactory experiences of one-to-one work (usually too little contact, or contact that was too rushed or superficial).

In a subsequent Home Office study by Sarah Partridge (2004), interviews with a small sample of offenders revealed that they too favoured continuity over a fragmented style of supervision:

> Offenders were unanimous about the importance of continuity of contact with the same case manager, particularly during the initial stages of their supervision. They reported being more likely to trust their case manager, address their problems and ask for help if they saw the same person over a period of time – indicating the importance of the case manager as a stable, human link during the order. (2004: 9)

Partridge found that the greater the degree of fragmentation they experienced, the more offenders were likely to be confused about who was overseeing their order and who to contact in a crisis. Offenders reported that it took time for them to gain confidence with a new member of staff and that they became easily disillusioned by having to explain their 'history' repeatedly.

As a number of commentators have pointed out, these studies seem to echo the findings of the research literature on psychotherapeutic interven- tions with *non-offending* populations (e.g. Marshall and Serran, 2004; Burnett and McNeill, 2005). As Marshall and Serran have noted, a large body of research in this context illustrates that the ways in which a therapist behaves, as well as his or her 'personal style', plays a significant role in outcomes. They cite one study which calculated that at least 25% of the variance in treatment outcomes was attributable to the influence of 'process variables', such as the therapist's style and the client–therapist relationship (Lambert and Bergin, 1994). Although there is much less empirical research on the influence of process variables on successful treatment outcomes among offender populations, a series of studies by Marshall and his colleagues in respect of prison-based sex offender treatment is one notable exception (cited in Marshall and Serran, 2004).

This series of studies sought to elucidate the influence of the programme tutor's behaviour on the effectiveness of the treatment programme for sexual offenders which has been running in English prisons since 1991. The researchers were able to utilise video recordings of treatment sessions to this end. Having established that variations between programme tutors could be reliably identified from the video tapes by trained observers, they went on to examine whether the independent ratings of programme tutors were related to intermediate offender outcomes (as assessed by a battery of pre- and post-treatment psychometric tests). They found that there were four 'tutor variables' which had a positive impact on offenders' test scores: these were empathy, warmth, rewardingness and directiveness. Conversely, confrontation which was judged by observers to be aggressive or derogatory was correlated with negative outcomes.

Reviewing the findings of these and a number of other studies, Marshall and Serran (2004) conclude that, whilst offenders can be a difficult population to work with (not least because their participation in treatment programmes is often characterised by a degree of coercion), those who work with offenders can become more effective in a number of ways. In particular, they argue:

> offenders will be motivated to effectively participate in treatment when the therapist creates a supportive and encouraging environment. The generation of this type of environment is maximized when therapists adopt a warm, empathic style that is complemented by rewards and encouragement, and when clients view the therapists as having adopted this style. (2004: 315)

It therefore follows, they argue, that a balance must be struck between the typical, 'manualised' approach to treatment programmes, and the need for flexibility in delivery. Striking such a balance, they argue, is an achievable challenge (2004: 316).

Pro-social modelling

Marshall and Serran's research then indicates that the ways in which therapists behave can encourage (or inhibit) motivation to change on the part of offenders. Another body of research, led by Chris Trotter in Australia, has shown that therapists or supervisors can have a more direct influence on offenders' behaviour by modelling (i.e. demonstrating) and rewarding desired behaviours (Trotter, 1996; 1999). Trotter explains that the pro-social approach includes:

> Being punctual and reliable, being polite and friendly, being honest and open, understanding the client's point of view, expressing views about the value of social pursuits such as mixing with non criminal friends, good family relations and work, etc. (1996: 32)

In an early study in Victoria, Australia, 30 Community Corrections Officers were offered a five-day training course which included instruction in the principles of pro-social modelling and reinforcement, as well as problem-solving and empathy (Trotter, 1996). They were then asked to use this model whilst supervising their clients, and to participate in follow-up training. Trotter found that where case file notes reflected the use of the model supervisors had been trained to use, there was a positive impact on both compliance and reconviction rates. Further, statistical analysis indicated that of the three approaches, pro-social modelling was most clearly linked with lower reconviction rates. Not surprisingly Trotter concluded that pro-social modelling could be a very useful addition to the skills repertoire of those working with offenders.

In England and Wales, the pro-social modelling approach has been championed by academic researchers at the University of Cambridge, and was one of a number of approaches which was delivered and evaluated in the context of the community service 'Pathfinder' research funded by the Home Office as part of its Crime Reduction Programme (Rex et al., 2003a; Rex and Matravers, 1998). However, it is not a component of 'mainstream' training for those professionals who work with offenders.

Mentoring: Advise, Assist and Befriend?

One possible response to offending behaviour which has an unambiguous 'relational' component is mentoring. Mentoring takes us out of the 'professional territory' of probation officers and the like, however, and into the less formal 'helping' relationships between individuals who are often volunteers, and 'mentees' who are not, by definition, offenders.

Although there is no definitive definition of mentoring, the majority of definitions have in common the notion of a trusting relationship that involves a more experienced person helping and acting as a role model for someone who is less experienced (St. James-Roberts et al., 2005). Indeed, the roots of the concept have been traced back to the Ancient Greeks: in Homer's *Odyssey* 'Mentor' was the name of the person chosen by Odysseus to be the guardian of his son Telemachus (Newburn and Shiner 2005: 45). Typically, mentoring has been utilised in respect of young people who have a history of, or are deemed to be 'at risk' of, 'problem' behaviour or social exclusion.

The literature on mentoring tends to introduce a distinction between so-called 'naturally occurring' and 'formalised' or 'artificial' mentoring (e.g. Newburn and Shiner, 2005). In the context of preventive work with young people, mentoring tends to be of the latter type: that is, it is 'a relationship between two strangers, instigated by a third party, who intentionally matches the mentor with the mentee according to the needs of the younger person as a part of a planned intervention programme' (Freedman, 1993, cited in Newburn and Shiner, 2005: 46). However, it is the relatively informal and voluntary nature of the mentor/mentee relationship which distinguishes it from the more formal rehabilitative interventions conducted by professional – often criminal justice – personnel, of the type we examined in the above section and in other parts of the book (Tarling et al., 2002).

Arguably the earliest and best known example of a mentoring programme is *Big Brothers, Big Sisters of America* (BBBSA). Big Brothers, the original arm of this programme, was established in 1904, in New York; Big Sisters came a year later. The contemporary 'mission' of BBBS is 'to help children reach their potential through professionally supported, one-to-one relationships with mentors that have a measurable impact on youth' (www.bbbs.org). Children aged 6–18 are paired with adult volunteers and agree to meet every 1–2 weeks for a minimum of one year, with meetings averaging four hours (Newburn and Shiner, 2005).

In the UK context, mentoring has a comparatively short history, with its roots in 1990s London and the well-known Dalston Youth Project which was established by Crime Concern (a charitable organization) and a number of other partner agencies (Newburn and Shiner, 2005). Subsequently, however, mentoring has been enthusiastically adopted in England and Wales by the Youth Justice Board (YJB), a statutory body established under the 1998 Crime and Disorder Act. The use of 'mentoring projects' as a means to prevent offending was initially piloted by the Youth Justice Board in 1999–2001 and subsequently a further 80 projects were funded by the Board. Many of these latter projects were 'competency-focused': that is, set up to do more than simply 'befriend' the young person – for example, to teach basic literacy, numeracy, social and/or life skills with a view to improving the young person's future prospects. In the first round of YJB-funded mentoring projects (1999–2001) some 2049 young people aged 9–18 were matched with 1576 volunteer mentors (Tarling et al., 2002); in the second round 80 projects recruited and matched nearly 3000 young people with mentors (St. James-Roberts et al., 2005).

As we noted in Chapter 8, research on the effectiveness of mentoring is not extensive; neither are its results clear-cut. In a Home Office review of research on mentoring, Elliott-Marshall et al. (2005) concluded that while some American studies point to mentoring having some positive impact on behaviour, few good quality British studies have been carried out. In order to assess the impact of mentoring on recidivism, Jolliffe and Farrington (2007) conducted a meta-analysis based on 18 studies (most were US-based) in which mentoring was deployed in respect of individuals who were either deemed to be 'at risk' of offending or had been apprehended by the police. 'Mentored' and control groups were compared. Of the 18 studies assessed, seven showed that mentoring had a statistically significant positive impact on reoffending. A further finding was that the more successful programmes were those where the mentor and mentee spent more time together at each meeting and met more than once a week. Further, it was found that mentoring was only successful in reducing reoffending when it was one of a number of interventions provided.

Mentoring has also been associated with the achievement of some key 'intermediate' outcomes. For example, in the second YJB evaluation, whilst mentoring appeared not to impact significantly on the reoffending of mentees, it was found that it did help a substantial proportion of young people re-engage in education, training or employment; become more involved in community activities; and improve relationships with their families (St. James-Roberts et al., 2005: 110). Furthermore, of a sample of mentees who were interviewed about their experience, three-quarters said they thought mentoring has been 'very useful'. Seventy-seven per cent said they thought mentoring had helped them stop getting into trouble; 64% said they had been helped 'to get through a tough time'; and 61% attributed improvements in relationships with peers to mentoring (St. James-Roberts et al., 2005: 94).

Researchers, however, caution that mentoring *on its own* should not be expected to produce significant behavioural changes in young people. For one thing, a number of studies have found that not all young people referred to mentoring schemes choose to take part in them (e.g. see St. James-Roberts et al., 2005: 11). For another, it is arguably unlikely that *any* relatively short-term intervention is sufficient to tackle, with long-term effects, the multiple needs of the young people who are typically referred to mentoring schemes. Nevertheless, St. James-Roberts et al. (2005: 114) conclude that there are at least three features of mentoring which distinguish this activity from other forms of intervention and are, in their view, worth preserving. These are as follows:

- the deliberate combination of a relationship that is at once unequal and caring/befriending
- as part of the mentor role, a combination of advocacy without statutory authority, responsibility or power
- a trusting relationship between mentor and mentee.

'Therapeutic Jurisprudence': Rethinking the Role of the Criminal Courts

Therapeutic Jurisprudence (TJ), with its roots in the late-1980s work of law professors David Wexler and Bruce Winick, has been defined as 'the study of the role of the law as a therapeutic agent' (Wexler and Winick, 1996: xvii). For Wexler and Winick, legal rules, procedures and actors (such as lawyers and sentencers) are 'social forces' that have the potential to produce either 'therapeutic' or 'antitherapeutic' consequences. TJ, they explain, seeks to maximise the law's therapeutic potential and minimise its antitherapeutic potential, without subordinating due process or other justice values.

One of the key areas in which ideas associated with TJ have been applied is in respect of the role of sentencers in the criminal courts (see Winick and Wexler 2003). Traditionally, sentencers have had little or no involvement in sentence implementation. Indeed, Zimmerman (cited in Rottman and Casey 1999: 13) captures the traditional role of the sentencer as that of the 'disinterested, dispassionate magistrate'. However, within the framework of TJ, it has been suggested that sentencers can potentially play a valuable role in encouraging and enhancing offenders' motivation and compliance in respect of rehabilitative initiatives (e.g. see McGuire, 2003 for an overview). Rottman and Casey (1999) have described the ways in which courts in the USA have been experimenting with a more proactive and problem-solving orientation, in which an effort is made to maximise the potential of the courtroom as a site for encouraging positive change in offenders. They argue that, in this jurisdiction, a more proactive, problem-solving orientation has emerged in the face of growing exposure to social problems around drug misuse, mental illness and family breakdown, coupled with rising demand from the public and communities for a 'more responsive and involved judiciary' (Rottman and Casey, 1999: 13).

Drug Courts

Drug Courts – or Drug Treatment Courts as they tend to be known in the USA – are the best known example of 'problem-solving courts': that is, courts for which TJ provides the underlying legal theory (Rottman and Casey 1999).[2] Drug Treatment Courts were initially established in the USA in the late 1980s by sentencers who were frustrated at the limited range and effectiveness of existing measures for dealing with those whose offending was related to the misuse of drugs (Hora et al., 1999; McIvor et al., 2006). In the space of just seven years, Drug Treatment Courts in the USA grew from one (established in 1989 in Miami, Florida) to in excess of 125 operating in 45 states (Hora et al., 1999: 115). Despite this proliferation, however, Hora et al., (1999: 113) argue that it is possible to encapsulate the 'essential elements' of the US Drug Treatment Courts (DTCs) in terms of the following five elements:

- immediate intervention
- a non-adversarial, collaborative adjudication process
- a hands-on approach to the defendant's treatment on the part of the judge
- treatment programmes with clearly defined rules and structured goals
- the concept of the DTC Team, made up of judge, prosecutor, defence counsel, treatment provider and corrections personnel.

Summarising the orientation of the Drug Treatment Court model, they conclude that:

> A DTC's therapeutic orientation compels the court and its participants to pursue and utilize *relationships*, methods and ideas which will reinforce and support the goal of getting the individual to stop using drugs. (1999: 137, emphasis added)

Central to the DTC approach, they explain, is the fact that only one judge will deal with the defendant's case. In the context of frequent, mandatory court appearances, the judge and the defendant develop a one-to-one 'working alliance' which allows the judge to become a key figure and powerful motivator in the rehabilitation process. Backed by the authority and sanctioning power of the court, the judge provides the defendant with the incentive to stay in treatment. Hora et al. maintain that without judicial leadership involving the active monitoring of progress, the DTC would not be effective (1999: 160).

Subsequently the Drug Court model has spread to a number of jurisdictions, including Australia, Canada and the UK. For illustrative purposes we will describe the UK's first Drug Court, which was established in Glasgow in 2001, initially on a pilot basis, and evaluated by a team of researchers based at Stirling University (McIvor et al., 2006).

Echoing the team approach described by Hora et al., the Glasgow Drug Court was developed with a dedicated court team consisting of Sheriffs (sentencers), a Sheriff Clerk, a court officer and a Procurator Fiscal (prosecutor) and Co-ordinator, supported by a Supervision and Treatment Team responsible for all aspects of assessment, supervision, testing, treatment and the provision of court reports. The Drug Court was set up to target male and female offenders aged 21 and over with an established pattern of offending and serious drug misuse. All Orders made by the Drug Court are subject to drug testing (urinalysis) and reviews led by Sheriffs, at least monthly (McIvor et al., 2006).

The Glasgow Drug Court also adopts the hands-on approach of US judges in the DTCs: indeed, a key aspect of the role of the Drug Court Sheriffs is the oversight and monitoring of the Orders they impose. As McIvor et al. (2006: 56) explain, this in effect means that Sheriffs 'adopt the roles of motivator, enforcer and sanctioner', and the cornerstone of the review hearing is 'direct dialogue between the bench and the offender'. Research on the operation of the Drug Court in its pilot phase included observation by the research team of 229 reviews, as well as interviews with key actors in the process. The researchers found that not only did Sheriffs consider their review function as central to the process; but also that Supervision and Treatment Team members reported that the review process had a positive impact on offenders' motivation, and felt that offenders responded well to the positive comments of Sheriffs. The research team reported that in the context of reviews, offenders were 'generally responsive, co-operative and honest' (McIvor et al., 2006: 62).

Indeed, offenders generally believed that reviews influenced their compliance with Orders: they experienced engaging in dialogue with Sheriffs in positive terms (often in contrast to previous experiences of being in court) and valued the chance to build rapport with 'their' Sheriff (McIvor et al., 2006).

Of the 150 offenders made subject to a Drug Court Order during the pilot period, a higher proportion (31%) of Orders were completed successfully than were terminated for reasons of non-compliance or ineffective treatment (29%). The researchers conclude that this indicates a degree of success for the Glasgow Drug Court, given the histories of offending and drug use which characterised its client group. Successful completion of an Order was also associated with a lower frequency of reconviction in the two years from the date of the Order, compared with the two years preceding it.

Re-entry courts

In the UK context, Drug Courts are a relatively recent initiative, and currently indications are that the model is proving popular and likely to spread. There are also indications of effectiveness. The results of a pilot scheme which examined the setting up of two dedicated drug courts in Leeds and London indicated that continuity of magistrates had a statistically significant impact on key outcomes: offenders were less likely to miss a court hearing, more likely to complete their sentence and less likely to be reconvicted (Matrix Knowledge Group, 2008). Meanwhile, in the USA, the Drug Court model has been used as a template for the development of new TJ-inspired approaches to the reintegration or 're-entry' of ex-prisoners. Where the Drug Court casts sentencers in the role of 'treatment managers', the 'reentry court' casts them as 'reentry managers' who oversee the offender's transition from custody to the community. As Maruna and LeBel (2003) explain, the re-entry court experiment is still in its infancy, and pilot sites in various US states differ significantly in their approaches. However, in general terms the re-entry court uses the authority of the court to apply graduated sanctions and positive reinforcement, and to marshal resources to support the ex-prisoner's reintegration. The core elements of the model, they explain, include *assessment and strategic re-entry planning*, involving the offender, sentencers and other key partners; *regular review meetings*, involving the offender and his circle of supporters; and *accountability to the community* through the involvement of citizen advisory boards and other community groups. Rewards for success include the possibility of early release from parole obligations, and 'graduation ceremonies' similar to those used in some Drug Courts (Maruna and LeBel, 2003: 2).

Maruna and LeBel argue that the re-entry court represents a promising development: not least because, in contrast to traditional parole, the notion of rewarding success is intrinsic to its design. Indeed, all re-entry courts are required to outline milestones in the re-entry process (such as the completion of voluntary work) which will automatically trigger recognition and appropriate rewards. As they note, rewarding positive achievements, rather than punishing violations, is an unusual but welcome role for the criminal courts. The re-entry court also stands in contrast to traditional parole by virtue of its attempts to involve members of the community in the reintegration process. For Maruna and LeBel, the community, not just the court, is an essential participant in the re-entry process: not only must the offender negotiate his or her *physical* re-entry into the community on release; but she or he must also accomplish some sort of 'relational reintegration' back into the wider *moral* community. This of course implies reacceptance of the offender by the community as a law-abiding citizen, which for many offenders is a significant hurdle to negotiate.

Restorative Justice Approaches: Offenders, Victims and Communities

So far this chapter has focused on the importance and potential effectiveness of relationships between offenders and professional (or in the case of mentoring, volunteer or quasi-professional) 'helpers' – in the pursuit of rehabilitation. But Maruna and LeBel usefully remind us that when we think about rehabilitation in its symbolic sense (see Chapter 1), a number of other stakeholders – and relationships – come into view. These stakeholders include family members and other supporters, but also victims and members of the wider community, with whom the offender's rehabilitation must arguably be negotiated. Restorative justice is an umbrella term for a group of approaches which seeks to resolve conflicts (broadly conceived) by bringing together those with a stake in resolving that conflict and deciding how to move on from it. This 'essence' of restorative justice is neatly captured in Marshall's popular definition:

> Restorative Justice is a process whereby parties with a stake in a specific offence collectively resolve how to deal with the aftermath of the offence and its implications for the future. (Marshall, 1999: 5)

As a response to offending, restorative justice differs from most other approaches in that it is not solely focused on what is done to or with the offender. Indeed, the current restorative justice 'boom' is commonly understood in the context of a victim's movement which has sought over a number of years to raise the profile of crime victims, forefront their needs and promote their involvement in justice processes in a number of ways (e.g. Dignan, 2005). Nonetheless, the objectives of restorative justice do include offender-focused ones such as encouraging offenders to assume responsibility for their actions;

seeking to reintegrate offenders into their communities; and reducing the likelihood of reoffending (see generally Johnstone, 2002; Robinson and Shapland, 2008). And, as an approach to securing such outcomes, its novelty lies in the value and importance it places on the involvement of other stakeholders – specifically 'non-professionals', including victims, supporters of offenders and victims, and sometimes members of the wider community in which offenders and victims reside.

Although there is no definitive typology of restorative justice practices (see McIvor, 2004 or Dignan, 2005 for examples), the most common operational examples of restorative justice can be classified under two main headings. First, **victim–offender mediation (VOM)** involves contact between offender and victim and is facilitated by a specially trained, neutral 'mediator'. Contact between the two parties may be direct (i.e. face-to-face) or indirect, involving the relaying of questions and/or information by the mediator. Recent research indicates that victim–offender mediation is currently the most common form of restorative justice practice in both the USA and Europe. **Restorative conferencing** differs from VOM principally in that it tends to involve members of the wider community as well as the victim and offender. Dignan (2005) draws a distinction between two main variants: family group conferencing, and police-led community conferencing. *Family group conferencing* originated in New Zealand as a means of dealing with offending by young people, and as an antidote to criminal justice processes which tended to offer little opportunity for victim involvement, and which were perceived as potentially discriminatory in respect of indigenous populations (Maxwell and Morris, 1993). *Police-led community conferencing*, in contrast, originated in the early 1990s in the small town of Wagga Wagga in New South Wales, Australia. Subsequently, this particular conferencing model spread not just to other parts of Australia, but also to the USA, and the UK (see further below). These two models differ on a number of important dimensions, but one of the key differences is that police-led conferencing, unlike family group conferencing, has been heavily influenced by Braithwaite's (1989) theory of reintegrative shaming.

Braithwaite's theory of reintegrative shaming

In the context of the present chapter, Braithwaite's theory is important because as well as being explicitly oriented toward offender rehabilitation, it also affords a central role to *relationships* as a conduit to rehabilitative outcomes. Braithwaite defines 'reintegrative shaming' as:

> disapproval dispensed within *an ongoing relationship* with the offender based on respect … shaming which focuses on the evil of the deed rather than on the offender as an irreclaimably evil person (Braithwaite, 1993: 1, emphasis added).

This he contrasts with the 'stigmatic' shaming typically dispensed by the criminal courts – and with what he views as the equally stigmatic delivery of rehabilitative programmes by professionals who 'come in to do things to or for people' (1999: 68).

Braithwaite proposed that reintegrative shaming could be an effective means of inducing guilt and eliciting remorse on the part of the offender, as well as a precursor to forgiveness, acceptance and reintegration within the law-abiding community. It is in respect of these processes that the offender's 'significant others' or 'community of care' play an important role: it is theorised that their disapproval of the offence ('moral censure') is likely to mean more to the offender than that of a magistrate or judge, in whose esteem the offender has little or no personal investment (Braithwaite, 1989: 87). In his later work, Braithwaite also acknowledged a role for the victim in the shaming process which involved drawing the offender's attention to the 'collateral damage' caused by the offence: damage which might include fear, personal injury and/or material loss (Braithwaite and Mugford, 1994). Faced with the victim's personal testimony, it is argued, the offender is less likely to be able to employ 'techniques of neutralization' (Sykes and Matza, 1957) which serve to minimise the harm caused by offending, and more likely to have to face up to the consequences of his or her actions.

In the context of a restorative justice conference, then, reintegrative shaming is enabled by inviting participants (victims and supporters of both parties) to express their emotions and views directly to the offender. But importantly, according to Braithwaite's theory, the community's 'judgement' is not a prelude to pain or retributive punishment: rather it is intended to perform an educative and reintegrative function. In this context we encounter the notion of 'responsibilisation' which was introduced at the end of Chapter 7. The concern is to persuade offenders to *share* the community's judgement of their behaviour, and to act in future with that judgement in mind. For Braithwaite, reintegrative shaming is about 'conscience-building' and it can be 'a reaffirmation of the morality of the offender'. It is this new or reconstituted morality or conscience which, he argues, subsequently serves to inhibit future offending behaviour (1989: 72–3). In this process, the offender can achieve 'symbolic' reintegration or rehabilitation: that is, he or she can earn (re-)acceptance or 'requalification' as a law-abiding member of the community. For Braithwaite, reintegration principally implies the 'decertification of deviance' which, it is argued, may be underlined by the acceptance of an offender's apology, offers of forgiveness, and/or the signing of an agreement. It may also be achieved through the offender's performance of reparative work – which may form part of such an agreement – upon which forgiveness or re-acceptance may be conditional (Braithwaite and Mugford, 1994: 141).

Developing social capital

There are, however, other ways of thinking about the rehabilitative potential of restorative justice through a 'relational lens'. One is with reference to the concept of social capital, which we encountered in Chapter 8. Bazemore is one of a number of writers who have argued that restorative justice – and conferencing in particular – offers valuable opportunities for offenders to generate the development of social capital (Halpern, 2005; Bazemore et al., 2000; Bazemore and O'Brien, 2002; Kurki, 2003).

The potential role of social capital in offender rehabilitation has been the subject of research in several countries on both desistance (or 'naturalistic' rehabilitation) (e.g. Maruna, 2001; Farrall, 2002; Farrall and Maruna, 2004) and the resettlement (or 're-entry') of ex-prisoners (e.g. Travis and Petersilia, 2001; Maruna and LeBel, 2003; Maruna et al., 2004). Both literatures have highlighted the typically low levels of (positive) social capital enjoyed by offenders, and have emphasised the key roles played by families, communities and social networks in encouraging ex-offenders to avoid offending. For example, Travis and Petersilia have argued that 're-entry activities' should take place as close as possible to the local communities to which offenders will ultimately return, because it is here that the 'positive power of social networks' can be found and exploited (2001: 309). Laub and Sampson (2003) highlight the importance of partners and jobs in their longitudinal study of desistance in persistent young offenders in the USA (see also Farrall, 2002).

In the context of restorative conferencing, it has been argued that the potential to generate or mobilise social capital can be maximised or 'strategised' by seeking to ensure that those most closely connected to the offender are present, as well as those likely to be relevant 'resource persons' for the offender. It is also hypothesised that the possibilities for increasing social capital increase as the number of conference participants grows (Bazemore and O'Brien, 2002: 51–2).

But of course staging restorative justice events offers no guarantee that either reintegrative shaming or the building of positive social capital will occur in any particular case. As Robinson and Shapland (2008) have observed, restorative justice conferences may be scripted with a view to eliciting the sorts of relational dynamics we have discussed here, but they are not choreographed, and therefore will not necessarily achieve that potential. So for example in their evaluation of pilot restorative justice schemes which involved observation of some 280 conferences, reintegrative shaming (as described by Braithwaite) was by no means always observed; nor was social capital always acquired or developed. However, they did see some moving examples of what appeared to be genuine expressions of remorse on the part of offenders when faced with the accounts of 'their' victims; and in many cases victims were able to accept the apologies offered by offenders, helping both parties to move on from the offence (see also Shapland et al., 2006; 2007).

They also reported some examples of the mobilisation or generation of social capital: that is, the apparent establishment of social connections likely to offer offenders instrumental (as well as, in many cases, emotional) support. For example, in some cases offenders were reunited with family members following a period of estrangement, and sometimes such reunions were characterised by explicit offers of practical help (e.g. accommodation and help finding employment). Further, in a number of other cases victims or their supporters offered similar types of help to offenders, even though there had been no prior relationship between the parties.

Circles of Support and Accountability: Reintegrating the 'Worst of the Worst'?

One group of offenders for whom notions of reintegration and community acceptance are particularly problematic are those who have been convicted of sexual offences. In recent years many jurisdictions have sought to strengthen measures to control and manage the risks posed by sexual offenders, and in some instances this has included calls to notify communities about the existence of such offenders in their neighbourhoods. For example, 'Megan's Law' in the USA has enabled the public to have internet access to the personal details and addresses of known sexual offenders, with a view to protecting children from harm.[3] A rather different approach to managing the risks posed by sexual offenders in the community, however, is *Circles of Support and Accountability* (COSA). This model has its roots in Canada – and specifically the Mennonite congregation of a small, urban city in which a notorious paedophile was released from federal prison in 1994. The case of Charlie Taylor – described by Wilson et al. (2007a) – provided the impetus for a new approach to the management of sexual offenders in the community: an approach which sought to preserve community safety whilst also ensuring that the offender himself had adequate support and could be safely reintegrated into that community. The COSA model was formalised in 1996 and has subsequently spread not just across Canada, but also to a number of US jurisdictions (Wilson et al., 2007a). In the UK, the COSA model has been tested and evaluated in the Thames Valley (Newell et al., 2005) and at the time of writing is being developed elsewhere.

COSA has been described as a *restorative* approach, reflecting its dual concern with meeting the needs of victims, offenders and communities (Cesaroni, 2001; Quaker Peace and Social Witness, 2005; Wilson et al. 2007a). Wilson et al. describe the COSA model thus:

> The goal of COSA is to promote successful reintegration of released men into the community by providing support, advocacy, and a way to be meaningfully accountable in exchange for living *safely* in the community ... Simply put, COSAs promote safety for

victims (past or potential) by validating their needs for healing and continued safety while, at the same time, supporting ex-offenders with their daily needs and holding them accountable for behaving responsibly. In return for remaining accountable, the ex-offender's rights as a citizen are protected. (Wilson et al., 2007a: 8; emphasis in original)

In the context of COSA, accountability means that the offender must accept that his past behaviour was unacceptable and caused harm; he must also demonstrate a commitment to desistance. If an offender chooses to leave the circle, the police are notified (Cesaroni, 2001). Thus, the offender's rights as a citizen are *contingent* on his willingness to cooperate with the terms of an explicit agreement to cooperate with the COSA. What is of particular interest in the context of the current chapter is the mechanisms through which accountability is maintained: namely, through the mechanism of the relationships formed between the 'core member' of the circle (i.e. the offender) and its other members.

A central feature of COSA is its involvement of community members – usually volunteers – albeit that their role is variable in different jurisdictions. In Canada, where the model originated, COSA is a community-driven but professionally supported model. In the UK (Thames Valley), COSAs also depend upon volunteers but are managed by professionals and have been piloted (with Home Office funding) to support the statutory agencies which are responsible for the management of high-risk sex offenders living in the community (Quaker Peace and Social Witness, 2005). Describing the Canadian model, Wilson et al. report that COSAs 'work' via the mechanism of relationships which are forged between the circle and the core member:

COSA volunteers seek relationships not based on professional respect and distance, but in terms of friendships [...] the 'currency' of a Circle's influence on the prosocial behaviour of a Core Member is founded on relationships of trust and friendship that are, at times, different from those founded on authority and professionalism. (2007a: 11)

Initially the circle meets weekly and, in addition, there is informal contact between the core member and circle members on a daily basis. This may be a telephone call or an informal meeting. Often, formal circle meetings develop into or are complemented by informal gatherings, such as visits to the cinema or meals together. Additionally, circle members are 'on call' to respond to any crisis experienced by the core member (Cesarini, 2001).

Not surprisingly, one of the biggest challenges faced by Canadian COSA projects has been the recruitment of volunteers who are both suitable for this kind of role, and willing to take on the responsibilities (and necessary training) involved. Wilson et al. (2007a) report that to date the majority of volunteers have come from faith communities, reflecting the project's origins in the actions of a single Mennonite minister, as noted above. A survey of volunteers[4] revealed that about two-thirds became involved with the project because of an interest in working with sexual offenders, and 30% were motivated by a desire to 'give something back' to their community. Volunteers had an average age of 55, and among the 75% who were not retired, about half (48%) were employed in 'helping' professions (Wilson et al., 2007b).

The same survey also revealed some interesting feedback about offenders' experiences of involvement with COSA. When asked to describe their relationships with circle volunteers, 90% of offenders reported that they got along with everyone and 86% said that volunteers were very supportive of them.[5] Respondents indicated that circle volunteers had helped them with practical tasks such as finding employment or obtaining identification papers, as well as providing emotional support and opportunities to socialise. When asked how they might have managed without the circle, the vast majority said that they would have found it harder to adjust to the community and two-thirds thought they would have returned to crime (Wilson et al., 2007b: 296). Indeed, an outcome evaluation which compared 60 COSA offenders with a matched comparison group of 60 similar offenders who did not participate in the project revealed that the COSA group reoffended at a rate that was considerably lower than the comparison group.[6] In respect of sexual recidivism specifically, the comparison group were three times as likely to reoffend, committing ten offences in an average of 18.54 months, compared with three offences in the COSA group in an average of 22.1 months. Further, in each of the cases of sexual reoffending by COSA members, the new offence was less serious than the original one for which they had been convicted. This was not the case for the comparison group (Wilson et al., 2007c). Similarly positive results have been reported by the Thames Valley COSA project in the UK (Quaker Peace and Social Witness, 2005).

Conclusion

In this chapter we have described a number of contemporary and emerging approaches which have sought to develop or utilise relationships of various kinds in the interests of offender rehabilitation. The relationships in question have included those between offenders and criminal justice professionals – some of whom have not traditionally been associated with rehabilitative processes – and also relationships forged between offenders and non-professionals, including community volunteers. In the course of this chapter we have also considered the more general issue of the offender's relationship with the wider community, which always provides the broad context in which rehabilitation must take place.

One important feature that the approaches described in this chapter share is that they do not generally constitute 'stand-alone' interventions; that is, they are not intended to exclude other, potentially complementary approaches. Thus, for example, the supervisory relationship between offender and probation officer is likely to provide the context for other, time-limited interventions (such as groupwork programmes) and the COSA project in the Thames Valley is explicitly described as 'complementing' the intensive psychological interventions delivered by treatment professionals, as well as the statutory multi-agency public protection arrangements (MAPPA) which govern the management of sexual offenders in England and Wales[7] (Quaker Peace and Social Witness, 2005). In a similar vein, court initiatives which have drawn inspiration from 'therapeutic jurisprudence' complement the provision of specialist help for (most commonly) drug misuse problems.

With a few exceptions, the approaches considered in this chapter have not yet attracted the kinds of rigorous independent research which we have encountered in earlier chapters; for example, in respect of offending behaviour programmes (see Chapter 7). This inevitably means that any claims to effectiveness must be treated with some caution. But it should also be borne in mind that, understood as just one element of a rehabilitative process, the approaches considered in this chapter do not *by themselves* necessarily claim to be capable of reducing reoffending. Indeed, it is arguably the case that they are more concerned with the sorts of intermediate outcomes or 'non-reconviction benefits' we discussed in Chapter 4.

Indeed, the approaches described in this chapter provide a useful counterbalance to the idea that effective rehabilitation is simply a process of applying the 'right' intervention, with the singular aim of preventing reoffending. They also remind us that rehabilitation is a process which may have many strands: some of which may fall short of overt attempts to change people, focusing instead on building motivation, strengths and resources which can help or encourage people towards offence-free lives.

Questions to Consider

1 What do the approaches described in the chapter have in common? Are there important differences between them?
2 What do you see as the main weaknesses of these approaches?
3 Is it realistic or legitimate to aim for the reintegration of sexual offenders in the community?
4 Which, if any, of the approaches described in this chapter do you think is likely to develop and/or spread? Why?

Suggested Further Reading

A number of articles by Gordon Bazemore explore the notion of 'relational reha-bilitation'. Shadd Maruna's excellent book *Making Good: How Ex-Convicts Reform and Rebuild Their Lives* (2001) is a classic study of offenders' own accounts of 'going straight', and includes many case studies which illustrate well the relational context of rehabilitation and desistance. Stephen Farrall's book *Rethinking What Works With Offenders* (2002) presents the findings of a longitudinal study of 199 offenders on probation which also provides some useful ammunition for a 'relational' approach. There is a burgeoning literature on restorative justice but Robinson and Shapland (2008) specifically explore the relationship between restorative justice and offender rehabilitation.

Notes

1 In this chapter we draw on Gordon Bazemore's (1999) notion of 'relational reha-bilitation', developed in the context of his research in the field of restorative justice and subsequently explored by Raynor and Robinson (2005: Chapter 7).
2 It has been observed, however, that the Drug Treatment Court movement in the USA emerged relatively independently of – albeit in parallel with – growing acade-mic interest in TJ (Hora et al., 1999).
3 Megan's Law is named after seven-year-old Megan Kanka, who was raped and killed by a known child molester who had moved to the New Jersey neighbourhood in which the Kankas lived. In the wake of the offence, the Kanka family sought to enable local communities to be warned about sex offenders in their area. All US states now have a form of Megan's Law.
4 The response rate was 57/84 volunteers surveyed.
5 The response rate was 24/37 offenders surveyed.
6 In this study 'reoffending' was defined as being charged or convicted of an offence or for breach of a condition imposed by the court.
7 Discussion of the MAPPA framework is beyond the scope of this chapter, but see Wood and Kemshall (2007).

TEN

Conclusion: Rehabilitation in the Twenty-first Century

In the opening chapter of their recent book, Ward and Maruna (2007) debate the currency of the term *rehabilitation* in the twenty-first century context. They argue that rehabilitation is a notion which, for some, has become a 'dirty word'; and one which has been to some extent at least superseded or eclipsed by 'newer, shinier' terms like *desistance, resettlement* and *reintegration*. Ward and Maruna are surely right to observe that, for some – among them some offenders – the very idea of rehabilitation has negative connotations. These derive principally from its historical association with a *medical model* of crime causation; and with forms of punishment which either jeopardise justice for offenders, stigmatise them and render them passive recipients of 'expert' intervention; or else let them off too lightly, enabling offenders to avoid 'real' punishment. We discussed these issues in Chapters 1, 2 and 3.

In this book we have advocated a broader conceptualisation of rehabilitation: one which takes us beyond what Rotman (1990) would call 'authoritarian' models and modes of intervention to include 'anthropocentric' ones as well (see Chapter 1). On the one hand, we have acknowledged the negative and sometimes damaging potential of rehabilitation, and have sought to illustrate how this has been realised at certain points in history and in particular contexts. But we have also argued that there are more positive ways of seeing (and doing) rehabilitation, examples of which can be found throughout the book. We encountered one such example in Chapter 6, where we considered ways in which offender assessment can be approached with reference to positives like motivations and strengths, as well as or instead of risks and needs. In its broadest sense, we would argue that rehabilitation is a notion which implies change: but just what kind of change, how it should be achieved and in what contexts is the subject of continuing debate.

Our view is that the so-called 'receptacle model' of rehabilitation, 'where the professional counsels the relatively passive offender into avoiding future crime' (Bazemore and O'Brien, 2002: 39), is not one which should be pursued in the twenty-first century. For us, rehabilitation is a process which can include 'therapeutic' interventions which aim to help change offenders' behaviour, but it is a process which can also include attempts to change aspects of their environment. It can include attempts by external bodies/agencies to intervene or facilitate change, but also the self-directed efforts of the individual offender, supported by his or her significant others. Further, we think that individuals seeking to change their behaviour or overcome 'offending identities' have a right to be supported in those processes, particularly when they have been damaged by the experience or institutions of punishment. We also take the view that rehabilitation *does ideally* mean the cessation of offending, but that there may be important intermediate outcomes in the process which fall short of desistance. And, ideally, behavioural change will be accompanied by the reacceptance of the rehabilitated person by others in his or her community. So rehabilitation in its fullest sense should have both the behavioural and symbolic dimensions we described in Chapter 1.

Ward and Maruna are also right to observe that we have, in the twenty-first century, acquired some new ways of talking about what has traditionally been called rehabilitation, but like them we think it is a term worthy of retention. We think this largely because without it there is a risk that we may lose sight of the past, and fail to recognise what they call 'old wine in new bottles' (Ward and Maruna, 2007: 5). As we have seen, the history of rehabilitation is one characterised by a degree of circularity or reinvention: that is, the re-discovery of ideas, theories and practices which have been tried before and subsequently fizzled out or otherwise been found wanting. This has been the case, as we have seen, for psychological, social *and* relational approaches: all have a long history; all have at one or more time been de-emphasised, and all are at present enjoying something of a 'revival' (see Chapters 7, 8 and 9 respectively). Indeed, we might say that in the early years of the twenty-first century, all of these approaches have themselves been rehabilitated. But another reason why we think that rehabilitation has continuing value is that, for us, it expresses a positive potential which is lacking in certain more recent terms. *Offender management* is one such example (e.g. Home Office, 2006a). For us, this notion is at best bland and at worst pessimistic.

Questions remain, however, about the future of rehabilitation. On the one hand, as we saw in Chapter 3, there has in England and Wales been something of a revival or re-legitimation of rehabilitation in penal policy, evidenced for example in the Criminal Justice Act 2003 which has put rehabilitation on a statutory footing as one of five 'purposes of sentencing'. However, at the same time there is little doubt that we are witnessing a 'new punitiveness' in punishment (Pratt et al., 2005) which is resulting not only in more sentences of imprisonment, for longer periods, and plans for more and larger prisons; but also community penalties with more conditions and restrictions than at any time in the past (e.g. Ministry of Justice, 2008). In this context, it is difficult to see rehabilitation as a priority for policymakers or sentencers (Lewis, 2005). A related concern stems from the ways in which rehabilitation tends to be justified in contemporary policy. This is a theme we discussed in Chapter 1. Evidence from contemporary policy documents points toward an unreservedly utilitarian justification for rehabilitative measures: that is, one which emphasises its crime reduction benefits and, ultimately, its contribution to the overarching policy objectives of risk management and public protection. Rarely if ever do we see in official discourse the justification of rehabilitative measures on humanitarian or rights-based grounds. It is no longer offenders themselves who are seen as the main beneficiaries of rehabilitation, but rather communities and potential victims. As Garland has observed, rehabilitative interventions can only be justified in the contemporary context to the extent that they are compatible with the interests of these other stakeholders. Such interventions:

> hold themselves out as being for the benefit of future victims rather than for the benefit of the offender. It is future victims who are now 'rescued' by rehabilitative work, rather than the offenders themselves. (Garland, 2001: 176)

Indeed, in England and Wales penal policy is currently seeking to 're-balance the criminal justice system in favour of the victim' – a policy turn which implies that we perhaps ought to be doing less, not more, for offenders; albeit that improving services for victims does not in fact necessitate the downgrading of services for offenders (Home Office, 2006b). We, however, agree with Rotman (1990) that the minimum society owes to offenders who have been imprisoned is a duty to undo any damage caused by incarceration. In the twenty-first century context which is seeing a seemingly limitless expansion of carceral punishment, this means that the need for rehabilitative services has perhaps never been greater (see also McNeill, 2006).

A problem of course with a reliance on utilitarian justifications for rehabilitation is that, as we saw in Chapter 5, answers to the question 'What Works?' (in respect of reducing reoffending) remain somewhat elusive. As Peter Raynor has observed, this means that we could be on the verge of a drift back towards 'nothing works': as he rightly points out, this has proved in the past to be a 'powerful, resilient and simplistic doctrine' which could prove (once again) difficult to shake off (Raynor, 2008: 75). If this were to happen, rehabilitation's foothold in penal policy could be in serious jeopardy. In our view, however, a continuing culture of curiosity among practitioners and researchers (as discussed in Chapters 4, 5 and elsewhere) is the best defence for rehabilitation, and this should include research which takes into account the views of those subject to rehabilitative practices: i.e. offenders themselves. We do not believe that there are any 'magic bullets' in offender rehabilitation, and this conclusion is supported by decades of research. We do however believe that it is imperative to continue to ask the question: 'what works – and with whom?'

Questions to Consider

1 What factors are likely to affect the future of rehabilitation?
2 Has rehabilitation shed its negative image in the twenty-first century?
3 What justifications for rehabilitation are in your view most valid?

Suggested Further Reading

Discussions of the standing of rehabilitation in the twenty-first century can be found in Garland (2001), Lewis (2005), McNeill (2006) and Raynor and Robinson (2005: Chapter 8). For a more in-depth discussion of the contemporary status of and justifications for rehabilitation in England and Wales, see Robinson (2008).

References

Adams, K., Bennett, K.J., Flanagan, T.J., Marquart, J.W., Cuvelier, S.J., Fritsch, E., Gerber, J., Longmire, D.R. and Burton, Jr. V.S. (1994) 'A large-scale multidimensional test of the effect of prison education programs on offenders' behavior', *The Prison Journal*, **74**, 4: 433–49.

Advisory Council on the Treatment of Offenders, Sub-committee on the Organisation of After-Care (1963) *The Organisation of After-Care*. London: HMSO.

Allen, F. A. (1959) 'Criminal justice, legal values and the rehabilitative ideal', *Journal of Criminal Law, Criminology and Police Science*, **50**, 3: 226–32.

American Friends Service Committee (1971) *Struggle for Justice: A Report on Crime and Punishment in America*. New York: Hill and Wang.

Andrews, D. (1995) 'The psychology of criminal conduct and effective treatment', in J. McGuire (ed.) *What Works: Reducing Reoffending*. Chichester: Wiley.

Andrews, D. and Bonta, J. (1995) *The Level of Service Inventory – Revised: Manual*. New York: Multi-Health Systems Inc.

Andrews, D. and Dowden, C. (2005) 'Managing correctional treatment for reduced recidivism: A meta-analytic review of programme integrity', *Legal and Criminological Psychology*, 10: 173–87.

Andrews, D.A., Zinger, I., Hoge, R.D., Bonta, J., Gendreau, P. and Cullen, F.T. (1990a) 'Does correctional treatment work? A clinically relevant and psychologically informed meta-analysis', *Criminology*, **28**, 3: 369–404.

Andrews, D., Bonta, J. and Hoge, R. (1990b) 'Classification for effective rehabilitation', *Criminal Justice and Behavior*, **17**, 1: 19–52.

Audit Commission (2002) *Route to Justice: improving the pathway of offenders through the criminal justice system*. London: Audit Commission (http://www.audit-commission. gov.uk/Products/NATIONAL-REPORT/99EDE976-8893-44b3-8D1A-631B36174 EE9/criminaljustice.pdf)

Baker, K. (2004) 'Is *Asset* really an asset? Assessment of young offenders in practice', in R. Burnett and C. Roberts (eds) *What Works in Probation and Youth Justice*. Cullompton: Willan.

Baker, K., Jones, S., Roberts, C. and Merrington, S. (2003) *The Evaluation of the Validity and Reliability of the Youth Justice Board's Assessment for Young Offenders*. London: Youth Justice Board.

Bandura, A. (1975) *Social and Personality Development*. New York: Holt, Rinehart & Winston.

Bazemore, G. and O'Brien, S. (2002) 'The quest for a restorative model of rehabilitation: theory-for-practice and practice-for-theory', in L. Walgrave (ed.), *Restorative Justice and the Law.* Cullompton: Willan.

Bazemore, G. (1999) 'After shaming, whither reintegration: restorative justice and relational rehabilitation', in G. Bazemore and L. Walgrave (eds), *Restorative Juvenile Justice: Repairing the Harm of Youth Crime.* Monsey, NY: Criminal Justice Press.

Bazemore, G., Nissen, L. and Dooley, M. (2000) 'Mobilizing social support and building relationships: Broadening correctional and rehabilitative agendas', *Corrections Management Quarterly* **4**, 4: 10–21.

Beaumont, B., Caddick, B. and Hare-Duke, H. (2001) *Meeting Offenders' Needs.* Bristol: University of Bristol School for Policy Studies.

Beccaria, C. (1963) [1764] *On Crimes and Punishment* (Trans. H. Paolucci). Indianapolis: Bobbs-Merrill.

Beck, A.T. (1976) *Cognitive Therapy and Emotional Disorders.* New York: International Universities Press.

Becker, H. S. (1963) *Outsiders: Studies in the Sociology of Deviance.* Toronto: The Free Press of Glencoe.

Beckett, R.C., Beech, A.R., Fisher, D. and Fordham, A.S. (1994) *Community-based Treatment for Sex Offenders: An Evaluation of Seven Treatment Programmes.* London: Home Office.

Bennett, T. (1998) *Drugs and Crime: The Results of Research on Drug Testing and Interviewing Arrestees.* Home Office Research Study 183. London: Home Office.

Bhui, H.S. (1999) 'Race, racism and risk assessment', *Probation Journal,* **46**, 3: 171–81.

Blunkett, D. (2004) *Reducing Crime – Changing Lives: The Government's plans for Transforming the Management of Offenders.* London: Home Office.

Bochel, D. (1976) *Probation and After-Care: Its Development in England and Wales,* Edinburgh: Scottish Academic Press.

Bonta, J. and Andrews, D. (2003) 'A commentary on Ward and Stewart's model of human needs', *Psychology, Crime and Law,* 9: 215–18.

Bonta, J. and Wormith, S. (2007) 'Risk and need assessment', in G. McIvor and P. Raynor (eds), *Developments in Social Work with Offenders.* London: Jessica Kingsley.

Bonta, J. (1996) 'Risk-needs assessment and treatment', in A.T. Harland (ed.), *Choosing Correctional Options That Work.* London: Sage.

Bottoms, A. E. (1977) 'Reflections on the Renaissance of dangerousness', *Howard Journal of Criminal Justice,* **16** (2): 70–96.

Bottoms, A. E. and McWilliams, W. (1979) 'A Non-treatment paradigm for probation practice', *British Journal of Social Work,* **9**, 2: 159–202.

Bourdieu, P. (1992) *An Invitation to Reflexive Sociology.* Chicago: University of Chicago Press.

Braithwaite, J. and Mugford, S. (1994) 'Conditions of successful reintegration ceremonies', *British Journal of Criminology* **34**, 2: 139–71.

Braithwaite, J. (1989) *Crime, Shame and Reintegration.* Cambridge: Cambridge University Press.

Braithwaite, J. (1993) 'Shame and modernity', *British Journal of Criminolgy,* 33, 1, 1–18.

Braithwaite, J. (1999) 'Restorative justice: assessing optimistic and pessimistic accounts', in M. Tonry (ed.) *Crime and Justice: A Review of Research,* 25, Chicago: University of Chicago Press.

Bridges, A. (1998) *Increasing the Employability of Offenders: An Inquiry into Probation Service Effectiveness.* Probation Studies Unit Report No. 5. Oxford: University of Oxford Centre for Criminological Research.

Briggs, S. and Turner, R. (2003) *Barriers to Starting Programmes: Second Phase Report.* National Probation Service (West Yorkshire).

Brody, S. R. (1975) *The Effectiveness of Sentencing.* Home Office Research Study 35. London: HMSO.

Bryant, M., Coker, J., Estlea, B., Himmel, S. and Knapp, T. (1978) 'Sentenced to Social Work', *Probation Journal,* **25**, 4: 110–14.

Burgess, A. (1962) *A Clockwork Orange.* London: Heinemann.

Burnett, R. (1996) *Fitting Supervision to Offenders: Assessment and Allocation Decisions in the Probation Service.* Home Office Research Study 153. London: Home Office.

Burnett, R. and McNeill, F. (2005) 'The place of the officer–offender relationship in assisting offenders to desist from crime', *Probation Journal,* **52**, 3: 221–42.

Burrows, J., Clarke, A., Davison, T., Tarling, R. and Webb, S. (2000) *The Nature and Effectiveness of Drugs Throughcare for Released Prisoners.* Research Findings 109. Home Office Research, Development and Statistics Directorate. London: Home Office.

Burt, C. (1925) *The Young Delinquent.* London: University of London Press.

Butler Committee (1975) *Report of the Committee on Mentally Abnormal Offenders.* Home Office and Department of Health and Social Security. Cmnd 6244. London: HMSO.

Cann, J. (2006) *Cognitive Skills Programmes: Impact on Reducing Reconviction among a Sample of Female Prisoners.* Home Office Research Findings 276. London: Home Office.

Cann, J., Falshaw, L., Nugent, F. and Friendship, C. (2003) *Understanding What Works: Accredited Cognitive Skills Programmes for Adult Men and Young Offenders.* Home Office Research Findings 226. London: Home Office.

Carlen, P. (1989) 'Crime, inequality and sentencing', in P. Carlen and D. Cook (eds), *Paying for Crime.* Milton Keynes: Open University Press.

Carlisle, J. (1997) 'Accommodation issues for prisoners', *Prison Service Journal,* 114: 12–13.

Carter, P. (2003) *Managing Offenders, Reducing Crime.* London: Home Office.

Cavadino, M. and Dignan, J. (1997) *The Penal System: An Introduction* (2nd Edition), London: Sage.

Cavadino, M. and Dignan, J. (2006) *Penal Systems: A Comparative Approach.* London: Sage Publications.

Cavadino, M. and Dignan, J. (2007) *The Penal System: An Introduction,* 4th edn. London: Sage.

Cavadino, M., Crow, I. and Dignan, J. (1999) *Criminal Justice 2000: Strategies for a New Century.* Winchester: Waterside Press.

Cesaroni, C. (2001) 'Releasing sex offenders into the community through "Circles of Support" – a means of reintegrating the "worst of the worst"', *Journal of Offender Rehabilitation,* **34**, 2: 85–98.

Chapman, T. and Hough, M. (1998) *Evidence Based Practice.* London: Home Office.

Chitty, C. (2005) 'The impact of corrections on re-offending: conclusions and the way forward', in G. Harper and C. Chitty (eds), *The Impact of Corrections: A Review of 'What Works'.* Home Office Research Study 291 (2nd edn). London: Home Office.

Clarke, A., Simmonds, R. and Wydall, S. (2004a) *Delivering Cognitive Skills Programmes in Prison: A Qualitative Study.* Home Office Online Report 27/04. London: Home Office.

Clarke, A., Simmonds, R. and Wydall, S. (2004b) *Delivering Cognitive Skills Programmes in Prison: A Qualitative Study.* Home Office Research Findings 242. London: Home Office.

Coker, J. (1984) 'Sentenced to social work?: the revival of choice', *Probation Journal*, **31**, 4: 123–25.

Colbourne, T. (2001) 'Training prisoners for the real world: prison work does little for prisoners' employment prospects', *Prison Service Journal*, 134: 30–1.

Colledge, M., Collier, P. and Brand, S. (1999) *Programmes for Evaluators: Guidance for Evaluators.* Crime Reduction Programme, Guidance Note 2. Research Development and Statistics Directorate. London: Home Office.

Cook, T. D. and Campbell, D. T. (1979) *Quasi-Experimentation.* Chicago: Rand-McNally.

Copas, J. and Marshall, P. (1998) 'The Offender Group Reconviction Scale: a statistical reconviction score for use by probation officers', *Applied Statistics*, 47: 159–71.

Copas, J., Ditchfield, J. and Marshall, P. (1994) 'Development of a new reconviction prediction score', *Home Office Research Bulletin*, 36: 30–37.

Coyle, A. (1992) 'The responsible prisoner: rehabilitation revisited', *The Howard Journal*, **31**, 1: 1–7.

Crawford, A. and Newburn, T. (2003) *Youth Offending and Restorative Justice.* Cullompton, Devon: Willan.

Crawford, A. (2003) '"Contractual governance" of deviant behaviour', *Journal of Law and Society*, **30**, 4: 479–505.

Crow, I. (2006) *Resettling Prisoners: A Review.* National Offender Mangement Service and University of Sheffield. York: York Publishing Services.

Crow, I. (1996) 'Employment, training and offending', in M. Drakeford and M. Vanstone (eds), *Beyond Offending Behaviour.* Aldershot: Arena.

Crow, I. (2000) 'Evaluating initiatives in the community', in V. Jupp, P. Davies and P. Francis, *Doing Criminological Research.* London: Sage.

Crow, I., Richardson, P., Riddington, C. and Simon, F. (1989) *Unemployment, Crime and Offenders*, London: Routledge.

Crow, I., Cavadino, M., Dignan, J., Johnston, V. and Walker, M. (1996) *Changing Criminal Justice: The Impact of the Criminal Justice Act 1991 in Four Areas of the North of England.* Centre for Criminological and Legal Research, University of Sheffield.

Crow, I. and Semmens, N. (2008) *Researching Criminology.* Maidenhead: Open University Press.

Cullen, E. (1994) 'Grendon: the therapeutic prison that works', *Journal of Therapeutic Communities*, **15**, 4: 301–10.

Cullen, E. (1998) *Grendon and Future Therapeutic Communities in Prison.* London: Prison Reform Trust.

Cullen, F.T. and Gilbert, K.E. (1982) *Reaffirming Rehabilitation.* Cincinnati, Ohio: Anderson Publishing.

Currie, E. (1996) *Is America Really Winning the War on Crime and Should Britain Follow Its Example?* NACRO 30th Anniversary Lecture. London: NACRO.

Davies, M. (1969) *Probationers in Their Social Environment: A Study of Male Probationers aged 17–20.* Home Office Research Study 2. London: Home Office.

Davies, M. (1974) *Prisoners of Society: Attitudes and After-care.* London: Routledge and Kegan Paul.

Davies, K., Lewis, J., Byatt, J., Purvis, E. and Cole, B. (2004) *An Evaluation of the Literacy Demands of General Offending Behaviour Programmes.* Home Office Research Findings 233. London: Home Office.

Day, A., Tucker, K. and Howells, K. (2004) 'Coerced offender rehabilitation – a defensible practice?' *Psychology, Crime and Law*, **10**, 3: 259–69.

Dearden, J. S. (2004) *John Ruskin.* Buckinghamshire: Shire Publications.

Departmental Committee on Prisons (1895) *Report from the Departmental Committee on Prisons* (The Gladstone Report). London: HMSO.

Department for Education and Skills (2005) *Reducing Re-Offending Through Skills and Employment*. Cm 6702. London: The Stationery Office.

Department for Education and Skills (2006) *Reducing Re-Offending Through Skills and Employment: Next Steps*. London: Department for Education and Skills, the Home Office and the Department for Work and Pensions on behalf of HM Government (at www.dfes.gov.uk/offenderlearning)

Dignan, J. (2005) *Understanding Victims and Restorative Justice*. Maidenhead: Open University Press.

Ditchfield, J. and Marshall, P. (1990) 'A review of recent literature evaluating treatments for sex offenders in prison', *Prison Service Journal*, No. 81: 24–8.

Duff, A. (2001) *Punishment, Communication, and Community*. Oxford: Oxford University Press.

Duff, A. and Garland, D. (eds) (1994) *A Reader on Punishment*. Oxford: Oxford University Press.

Duff, R. A. (2005) 'Punishment and rehabilitation – or punishment as rehabilitation', *Criminal Justice Matters*, No. 60: 18–19.

Ekblom, P., Law, H., and Sutton, M. (1996) *Safer Cities and Domestic Burglary*. Home Office Research Study 164. London: Home Office.

Elliott-Marshall, R., Ramsay, M. and Stewart, D. (2004) 'Alternative approaches to integrating offenders into the community', in G. Harper and C. Chitty, *The Impact of Corrections on Re-Offending: A Review of 'What Works'*. Home Office Research Study 291. London: Home Office Research, Development and Statistics Directorate.

Evans, R. (1968) 'The labour market and parole success', *Journal of Human Resources*, **3**, 2: 201–12.

Eysenck, H. J. (1978) 'An exercise in mega-silliness', *American Psychologist*, **33**: 517.

Falshaw, L., Friendship, C. and Bates, A. (2003a) *Sexual Offenders – Measuring Reconviction, Reoffending and Recidivism*. Home Office Research, Development and Statistics Directorate Research Findings 183. London: Home Office.

Falshaw, L., Friendship, C., Travers, R. and Nugent, F. (2003b) *Searching for 'What Works': An Evaluation of Cognitive Skills Programmes*. Home Office Research Findings 206. London: Home Office.

Farabe, D., Prendergast, M.L. and Anglin, M.D. (1998) 'The effectiveness of coerced treatment for drug-abusing offenders', *Federal Probation* 62: 3–10.

Farrall, S. (2002) *Rethinking What Works with Offenders*. Cullompton: Willan.

Farrall, S. and Maruna, S. (2004) 'Desistance-focused criminal justice policy research', *The Howard Journal*, **43**, 4: 358–67.

Farrington, D.P. (1989) *Cambridge Study in Delinquent Development: Long-term Follow-up*. Cambridge University, Institute of Criminology.

Farrington, D. P. and Morris, A. M. (1983) 'Sex, sentencing and reconviction', *British Journal of Criminology*, **23**, 3: 229–48.

Fattah, E.A. (1997) *Criminology: Past, Present and Future: A Critical Overview*. London: Macmillan.

Fisk, K. (1998) 'Arkwright: Cotton King or Spin Doctor', *History Today*, **48**, 3: 25–30.

Fitzpatrick, S. and Klinker, S. (2000) *Research on Single Homelessness in Britain*. York: Joseph Rowntree Foundation.

Fleet, F. and Annison, J. (2003) 'In support of effectiveness: facilitating participation and sustaining change', in W-H. Chui and M. Nellis (eds), *Moving Probation Forward: Evidence, Arguments and Practice*. Harlow: Pearson Longman.

Fletcher, D.R., Woodhill, D. and Herrington, A. (1998) *Building Bridges into Employment and Training for Ex-Offenders*. York: York Publishing Services.

Folkard, M. S., Smith, D. E. and Smith, D. D. (1976) *Intensive Matched Probation and After-Care Treatment, Vol. II*. Home Office Research Study 36. London: HMSO.

Foucault, M. (1977) *Discipline and Punish: The Birth of the Prison*. London: Penguin.

Friendship, C., Beech, A. R. and Browne, K. D. (2002a) 'Reconviction as an outcome in research: a methodological note', *British Journal of Criminology*, **42**: 442–44.

Friendship, C., Blud, L., Erikson, M. and Travers, R. (2002b) *An Evaluation of Cognitive Behavioural Treatment for Prisoners*. Home Office Research Findings 161. London: Home Office.

Friendship, C., Mann, R, and Beech, A. (2003) *The Prison-Based Sex Offender Treatment Programme – An Evaluation*. Findings 205. Research, Development and Statistics Directorate. London: Home Office.

Friendship, C., Street, R., Cann, J. and Harper, G. (2005) 'Introduction: the policy context and assessing the evidence', in G. Harper and C. Chitty (eds), *The Impact of Corrections on Re-Offending: A Review of 'What Works'*. Home Office Research Study 291. London: Home Office.

Gaes, G.G., Flanagan, T.J., Motiuk, L. and Stewart, L. (1999) 'Adult correctional treatment', in M. Tonry and J. Petersilia (eds), *Crime and Justice: A Review of Research*, 26, 361–426. University of Chicago Press: Chicago.

Garland, D. (1985) *Punishment and Welfare: A History of Penal Strategies*. Aldershot: Gower.

Garland, D. (1996) 'The limits of the sovereign state: strategies of crime control in contemporary society, *British Journal of Criminology*, 36, 4: 445–71.

Garland, D. (1997) 'Of crimes and criminals: the development of criminology in Britain', in M. Maguire, R. Morgan and R. Reiner (eds), *The Oxford Handbook of Criminology*, 2nd edn. Oxford: Clarendon Press.

Garland, D. (2001) *The Culture of Control: Crime and Social Order in Contemporary Society*. Oxford: Oxford University Press.

Gelsthorpe, L. (2001) 'Accountability: difference and diversity in the delivery of community penalties', in A. Bottoms, L. Gelsthorpe and S. Rex (eds), *Community Penalties: Change and Challenges*. Devon: Willan.

Gelsthorpe, L. and Sharpe, G. (2006) 'Criminological research: typologies versus hierarchies', *Criminal Justice Matters*, No. 62.

Gelsthorpe, L. and Morgan, R. (eds.) (2007) *Handbook of Probation*. Cullompton, Devon: Willan Publishing.

Genders, E. and Player, E. (1995) *Grendon: A Study of a Therapeutic Community*. Oxford: Clarendon Press.

Gendreau, P. and Ross, R. (1979) 'Effective correctional treatment: bibliotherapy for cynics', *Crime & Delinquency*, **25**, 4: 463–89.

Gendreau, P., Goggin, C. and Smith, P. (1999) 'The forgotten issue in effective correctional treatment: program implementation', *International Journal of Offender Therapy and Comparative Criminology* 43: 180–87.

Giddens, A. (2006) *Sociology*, 5th edn. Cambridge: Polity Press.

Gill, M. (1997) 'Employing ex-Offenders: a risk or an opportunity?', *Howard Journal*, **36**, 4: 337–51.

Glass, G.V., McGaw, B. and Smith, M.L. (1981) *Meta-Analysis in Social Research*, London: Sage.

Glover, E. (1955) 'Prognosis or prediction: a psychiatric examination of the concept of "Recidivism"', *British Journal of Delinquency*, **6**, 21: 116–25.

Godwin, E. (1793) *Enquiry Concerning Political Justice and its Influence on Morals and Happiness. Two Volumes*. London: Robinson. (Cited in Ignatieff, 1978: 117)

Goggin, C. and Gendreau, P. (2006) 'Quality services in rehabilitation programmes', in C. Hollin and E. Palmer (eds), *Offending Behaviour Programmes*. Chichester: Wiley.

Goldblatt, P. and Lewis, C. (1998) *Reducing Offending: An assessment of Research Evidence on Ways of Dealing with Offending Behaviour*. Home Office Research Study 187. London: Home Office.

Goring, C. (1913) *The English Convict: A Statistical Study*. London: HMSO.

Gormally, B., Lyner, O., Mulligan, G. and Warden, M. (1981) *Unemployment and Young Offenders in Northern Ireland*. Belfast: NIACRO.

Gossop, M., Marsden, J. and Stewart, D. (1998) *NTORS at One Year. The National Treatment Outcomes Research Study: Changes in Substance Use, Health and Criminal Behaviours at One Year after Intake*. London: Department of Health.

Gossop, M., Marsden, J. and Stewart, D. (2000) 'The UK National Treatment Outcome Research Study and its implications', *Drug and Alcohol Review*, **19**: 5–7.

Grubin, D. and Thornton, D. (1994) 'A national programme for the assessment and treatment of sex offenders in the English prison system', *Criminal Justice and Behavior*, 21: 55–71.

Gunn, J. and Robertson, G. (1987) 'A ten year follow-up of men discharged from Grendon Prison', *British Journal of Psychiatry*, 151: 674–8.

Hall, J. (2003) *Mentoring and Young People: A Literature Review*. Glasgow: Scottish Council for Research in Education.

Halpern, D. (2005) *Social Capital*. Cambridge: Polity Press.

Hannah-Moffat, K. (1999) 'Moral agent or actuarial subject: risk and Canadian women's imprisonment', *Theoretical Criminology*, 3 (1): 71–94.

Harman, K. and Paylor, I. (2005) 'An Evaluation of the CARAT Initiative', *The Howard Journal of Criminal Justice*, **44**, 4: 357–73.

Harper, G. and Chitty, C. (eds) (2005) *The Impact of Corrections on Re-offending: A Review of 'What Works'*. Home Office Research Study 291, 2nd edn. London: Home Office.

Harper, G., Man, L-H., Taylor, S. and Niven, S. (2005) 'Factors associated with offending', in G. Harper and C. Chitty (eds), *The Impact of Corrections on Re-offending: A Review of 'What Works'*. Home Office Research Study 291, 2nd edn. London: Home Office.

Harraway, P. C., Brown, A. J., Hignett, C. F., Wilson, C. O., Abbot, J. S., Mortimer, S. A. and Keegan, A. C. (1985) *The Demonstration Unit, 1981–85*. London: Inner London Probation Service.

Haslewood-Pocsik, I., Merone, L. and Roberts, C. (2004) *The evaluation of the Employment Pathfinder: lessons from Phase 1 and a survey for Phase 2*. Online Report 22/04. London: Home Office.

Hedderman, C. (2004) 'The "criminogenic" needs of women offenders', in G. McIvor (ed.), *Women Who Offend*. London: Jessica Kingsley.

Hedderman, C., Ellis, T. and Sugg, D. (1999) *Increasing Confidence in Community Sentences: The Results of Two Demonstration Projects*. Home Office Research Study 194, Research, Development and Statistics Directorate. London: Home Office.

Hedderman, C. and Sugg, D. (1996) *Does Treating Sex Offenders Reduce Reoffending?* Research Findings 45, Home Office Research and Statistics Directorate. London: Home Office.

Henry S. and Milovanovic D. (1996) *Constitutive Criminology*, London: Sage.

HM Chief Inspector of Prisons (1997) *Report of an Inspection of HMP Grendon and Springhill*. London: Home Office.

HM Chief Inspector of Prisons (1998) *Report of Her Majesty's Chief Inspector of Prisons, 1996–97*. London: HMSO.

HM Chief Inspector of Prisons (2007) *Report on an Unannounced Short Follow-up Inspection of HMP Grendon, 31 October–2 November 2006*. London: HM Inspectorate of Prisons.

HM Inspectorates of Prisons and Probation (2001) *Through the Prison Gate*. London: Home Office.

HM Prison Service (1993) *National Framework for the Throughcare of Offenders in Custody to the Completion of Supervision in the Community*. London: HM Prison Service.

HM Prison Service (1998a) *The Review of the Prison Service Drug Strategy: 'Drug Misuse in Prison'*. London: HM Prison Service.

HM Prison Service (1998b) *Tackling Drugs in Prison: The Prison Service Drug Strategy*. London: HM Prison Service.

HM Prison Service (1999) *Corporate Plan 1999–2000 to 2001–2002*. London: HM Prison Service.

HM Prison Service (undated) *Grendon: a therapeutic prison*. London: HM Prison Service.

Hobson, J. and Shine, J. (1998) 'The measurement of psychopathy in a UK prison population referred for long-term psychotherapy', *British Journal of Criminology*, 38, 3: 504–15.

Hollin, C. and Palmer, E. (2006a) 'Criminogenic need and women offenders: a critique of the literature, *Legal and Criminological Psychology*, 11: 179–95.

Hollin, C. and Palmer, E. (2006b) 'Offending behaviour programmes: controversies and resolutions', in C. Hollin and E. Palmer (eds), *Offending Behaviour Programmes*. Chichester: Wiley.

Hollin, C. and Palmer, E. (2006c) 'Offending behaviour programmes: history and development', in C. Hollin and E. Palmer (eds), *Offending Behaviour Programmes*. Chichester: Wiley.

Hollin, C. (1995) 'The meaning and implications of "programme integrity"', in J. McGuire (ed.), *What Works: Reducing Reoffending*. Chichester: Wiley.

Hollin, C. (2004) 'To treat or not to treat? An historical perspective', in C. Hollin (ed.), *The Essential Handbook of Offender Assessment and Treatment*. Chichester: Wiley.

Hollin, C. (2006) 'Offending behaviour programmes and contention: evidence-based practice, manuals, and programme evaluation', in C. Hollin and E. Palmer (eds), *Offending Behaviour Programmes*. Chichester: Wiley.

Hollin, C., McGuire, J., Palmer, E., Bilbly, C., Hatcher, R. and Holmes, A. (2002) *Introducing Pathfinder Programmes into the Probation Service*. Home Office Research Findings 177. London: Home Office.

Hollin, C., Palmer, E., McGuire, J., Hounsome, J., Bilbly, C. and Clarke, C. (2004) *Pathfinder Programmes in the Probation Service: A Retrospective Analysis*. Home Office Online Report 66/04. London: Home Office.

Hollin, C. R. (2008) 'Evaluating offending behaviour programmes: Does randomization glister?' *Criminology and Criminal Justice*, 8, 1: 89–106.

Home Office (1971) *The Sentence of the Court: A Handbook for Courts on the Treatment of Offenders*. London: HMSO

Home Office (1978), 'A survey of the South-East prison population', *Research Bulletin No. 5*, pp. 12–14. London: Home Office Research Unit.

Home Office (1990a) *Partnership in Dealing with Offenders in the Community*. London: Home Office.

Home Office (1990) *Provision for Mentally Disordered Offenders*. Home Office Circular 66/90. London: Home Office.

Home Office (1995a) *Tackling Durgs Together: A Strategy for England* 1995–1998, Cm. 2846.

Home Office (1995b) *Drug Misuse in Prisons*, London: Home Office.

Home Office (1995) *Strengthening Punishment in the Community: A Consultation Document*, Cm 2780, London: HMSO.

Home Office (1998) *Effective Practice Initiative: A National Implementation Plan for the Effective Supervision of Offenders*, Probation Circular 35/1998. London: Home Office.

Home Office (1999) *Effective Practice Initiative: A Joint Risk/Needs Assessment System for the Prison and Probation Services*. Probation Circular 16/1999. London: Home Office.

Home Office (2000) *What Works Strategy for the Probation Service*. Probation Circular 60/2000.

Home Office (2004) *Reducing Re-offending: National Action Plan*. London: Home Office.

Home Office (2005) *Probation Circular 25/2005: Criminal Justice Act 2003: Implementation on 4 April*. London: Home Office.

Home Office (2006a) *The NOMS Offender Management Model*. London: Home Office.

Home Office (2006b) *Rebalancing the Criminal Justice System in Favour of the Law-Abiding Majority: Cutting Crime, Reducing Re-offending and Protecting the Public*. London: Home Office.

Hora, P.F., Schma, W.G. and Rosenthal, J.T.A. (1999) 'Therapeutic jurisprudence and the drug treatment court movement: revolutionizing the criminal justice system's response to drug abuse and crime in America', *Notre Dame Law Review* 74: 439. http://www.quaker.org.uk/shared_asp_files/uploadedfiles/82f718a7-9344-4a5c-a4a7-4b053ff22239_circlesofsupport-first3yrs.pdf

Horkheimer, M. and Adorno, T. W. (1973) *Dialectic of the Enlightenment*. London: Allen Lane.

Hough, M. and Allen, R. (2006) 'Probation work and NOMS', *Criminal Justice Matters*, No. 62. London: Centre for Crime and Justice Studies.

Hough, M., Clancy, A., McSweeney, T. and Turnbull, P.J. (2003) *The Impact of Drug Treatment and Testing Orders on Offending: Two-year Reconviction Results*. Home Office Research Findings 184. London: Home Office.

Howard, J. (1929) [1777] *The State of the Prisons*. London: J.M. Dent and Sons.

Howard, P. (2006) *The Offender Assessment System: An Evaluation of the Second Pilot*. Home Office Research Findings 278. London: Home Office.

Hudson, B. (1987) *Justice Through Punishment*, London: Macmillan.

Hudson, B. (2001) 'Human rights, public safety and the probation service: defending justice in the risk society', *Howard Journal*, **40**, 2: 103–13.

Hudson, B. (2003) *Understanding Justice*, 2nd edn. Buckingham: Open University Press.

Hullin, R. (1978) 'The effect of two randomly allocated court procedures on truancy', *British Journal of Criminology*, **18**, 3: 232–44.

Hullin, R. (1985) 'The Leeds Truancy Project', *Justice of the Peace*, 488–91.

Humphrey, C., Carter, P. and Pease, K. (1992) 'A reconviction predictor for probationers', *British Journal of Social Work*, 22: 33–46.

Hurry, J. and Moriaty, V. (2004) *Education, Training and Employment: The National Evaluation of the Youth Justice Board's Education, Training and Employment Projects*. London: Youth Justice Board.

Hutchinson, S. (2006) 'Countering catastrophic criminology: reform, punishment and the modern liberal compromise', *Punishment and Society*, 8, 4: 443–67.

Ignatieff, M. (1978) *A Just Measure of Pain, The Penitentiary in the Industrial Revolution, 1750–1850*. London: Macmillan.

Izzo, R. L. and Ross, R. R. (1990) 'Meta-analysis of rehabilitation programs for juvenile delinquents', *Criminal Justice and Behaviour*, **17**, 1: 134–42.

Johnstone, G. (1996) *Medical Concepts and Penal Policy*. London: Cavendish Publishing Limited.

Johnstone, G. (2002) *Restorative Justice: Ideas, Values, Debates.* Cullompton: Willan.

Jolliffe, D. and Farrington, D. (2007) 'A rapid evidence assessment of the impact of mentoring in re-offending: a summary', *Home Office Online Report 11/07.*

Joseph Rowntree Foundation (1996) *The Housing Needs of Ex-Prisoners.* Findings: Housing Research No. 178. York: Joseph Rowntree Foundation.

JUSTICE, The Howard League for Penal Reform and the National Association for the Care and Resettlement of Offenders (1972) *Living It Down: The Problem of Old Convictions.* London: Stevens.

Keen, J., Oliver, P., Rowse, G. and Mathers, N. (2001) 'Residential rehabilitation for drug users: a review of 13 months' intake to a therapeutic community', *Family Practice,* **18**, 5: 545–48.

Kemshall, H. (1996) *Reviewing Risk.* London: Home Office.

Kemshall, H. (1998) *Risk in Probation Practice.* Aldershot: Ashgate.

Kemshall, H. (2001) *Risk Assessment and Management of Known Sexual and Violent Offenders: A Review of Current Issues* (Police Research Series Paper No. 140). London: Home Office.

Kemshall, H. (2002) 'Effective practice in probation: an example of "advanced liberal" responsibilisation?', *Howard Journal of Criminal Justice,* **41**, 1: 41–58.

Kemshall, H., Canton, R. and Bailey, R. (2004) 'Dimensions of difference', in A. Bottoms, S. Rex and G. Robinson (eds), *Alternatives to Prison: Options for an Insecure Society.* Cullompton: Willan.

Kendall, K. (2002) 'Time to think again about cognitive behavioural programmes', in P. Carlen (ed.), *Women and Punishment: The Struggle for Justice.* Cullompton: Willan.

Kendall, K. (2004) 'Dangerous thinking: a critical history of correctional cognitive behaviouralism', in G. Mair (ed.), *What Matters in Probation.* Cullompton: Willan.

Kershaw, C. (1998) 'Interpreting Reconviction Rates', *The Use and Impact of Community Supervision,* Research Bulletin No. 39, Special Edition, 9–16, Home Office Research and Statistics Directorate. London: Home Office.

King, J. F. S. (1964) *The Probation Service,* 2nd edn. London: Butterworths.

King, R. and Morgan, R. (1980) *The Future of the Prison System.* Aldershot: Gower.

Kuhn, T. S. (1970) *The Structure of Scientific Revolutions.* Chicago and London: The University of Chicago Press.

Kurki, L. (2003) 'Evaluating restorative justice practices', in A. von Hirsch, J. Roberts, A.E. Bottoms, K. Roach and M. Schiff (eds), *Restorative Justice and Criminal Justice: Competing or Reconcilable Paradigms?* Oxford: Hart Publishing.

Lambert, M. and Bergin, A.E. (1994) 'The effectiveness of psychotherapy', in A.E. Bergin and S.L. Garfield (eds), *Handbook of Psychotherapy and Behavior Change.* New York: John Wiley & Sons.

Laub, J.H. and Sampson, R.J. (2003) *Shared Beginnings, Divergent Lives: Delinquent Boys to Age 70.* Cambridge, Mass.: Harvard University Press.

Learmont, J. (1995) *Review of Prison Service Security in England and Wales and the Escape from Parkhurst Prison on Tuesday, 3rd January 1995.* Cm 3020. London: HMSO.

Lewis, S. (2005) 'Rehabilitation: headline or footnote in the new penal policy?', *Probation Journal,* **52**, 2: 119–35.

Lewis, S., Vennard, J., Maguire, M., Raynor, P., Vanstone, M., Raybould, S. and Rix, A. (2003) *The Resettlement of Short-Term Prisoners: An Evaluation of Seven Pathfinders.* RDS Occasional Paper No. 83. London: Home Office.

Lipsey, M. W. (1992) 'The effect of treatment on juvenile delinquents: results from meta-analysis', in F. Lösel, D. Bender and T. Bliesner (eds), *Psychology and Law: International Perspectives.* Berlin: Walter de Gruyter.

Lipsey, M. (1999) 'Can rehabilitative programs reduce the recidivism of juvenile offenders? An inquiry into the effectiveness of practical programs', *Virginia Journal of Social Policy and the Law*, 6: 611–41.

Lloyd, C., Mair, G. and Hough, M. (1994) *Explaining Reconviction Rates: A Critical Analysis*. Home Office Research Study136. London: Home Office.

Lombroso, C. (1876) *L'Uomo Delinquente*. Milan: Hoepli.

Maguire, M. (2004) 'The Crime Reduction Programme in England and Wales: reflections on the vision and the reality', *Criminal Justice*, **4**, 3: 213–37.

Maguire, M., Hutson, S. and Nolan, J. (2007) *Accommodation for Ex-Prisoners in the Southwest Region*. Glamorgan: University of Glamorgan and Government Office of the South West. http://noms.justice.gov.uk/news-publications-events/publications/strategy/Maguire_accomadation_report?version=1

Mair, G. (1991) 'What works – nothing or everything?', *Home Office Research Bulletin*, 30: 3–8.

Mair, G., Llayd, C., Nee, C., and Sibbett, R. (1994) *Intensive Probation in England and Wales: An evaluation*. Home Office Research Study 133. London: Home Office.

Mair, G. (ed.) (1997a) *Evaluating the Effectiveness of Community Penalties*. Aldershot: Avebury.

Mair, G. (1997b) 'Community penalties and the probation service', in M. Maguire, R. Morgan and R. Reiner (eds), *The Oxford Handbook of Criminology*, 2nd edn. Oxford: Clarendon Press.

Mair, G. (2004) *What Matters in Probation*. Cullompton: Willan.

Mair, G., Burke, L. and Taylor, S. (2006) '"The worst tax form you've ever seen"? Probation officers' views about OASys', *Probation Journal* 53, 1: 7–23.

Mair, G. and Copas, J. (1996) *Nothing Works and What Works – Meta-Analysis?* Unpublished paper received from first author, School of Law, Social Work and Social Policy, Liverpool, John Moores University.

Mair, G., Cross, N. and Taylor, S. (2007) *The Use and Impact of the Community Order and the Suspended Sentence Order*. King's College London: Centre for Crime and Justice Studies.

Mannheim, H. (1939) *The Dilemma of Penal Reform*. London: Allen and Unwin.

Mannheim, H. and Wilkins, L. T. (1955) *Prediction Methods in Relation to Borstal Training*. Studies in the Causes of Delinquency and the Treatment of Offenders No. 1. London: HMSO.

Manpower Services Commission (1976) *Action Research Programme for Disadvantaged People*. Sheffield: MSC.

Marshall, P. (1994) 'Reconviction of imprisoned sexual offenders', *Research Bulletin*, No. 36. London: Home Office Research and Statistics Department.

Marshall, P. (1997) *A Reconviction Study of HMP Grendon Therapeutic Community*. Research Findings 53. London: Home Office Research and Statistics Directorate.

Marshall, T.F. (1999) *Restorative Justice: An Overview*. London: Home Office.

Marshall, W.L. and Serran, G.A. (2004) 'The role of the therapist in offender treatment', *Psychology, Crime and Law*, **10**, 3: 309–20.

Martin, C. (1996) 'Coming clean: drugs research in a prison setting', *Criminal Justice Matters*, No. 24: 22–3, Institute for the Study and Treatment of Delinquency.

Martin, J. P. and Webster, W. (1971) *Social Consequences of Conviction*. London: Heinemann.

Martinson, R. (1974) 'What works? – questions and answers about prison reform, *The Public Interest*, **35**: 22–54.

Martinson, R. (1979) 'New findings, new views: a note of caution regarding sentencing reform', *Hofstra Law Review* (7), 243–58.

Maruna, S. (2001) *Making Good: How Ex-Convicts Reform and Rebuild Their Lives.* Washington D.C.: American Psychological Association.

Maruna, S. and LeBel, T. (2003) 'Welcome home? Examining the "reentry court" concept from a strengths-based perspective', *Western Criminological Review*, **4**, 2: 91–107.

Maruna, S. Immarigeon, R. and LeBel, T.P. (2004) 'Ex-offender reintegration: theory and practice', in S. Maruna and R. Immarigeon (eds), *After Crime and Punishment: Pathways to Offender Reintegration.* Cullompton: Willan.

Matrix Knowledge Group (2008) *Dedicated Drug Court Pilots: A Process Report.* Ministry of Justice Research Series 7/08. London: Ministry of Justice.

Matza, D. (1969) *Becoming Deviant.* Englewood Cliffs. NJ: Prentice Hall.

Maxwell, G. and Morris, A. (1993) *Family, Victims and Culture: Youth Justice in New Zealand.* Wellington: Social Policy and Administration and Victoria University of Wellington.

May Committee (1979) *Report of the Committee of Inquiry into the United Kingdom Prison Services.* Cmnd 7673, London: HMSO.

May, C. (2006) *The CARAT drug service in prisons: findings from the research database.* Findings 262. Research, Development and Statistics Directorate. London: Home Office.

McGuire, J. (ed.) (2002) *Offender Rehablition and Treatment.* Chichester: Wiley.

McGuire, J. (2003) 'Maintaining change: converging legal and psychological initiatives in a therapeutic jurisprudence framework', *Western Criminology Review*, **4**, 2: 108–23.

McGuire, J. and Priestley, J. (1985) *Offending Behaviour: Skills and Stratagems for Going Straight.* London: Batsford.

McGuire, J. and Priestley, P. (1995) 'Reviewing "what works": past, present and future', in J. McGuire (ed.), *What Works: Reducing Reoffending,* Chichester: Wiley.

McGuire, J. (1995) (ed.) *What Works: Reducing Reoffending,* Chichester: Wiley.

McGuire, J. (2000a) *Cognitive-Behavioural Approaches: An Introduction to Theory and Research.* London: HMIP.

McGuire, J. (ed.) (2002) *Offender Rehabilitation and Treatment.* Chichester: Wiley.

McGuire, J. (2001) 'Defining correctional programs', in L.L. Motiuk and R.C. Serin (eds), *Compendium 2000 on Effective Correctional Programming.* Ottowa: Correctional Service Canada.

McGuire, J. (2006) 'General offending programmes', in C. Hollin and E. Palmer (eds), *Offending Behaviour Programmes.* Chichester: Wiley.

McIvor, G. (1990) *Sanctions for Serious and Persistent Offenders: A Review of the Literature.* Stirling: Social Work Research Centre.

McIvor, G. (2004) 'Reparative and restorative approaches', in A. Bottoms, S. Rex and G. Robinson (eds), *Alternatives to Prison: Options for an Insecure Society.* Cullompton: Willan.

McIvor, G., Barnsdale, L., Eley, S., Malloch, M., Yates, R. and Brown, A. (2006) *The Operation and Effectiveness of the Scottish Drug Court Pilots.* Edinburgh: Scottish Executive.

McLintock, F. H. (1976), 'The Beeson Report: delinquency and unemployment in the North-East of England', in United Nations Social Defence Research Institute, *Economic Crises and Crime.* Rome: UNSDRI.

McMahon, G., Hall, A., Hayward, G., Hudson, C., and Roberts, C. (2004) *Basic Skills Programmes in the Probation Service: An Evaluation of the Basic Skills Pathfinder.* Home Office Research Findings 203. London: Home Office.

McNeill, F. (2006) 'A desistance paradigm for offender management', *Criminology and Criminal Justice*, **6**, 1: 39–62.

McWilliams, W. (1986) 'The English probation system and the diagnostic ideal', *The Howard Journal*, **25**, 4: 241–60.

McWilliams, W. and Pease, K. (1990) 'Probation practice and an end to punishment', *The Howard Journal*, 29, (1): 14–24.

Melossi, D. and Pavarini, M. (1981) *The Prison and The Factory, Origins of the Penitentiary System*, London: Macmillan.

Merrington, S. and Stanley, S. (2000) 'Doubts about the What Works initiative', *Probation Journal*, **47**, 4: 272–75.

Merrington, S. and Stanley, S. (2004) 'What Works? Revisiting the evidence in England and Wales', *Probation Journal*, **51** (1): 7–20.

Merrington, S. (2004) 'Assessment tools in probation: their development and potential', in R. Burnett and C. Roberts (eds), *What Works in Probation and Youth Justice*. Cullompton: Willan.

Ministry of Justice (2008) *Prison Policy Update: Briefing Paper.* London: Ministry of Justice.

Moore, R. (2007) *Adult Offenders' Perceptions of their Underlying Problems: Findings from the OASys Self-assessment Questionnaire.* Findings 284. London: Home Office.

Morgan, R. (1994) 'Imprisonment: current concerns and a brief history since 1945', in M. Maguire, R. Morgan and R. Reiner (eds), *The Oxford Handbook of Criminology*, 2nd edn. Oxford: Clarendon Press.

Morgan, R. (2003) 'Foreword', *HM Inspectorate of Probation Annual Report 2001/2002.* London: Home Office.

Morgan, R. and Liebling, A. (2007) 'Imprisonment: an expanding scene', in Maguire, M., Morgan, R. and Reiner, R. (eds), *The Oxford Handbook of Criminology, Fourth Edition.* Oxford: Oxford University Press.

MORI (1998) *Re-Branding the Probation Service.* Research Study Conducted for Association of Chief Officers of Probation. London: Association of Chief Officers of Probation.

Morris, P. and Beverley, F. (1975) *On Licence: A Study of Parole.* London: Wiley.

Motiuk, L. and Brown, S.L. (1993) *Validity of Offender Needs Identification and Analysis in Community Corrections.* Canada: Canada Correctional Service.

NACRO (1998) *Going Straight Home?* London: NACRO.

National Probation Service (2003) *What Works News*, Issue 14, August 2003.

Nellis, M. (1999) 'Towards "the field of corrections": modernizing the Probation Service in the late 1990s', *Social Policy and Administration*, 33, 3: 302–23.

Newburn, T. and Shiner, M. (2005) *Dealing with Disaffection: Young people, Mentoring and Social Exclusion.* Devon: Willan.

Newton, M. (1971) 'Reconviction after treatment at Grendon', *Chief Psychologist's Report, Series B*, No. 1. London: Office of the Chief Psychologist, Prison Department, Home Office.

Niven, S. and Olagundaye, J. (2002) *Jobs and Homes: A Survey of Prisoners Nearing Release.* Home Office Research Findings 173. London: Home Office.

Niven, S. and Stewart, D. (2005) *Resettlement Outcomes on Release from Prison in 2003.* Home Office Research, Development and Statistics Directorate, Findings 248. London: Home Ofice.

O'Brien, P. (2001) 'Just like baking a cake': women describe the necessary ingredients for successful reentry after incarceration', *Families in Society*, 82, 3: 287–95.

Office of the Deputy Prime Minister (2004) *Survey of English Housing, 2003–04.* http://www.communites.gov.uk/publications/housing/surveyenglish2

Ogloff, J.R.P. and Davis, M.R. (2004) 'Advances in offender assessment and rehabilitation: contributions of the risk-needs-responsivity approach', *Psychology, Crime and Law* 10, 3: 229–42.

Palmer, T. (1975) 'Martinson revisited', *Journal of Research in Crime and Delinquency*, **12**, 2: 133–52.

Palmer, E. (2003) *Offending Behaviour: Moral Reasoning, Criminal Conduct and the Rehabilitation of Offenders*. Cullompton, Devon: Willan.

Partridge, S. (2004) *Examining Case Management Models for Community Sentences*, Home Office Online Report 17/04, London: Home Office.

Paterson, A. (1951) *Paterson on Prisons*. London: Muller Ltd.

Patten, J. (1991) 'Making the punishment fit the frame', *The Guardian*, 20 February.

Pawson, R. and Tilley, N. (1994) 'What works in Evaluation research?', *British Journal of Criminology*, **34**, 3: 291–306.

Pawson, R. and Tilley, N. (1998) 'Caring communities, paradigm polemics, design debates', *Evaluation*, **4**, 1: 73–90.

Pawson, R. and Tilley, N. (1997) *Realistic Evaluation*. London: Sage Publications.

Pease, K. and Wolfson, J. (1979) 'Incapacitation studies: a review and commentary', *The Howard Journal*, **18**: 160–7.

Phillpotts, G. J. O. and Lancucki, L. B. (1979) *Previous Convictions, Sentence and Reconviction*. Home Office Research Study 53. London: HMSO.

Player, E. and Martin, C. A. (1996) *Preliminary Evaluation of the ADT Drug Treatment Programme at HMP Downview*. Research Findings 31. Research and Statistics Department. London: Home Office.

Porporino, F.J. and Robinson, D. (1992) *Can Educating Adult Offenders Counteract Recidivism?* Ottawa: Correctional Service of Canada.

Pratt, J., Brown, D., Brown, M., Hallsworth, S. and Morrison, W. (2005) *The New Punitiveness: Trends, Theories, Perspectives*. Cullompton: Willan.

Priestley, P., McGuire, J., Flegg, D., Barnitt, R., Welham, D. and Hemsley, V. (1984) *Social Skills in Prisons and the Community: Problem-Solving for Offenders*. London: Routledge.

Prochaska, J., DiClemente, C. and Norcross, J. (1992) 'In search of how people change: applications to addictive behaviours', *American Psychologist*, 47 (9): 1102–1114.

Putnam, R. (2000) *Bowling Alone: The Collapse and Revival of American Community*. New York: Simon and Schuster.

Quaker Peace and Social Witness (2005) *Circles of Support and Accountability in the Thames Valley: The First Three Years*. London: Quaker Communications.

Ramsay, M. (2003) *Prisoners' Drug Use and Treatment: Seven Studies*. Home Office RDS Findings 186. London: Home Office.

Raynor, P. (1988) *Probation as an Alternative to Custody*. Aldershot: Avebury.

Raynor, P. (1995) '"What works": probation and forms of justice', in D. Ward and M. Lacey (eds), *Probation: Working for Justice*. London: Whiting and Birch.

Raynor, P. (1997) 'Some observations on rehabilitation and justice', *Howard Journal of Criminal Justice*, **36**, 3: 248–62.

Raynor, P. (2004a) 'Rehabilitative and reintegrative approaches', in A. Bottoms, S. Rex and G. Robinson (eds), *Alternatives to Prison: Options for an Insecure Society*. Cullompton: Willan.

Raynor, P. (2004b) 'The Probation Service "Pathfinders": finding the path and losing the way?', *Criminal Justice*, **4**, 3: 309–25.

Raynor, P. (2007a) 'Community penalties: probation, "What Works", and offender management', in M., Maguire, R. Morgan and R. Reiner (eds), *The Oxford Handbook of Criminology*, 4th edn. Oxford: Oxford University Press.

Raynor, P. (2007b) 'Risk and need assessment in British probation: the contribution of LSI-R', *Psychology, Crime and Law*, **13**, 2: 125–38.

Raynor, P. (2008) 'Community penalties and Home Office research: On the way to 'nothing works'? *Criminology and Criminal Justice*, 8, 1: 73–87.

Raynor, P., Kynch, J., Roberts, C. and Merrington, S. (2000) *Risk and Need Assessment in Probation Services: An Evaluation*. Home Office Research Study 211. London: Home Office.

Raynor, P. and Robinson, G. (2005) *Rehabilitation, Crime and Punishment*. Basingstoke: Palgrave Macmillan.

Raynor, P. and Vanstone, M. (1994) 'Probation practice, effectiveness and the non-treatment paradigm', *British Journal of Social Work*, 24: 387–404.

Raynor, P. and Vanstone, M. (1996) 'Reasoning and rehabilitation in Britain: the results of the Straight Thinking on Probation (STOP) programme', *International Journal of Offender Therapy and Comparative Criminology*, 40 (4): 279–91.

Raynor, P. and Vanstone, M. (1997) *Straight Thinking on Probation (STOP): The Mid Glamorgan Experiment*. Probation Studies Unit Report No. 4. Oxford: University of Oxford Centre for Criminological Research.

Raynor, P. and Vanstone, M. (2002) *Understanding Community Penalties*. Maidenhead: Open University Press.

Rex, S. (1998) 'A new form of rehabilitation?' in A. von Hirsch and A. Ashworth (eds), *Principled Sentencing: Readings on Theory and Policy*, 2nd edn. Oxford: Hart Publishing.

Rex, S. (1999) 'Desistance from offending: experiences of probation', *Howard Journal of Criminal Justice*, **38**, 4: 366–83.

Rex, S. and Matravers, A. (eds) (1998) *Pro-Social Modelling and Legitimacy*. Cambridge: Institute of Criminology.

Rex, S., Gelsthorpe, L., Roberts, C. and Jordan, P. (2003a) *Crime Reduction Programme: An Evaluation of Community Service Pathfinder Projects: Final report 2002*. RDS Occasional Paper 87. London: Home Office.

Rex, S., Lieb, R., Bottoms, A. and Wilson, L. (2003b) *Accrediting Offender Programmes: A Process-based Evaluation of the Joint Prison/Probation Services Accreditation Panel*. Home Office Research Study 273. London: Home Office.

Richie, B. (2001) 'Challenges incercerated women face as they return to their communities: findings from life history interviews', *Crime and Delinquency*, **47**, 3: 368–89.

Roberts, C. (2004) 'Offending behaviour programmes: emerging evidence and implications for practice', in R. Burnett and C. Roberts (eds), *What Works in Probation and Youth Justice*. Cullompton: Willan.

Roberts, C.H. (1989) *Hereford and Worcester Probation Service Young Offender Project: First Evaluation Report*. Oxford: Department of Social and Administrative Studies.

Robinson, D. and Porporino, F.J. (2000) 'Programming in cognitive skills: the reasoning and rehabilitation programme', in C. Hollin (ed.), *Handbook of Offender Assessment and Treatment*. Chichester: Wiley.

Robinson, G. (2001) 'Power, knowledge and What Works in probation', *Howard Journal*, 40 (3): 235–54.

Robinson, G. (2002) 'Exploring risk management in the probation service: contemporary developments in England and Wales', *Punishment and Society*, **4**, 1: 5–25.

Robinson, G. (2003a) 'Risk and risk assessment', in W-H. Chui and M. Nellis (eds), *Moving Probation Forward: Evidence, Arguments and Practice*. Harlow: Pearson Education.

Robinson, G. (2003b) 'Implementing OASys: lessons from research into LSI-R and ACE', *Probation Journal*, **50**, 1: 30–40.

Robinson, G. (2005) 'What Works in offender management?', *Howard Journal of Criminal Justice*, **44**, 3: 307–18.

Robinson, G. (2008) 'Late-modern rehabilitation: the evolution of a penal strategy', *Punishment and Society*, 10(4): 429–45.

Robinson, G. and Shapland, J. (2008) 'Reducing recidivism: a task for restorative justice?' *British Journal of Criminology,* **48**, 3: 337–58.

Rock, P. (1996) *Reconstructing a Women's Prison: The Holloway Redevelopment Project, 1968–88.* Oxford: Clarendon Press.

Rose, D.R., Clear, T. and Scully, K. (1999, November 8) *Coercive mobility and crime: Incarceration and social disorganization.* Paper presented at the American Society of Criminology. Toronto, Ontario.

Rose, N. (2000) 'Government and control', *British Journal of Criminology,* 40: 321–39.

Ross, R.R. and Fabiano, E.A. (1985) *Time to Think: A Cognitive Model of Delinquency Prevention and Offender Rehabilitation.* Johnson City, TN: Institute of Social Sciences and Arts.

Ross, R.R., Fabiano, E.A., and Ewles, C.D. (1988) 'Reasoning and rehabilitation', *International Journal of Offender Therapy and Comparative Criminology,* 32 (1): 29–36.

Rotman, E. (1990) *Beyond Punishment: A New View of the Rehabilitation of Offenders,* Westport, Conn.: Greenwood Press.

Rottman, D. and Casey, P. (1999) 'Therapeutic jurisprudence and the emergence of problem-solving courts', *National Institute of Justice Journal,* July: 12–19.

Ruskin, J. (1968) *Notes on the General Principles of Employment for the Destitute and Criminal Classes.* (Cited in Dearden, 2004: 38–39)

Sampson, A. (1994) 'The future for sex offenders in prison', in E. Player and M. Jenkins (eds), *Prisons After Woolf: Reform Through Riot.* London: Routledge.

Saylor, W. G. and Gaes, G. G. (1997), 'Training inmates through industrial work participation and vocational and apprenticeship instruction'. Corrections Management Quarterly, 1 (2), 32–43.

Shapland, J., Atkinson, A., Atkinson, H., Chapman, B., Colledge, E., Dignan, J., Howes, M., Johnstone, J., Robinson, G. and Sorsby, A. (2006) *Restorative Justice in Practice: Findings from the Second Phase of the Evaluation of Three Schemes.* Home Office Research Findings 274. London: Home Office.

Shapland, J., Atkinson, A., Atkinson, H., Chapman, B., Dignan, J., Howes, M., Johnstone, J., Robinson, G. and Sorsby, A. (2007) *Restorative Justice: The Views of Victims and Offenders: The Third Report from the Evaluation of Three Schemes.* London: Ministry of Justice.

Shaw, S. (1980) *Paying the Penalty: An Analysis of the Cost of Penal Sanctions.* London: NACRO.

Shaw, M. and Hannah-Moffatt, K. (2000) 'Gender, diversity and risk assessment in Canadian corrections', *Probation Journal,* 47, 3: 163–72.

Sherman, L. W., Gottfredson, D. C., MacKenzie, D.L., Eck, J., Reuter, P. and Bushway, S.D. (1998) *Preventing Crime: What Works, What Doesn't, and What's Promising.* Washington: U.S. Department of Justice, National Institute of Justice.

Shinnar, S. and Shinnar, R. (1975) 'The effects of the criminal justice system on the control of crime: a quantitative approach', *Law and Society Review,* 9: 581–611.

Singleton, N., Pendry, E., Simpson, T., Goddard, E., Farrell, M., Marsden, J. and Taylor, C. (2005) *The Impact and Effectiveness of Mandatory Drug Testing in Prisons.* Findings 223. Research, Development and Statistics Directorate. London: Home Office.

Smith, D. (2005) 'Probation and social work', *British Journal of Social Work,* 35 (5): 621–37.

Smith, R. (2003) *Youth Justice: Ideas, Policy, Practice.* Devon: Willan.

Solomon, E., Eades, C., Garside, R. and Rutherford, M. (2007) *Ten Years of Criminal Justice Under Labour: An Independent Audit.* London: Centre for Crime and Justice Studies.

Sarno, C., Hough, M., Nee, C. and Herrington, V. (1999) *Probation Employment Schemes in Inner London and Surrey – An Evaluation*. Research Findings 89. Home Office Research, Development and Statistics Directorate. London: Home Office.

Saylor, W.G. and Gaes, G.G. (1997) 'Training inmates through industrial work participation and vocational and apprenticeship instruction', *Corrections Management Quarterly*, **1**, 2: 32–43.

Seiter, R. P. and Kadela, K. R. (2003) Prisoner reentry: What works, what does not, and what is promising, *Crime and Delinquency*. **49**, 3: 360–88.

Shiner, M., Young, T., Newburn, T. and Groben, S. (2004) *Mentoring Disaffected Young People: An Evaluation of Mentoring Plus*. York: Joseph Rowntree Foundation.

Silberman, M. and Chapman, B. (1971) 'After-care units in London, Liverpool and Manchester', in *Explorations in After-Care*, Home Office Research Unit Study 9. London: HMSO.

Social Exclusion Unit (2002) *Reducing Re-Offending by Ex-Prisoners*. London: Office of the Deputy Prime Minister.

Softley, P. (1978) *Fines in Magistrates' Courts*. Home Office Research Study 46. London: Home Office.

Soothill, K. (1974) *The Prisoner's Release: a Study of the Employment of Ex-prisoners*. London: Allen and Unwin.

Stewart, G. (1996) 'Housing', in M. Drakeford and M. Vanstone (eds), *Beyond Offending Behaviour*. Aldershot: Arena.

St. James-Roberts, I., Greenlaw, G., Simon, A. and Hurry, J. (2005) *National Evaluation of Youth Justice Board Mentoring Schemes 2001–2004*. London: Youth Justice Board.

Sykes, G.M. and Matza, D. (1957) 'Techniques of neutralization: a theory of delinquency', *American Sociological Review*, **22**, (6): 664–73.

Taggart, R. (1972) *The Prison of Unemployment*. Baltimore: Johns Hopkins University Press.

Tarling, R. (1979) 'The "incapacitation" effects of imprisonment', *Home Office Research Bulletin*, No. 7: 6–8.

Tarling, R., Davison, T. and Clarke, A. (2002) *The Youth Justice Board Youth Mentoring Intervention Programme: An Evaluation*. Institute for Social Research, Guildford University of Surrey Institute of Social Research.

Taylor, I., Walton, P. and Young, J. (1973) *The New Criminology: For a Social Theory of Deviance*. London: Routledge and Kegan Paul.

Taylor, I., Walton, P. and Young, J. (1975) *Critical Criminology*. London: Routledge and Kegan Paul.

Taylor, R. (1999) *Predicting Reconvictions for Sexual and Violent Offences Using the Revised Offender Group Reconviction Scale*. Home Office Research Findings 104. London: Home Office.

Tidmarsh, D., Wood, S. and Wing, J. K. (1972) *Camberwell Reception Centre: Summary of the Research Finding and Recommendations*. London: Institute of Psychiatry.

Tilt, R. (1997) 'Prison Service Drugs Strategy', *CJCC Newsletter*, Issue 7, Criminal Justice Consultative Council.

Travis, J. and Petersilia, J. (2001) 'Reentry reconsidered: a new look at an old question', *Crime & Delinquency*, **47**, 3: 291–313.

Trotter, C. (1996) 'The impact of different supervision practices in community corrections: cause for optimism', *Australian and New Zealand Journal of Criminology*, *29*: 29–46.

Trotter, C. (1999) *Working with Involuntary Clients*. London: Sage.

Turner, R. (2006) 'Developing understanding of Accredited Programmes Completions: the role of case-management and barriers to completion'. Unpublished report produced by the National Probation Service, West Yorkshire.

Underdown, A. (1998) *Strategies for Effective Offender Supervision: Report of the HMIP What Works Project.* London: Home Office.

Van Dine, S., Dinitz, S. and Conrad, J. P. (1977) 'The incapacitation of the dangerous offender: a statistical experiment'. *Journal of Research in Crime and Delinquency*, **14**, 1: 22–34.

Vanstone, M. (2000) 'Cognitive-behavioural work with offenders in the UK: A history of influential endeavour', *Howard Journal*, **39**, 2: 171–183.

Vanstone, M. (2004) *Supervising Offenders in the Community: A History of Probation Theory and Practice.* Aldershot: Ashgate.

Vennard, J. and Hedderman, C. (1998) 'Effective interventions with offenders', in P. Goldblatt and C. Lewis (eds), *Reducing Offending: An Assessment of Research Evidence on Ways of Dealing with Offending Behaviour.* Home Office Research Study 187. London: Home Office.

Vennard, J., Sugg, D. and Hedderman, C. (1997) *Changing Offenders' Attitudes and Behaviour: What Works?* Home Office Research Findings 61. London: Home Office.

Visher, C. A. and Travis, J. (2003) 'Transitions from prison to community: understanding individual pathways', *Annual Review of Sociology*, **29**, 89–113.

von Hirsch, A. (1976) *Doing Justice: The Choice of Punishments.* Report of the Committee for the Study of Incarceration. New York: Hill and Wang.

von Hirsch, A. and Ashworth, A. (1998) (eds), *Principled Sentencing: Readings on Theory and Policy*, 2nd edn. Oxford: Hart Publishing.

von Hirsch, A. and Maher, L. (1992) 'Should penal rehabilitationism be revived?', in A. von Hirsch and A. Ashworth (eds), *Principled Sentencing: Readings on Theory and Policy*, 2nd edn. Oxford: Hart Publishing.

Walmsley, R., Howard, L. and White, S. (1992) *The National Prison Survey 1991: Main Findings.* Home Office Research Study 128. London: HMSO.

Ward, T. and Brown, M. (2004) 'The good lives model and conceptual issues in offender rehabilitation', *Psychology, Crime and Law*, **10**, 3: 243–57.

Ward, T. and Maruna, S. (2007) *Rehabilitation.* London: Routledge.

Webster, R., Hedderman, C., Turnbull, P.J. and May, T. (2001) *Building Bridges to Employment for Prisoners.* London: Home Office Research Study 226. London: Home Office.

Weiss, C. H. (1998) *Evaluation: Methods for Studying Programs and Policies*, 2nd edn. Englewood Cliffs, NJ: Prentice Hall.

Wexler, D.B. and Winick, B.J. (1996) *Law in a Therapeutic Key: Developments in Therapeutic Jurisprudence.* Durham, NC: Carolina Academic Press.

Wilson, R.J., McWhinnie, A., Picheca, J.E., Prinzo, M. and Cortoni, F. (1997a) 'Circles of support and accountability: engaging community volunteers in the management of high-risk sexual offenders', *Howard Journal*, **46**, 1: 1–15.

Wilson, R.J., Picheca, J.E. and Prinzo, M. (2007b) 'Evaluating the effectiveness of professionally-facilitated volunteerism in the community-based management of high-risk sexual offenders: Part one – effects on participants and stakeholders', *Howard Journal*, **46**, 3: 289–302.

Wilson, R.J., Picheca, J.E. and Prinzo, M. (2007c) 'Evaluating the effectiveness of professionally-facilitated volunteerism in the community-based management of high-risk sexual offenders: Part two – a comparison of recidivism rates', *Howard Journal*, **46**, 4: 327–37.

Windlesham, D. (1993) *Responses to Crime, Volume 2: Penal Policy in the Making.* Oxford: Clarendon Press.

Winick, B.J. and Wexler, D.B. (eds) (2003) *Judging in a Therapeutic Key: Therapeutic Jurisprudence and the Courts.* Durham, NC: Carolina Academic Press.

Wolf, F. M. (1986) *Meta-Analysis: Quantitative Methods for Research Synthesis*. London: Sage Publications.

Women Prisoners Association (2004) Women Prisoners Association Resource Library Bibliography. New York: Women Prisoners Association. (available at http://www. wpaonline.org/WEBSITE/Bibliography/WPA_Annotated_Bibliography-Web.pdf

Wood, J. and Kemshall, H. (2007) *The Operation and Experience of Multi-Agency Public Protection Arrangements (MAPPA)*. Home Office Online Report 12/07.

Woodcock, J. (1994) *The Escape from Whitemoor Prison on Friday 9th September 1994 (The Woodcock Enquiry)*. Cm 2741. London: HMSO.

Woolf, Lord Justice and Tumim, S. (1991) *Prison Disturbances April 1990: Report of an Inquiry by the Rt Hon. Lord Justice Woolf (Parts I and II) and His Honour Judge Stephen Tumim Part III)*. Cm 1456. London: HMSO.

Worrall, A. and Hoy, C. (2005) *Punishment in the Community: Managing Offenders, Making Choices*. Cullompton: Willan.

Youth Justice Board (2005a) *Risk and Protective Factors*. London: Youth Justice Board.

Youth Justice Board (2005b) *Role of Risk and Protective Factors*. London: Youth Justice Board.

Zedner, L. (2004) *Criminal Justice*. Oxford: Oxford University Press.

Zimring, F. E. and Hawkins, G. (1995) *Incapacitation: Penal Confinement and the Restraint of Crime*. Oxford: Oxford University Press.

Index